Phenomenology and the
Science of Behaviour

This book is published within the *Advances in Psychology* Series, edited by John Cohen. The other titles in the Series are:

Behaviour and Perception in Strange Environments
HELEN E. ROSS

Early Learning in Man and Animal
W. SLUCKIN

Men at Work
C. R. BELL

Models of Thinking
FRANK GEORGE

Psychological Probability
JOHN COHEN

By the same author

Théorie de la Causalité Perceptive. Louvain, Publications Universitaires, 1962

Les Compléments Amodaux des Structures Perceptives (With A. Michotte and G. Crabbé). Louvain, Publications Universitaires, 1964

Psychologie des Animaux. Brussels, Dessart, 1966

La Problématique de la Psychologie. The Hague, Nijhoff, 1968

L'Evolution Régressive des Poissons Cavernicoles et Abyssaux. Paris, Masson, 1969

Atlas de la Vie Souterraine (With R. Tercafs). Brussels, De Visscher, 1972

Dictionnaire Général des Sciences Humaines (With A. Lempereur). Paris, Editions Universitaires, 1975

Phenomenology and the Science of Behaviour

An Historical and Epistemological Approach

GEORGES THINÈS

*Professor of Experimental and Comparative Psychology,
University of Louvain, Belgium*

London
GEORGE ALLEN & UNWIN
Boston   Sydney

First published in 1977

© George Allen & Unwin (Publishers) Ltd 1977

ISBN 0 04 121018 2

Printed in Great Britain
in 10 on 12 point Times Roman
by Willmer Brothers Limited, Birkenhead

To John Cohen
With affection and as a token
of twenty years of uninterrupted
friendship

Acknowledgements

This book reflects many fruitful discussions which I have had during the past three years with my scientific collaborators and with various persons who attended my seminars on the history of psychology and on problems of animal behaviour at the University of Louvain. I am particularly indebted to Dr René Zayan, with whom I spent many months discussing the main issues of this text and who contributed specially to the preparation of the last chapter. I am deeply grateful to Dr Susan Sara who read the manuscript critically and brought many useful amendments to the literary formulation.

I also wish to express my sincere thanks to Dr Liz Valentine, with whom I discussed various epistemological questions while lecturing at Bedford College, London University, and who kindly agreed to do the final reading of the manuscript.

I am also indebted to Professor John Cohen (Manchester University) and to Dr Colin McGinn (University College, London University) who made many useful suggestions on several of the topics treated.

Mrs Marie Bronchart-Lannoye, Miss Nicole Collen, Miss Agnès Lempereur and Miss Monique Soffié devoted much of their time to the preparation of the final typescript. Their invaluable help was greatly encouraging throughout the preparation of this book.

GEORGES THINÈS

Foreword

The author of this book is fortunate in that he is steeped in a dual tradition: first, that of the experimental study of human and animal behaviour, ranging from the perception of causality to the behaviour of blind fishes in subterranean lakes of Africa; and second, that of phenomenology and its pre-history from Brentano to Husserl. To most students of psychology and other biological sciences, in Britain and the US, experimental empiricism has assumed doctrinal proportions. The profound problems posed by phenomenological psychology lie beyond their ken, though there is today a quest for a deeper understanding of phenomena that cannot be satisfied by empiricism alone. Professor Thinès therefore performs a signal service in welding together these different traditions, thereby offering the student a broader conception of the human situation than would otherwise be possible.

Professor Thinès has succeeded in his task partly because of his remarkable grasp of the relevant historical literature in German and French as well as in English. He is well-versed equally in experimental psychology, ethology, physiology and phenomenology. Of particular interest, perhaps, is his re-discovery of Sherrington, in the chapter entitled 'Physiology of the Behavioural Field'. Here he demonstrates how much in common the great British physiologist had with continental thinkers.

Professor Thinès is nothing if not critical, but constructively so. The student who has access only to recent Anglo-American literature will find in these pages much to challenge his presuppositions, and a novel theoretical integration of apparently discrepant and discordant elements. The effort invested in studying this volume will be abundantly rewarded.

JOHN COHEN
Professor of Psychology
The University
Manchester
England

Preface

There is some triteness in saying that the subject-matter of psychology is complex. None the less, one still finds this remark at the conclusion of chapters on psychological topics, as if the psychologist were seeking an excuse for the very results he had reached. Such remarks are usually interpreted as the sign of a careful scientific attitude and of the critical mind of the theorist. It may also be interpreted as a kind of basic lack of certainty which originates in the very nature of psychological thinking. An expression like 'psychological thinking' or even 'psychological research' covers an astonishing number of activities, many of which could be incorporated under a different heading, depending on the point of view chosen.

It is debatable whether a field of knowledge which allows such a great diversity of 'points of view' can be considered as truly scientific. Most clinical psychologists are tempted to think that psychological work can be or even should be carried out without any mathematical treatment. Experimental psychologists, on the contrary, would feel uneasy if their results were expounded in everyday language, and they often tend to use mathematical formalism purely for the sake of mental satisfaction. Considering the historical evolution of Behaviourist theories, one is struck by the gradual 'recovery' of subjective aspects throughout the development of the successive systems along with continual attempts to give a central role to explanations based on crude mechanistic models. On the other hand, ethology, an approach to animal behaviour that remained largely descriptive for nearly twenty years, turns today to more abstract constructs. Confronted with such problems of method, the scientific psychologist will usually assert that these are only philosophical issues, to which the most diverse interpretations can be given without affecting the *facts* established by scientific research. It is extremely difficult to bring the pure laboratory psychologist to a critical evaluation of his own current procedures, and to convince him that his confidence in scientific methodology is, in the final analysis, an act of faith. In order to meet a fundamental requirement of psychological knowledge, the experimental approach would have to be bound up with the object under study, not only by some kind of logical necessity, in the way all explanatory theories are related to the facts they try to account for, but first of all by some *inherent* link.

1 Objectivity and methodological transposition

To throw full light on this point, it should be borne in mind that physical facts and physical methods *both* belong to what we call the realm of natural phenomena. As a consequence of this, the physicist has no choice: he can only deal with physical phenomena by referring to procedures which are themselves physical phenomena. The construct he calls a 'fact' remains valid at every moment of his investigation, including the initial question that led him to the particular experiment he is actually performing. But, from the point of view of epistemology, this constraint is at the same time a major advantage, because it ensures the relevance of the method to the problems studied. At the birth of laboratory psychology, the transposition of physical methods into the field of subjective research was considered a legitimate step in attempting to guarantee objectivity. One aim of this book is to unmask the basic misunderstanding which resulted from this important historical fact. It will be shown that a great deal of the nineteenth-century controversies about sensation, perception and consciousness resulted from assumptions about the nature of the psychological subject which were mechanical models devised to fit implicit Cartesian ideas. The concepts of 'consciousness' and 'subject' are hard to analyse in spite of the fact that they appear as a matter of course in psychological literature. It is our conviction that these concepts would gain in clarity if they referred to 'constitution', i.e. the active building up of the individual's own (or 'subjective') world according to perceptual and motor capacities. This idea, however, appeared only in later phenomenological psychology, since early phenomenologists referred to consciousness much in the sense of idealism, though they opposed the dualistic views of post-Kantian philosophy. It has still to be settled whether the abandonment of Cartesian dualism opened the way for an analysis of subjectivity bridging the gap between the 'constitutive' subject and the 'empirical' subject as conceived by experimental psychologists and – in a slightly different fashion – by biologists. A more detailed study of the systems which were precursory to the emergence of Gestalt psychology will throw some light on the factors which prevented a full appreciation of this well-known school. Turning to phenomenology, the task of the author will be to show that the critical analysis of psychology to which phenomenologists consistently proceeded should not be considered, as many would have it, as a purely philosophical dispute tending to deprive scientific psychology of its theoretical as well as its practical achievements. The main reason for referring to phenomenology is that phenomenology alone raised the question of whether psychology could be legitimately considered as the fundamental science. The fact is that this problem was raised when the system was still entirely embodied in philosophical speculation and had not yet evolved avowedly towards psychology as an autonomous field, viz. phenomenological psychology as distinct from transcendental reflection. But this would in turn raise the difficulties of *psychologism*, to which we shall return. The bearing of phenomenologically inspired epistemology on today's psychology considered as a science is, in our opinion, even more worthy of consideration than in the time of the first 'physiological psychology'. There is indeed no compelling reason to believe that present-day experimentalists are, on the whole, more aware of epistemological problems than their predecessors, at least if one considers the general background of their hypotheses. Besides, the increasing complexity of techniques has often masked the lasting influence of traditional views, not to mention mere re-formulations of ancient issues.

The very use of the word 'phenomenology' raises immediate suspicion in many scientific psychological circles. Either the term is understood to refer to a purely descriptive approach as opposed to controlled parametric procedures, or it is thought to be a return to introspective procedures. The scientific psychologist must become aware of the shallowness of such interpretations. Let us say that, if the phenomenologist often gave the impression of criticising experimental work without performing experiments himself, the scientific psychologist rejected phenomenological concepts with little regard for their actual meaning. If this book could contribute to mutual recognition, on the part of both experimentalists and phenomenologists, of the limits of their respective fields of research, its main purpose would be achieved.

2   The observer and the facts

The main difficulty in studying the meaning of psychological work, lies in the fact that the human subject is treated by the experimentalist as a 'passive observer', i.e. ultimately as a reactive system. On the other hand, he is treated by the clinical psychologist as a 'case' or, to put it in more general terms, as an individual person, claimed to be, as such, foreign to any formalistic reduction. We hope to show that the opponents of formalisation (including that particular kind of formalisation commonly referred to as the 'experimental approach') do not differ in accepting that a basic conception of subjectivity is an epistemological necessity. Like his experimental colleague, the clinical psychologist all too often obtains a result, because he has succeeded in framing the behavioural as well as the linguistic signs available to him in a system of reference at least as compelling as the requirements of a rigorous laboratory experiment. This amounts to saying that both the experimenter and the clinician use different vocabularies to describe so-called psychological 'facts', each of which may be equally foreign to the actual human situation, and each of which will finally be considered as established in virtue of the *pragmatic* powers of the method used.

The idea that a fact does not exist other than as the constructed product of a method is only true in physical science (and in all its natural derivatives) for the reason given earlier (p. 13), because physical phenomena and physical procedures *both* belong essentially to the natural world. In other words, devising new methods in natural science necessarily opens the way to new *facts*, a proposition which does not hold true when the object investigated is always a possible investigator. This leads us logically to a critical analysis of objective psychology in the classical sense. Our task in this respect will be to show that current psychological assumptions amount to extending the principle of causal induction from natural science to a field in which causal mechanisms cannot be proved to exist as a matter of course, except if one turns to the proximal field in physiology. Hence the emergence of a physiological psychology as an absolute model just at the very moment when psychology was attempting to free itself of its philosophical chains. Much is to be said about this historical evolution; if for centuries psychology had actually been a 'slave' of philosophy, it now had only changed masters. It must be added that the fundamental reference to physiology, which prevented the foundation of an authentically autonomous psychological science, was still, as such, a philosophical choice.

The epistemological implications of psychophysics and physiological psychology can only be fully unravelled when one considers the theory of consciousness which underlies early psychological research. It is obvious that the main stumbling-block here was the unavoidable use of language in order to obtain the necessary factual categories of inductive analysis. The rather dubious role of introspection in early scientific research gave rise to well-known reactions, among which are those of Brentano and the Graz school (Meinong, Stumpf, von Ehrenfels, to which the names of Mach and of Husserl himself may be added). The historical study of this school leads directly to the consideration of the parallel development of Gestalt psychology and of early phenomenology. The specific relations which existed for a time between the Graz experimentalists and the first form of phenomenology will be made clear by referring especially to Stumpf, a rather poorly known author in the Anglo-Saxon world, where it is customary to jump from Elementarism to Behaviourism through the rather narrow channel of biometrics and the Galtonian tradition. The first appearance of Husserl as a pupil of Stumpf, thus partly as an experimentalist, has been considered useful in order to show the true psychological orientation of his first reflections. This refers to a short period during which he was occupied with his *Philosophy of Arithmetic* (1891). The Graz school largely developed, after Brentano (whose *Psychology from an empirical standpoint* was published in 1873), the concept of the 'act of consciousness', attempting thereby to do away with the methodological difficulties of introspective procedures, and at the same time broadening the way in which intentionality made its appearance in psychological thinking. We apologise for this rather lengthy historical preamble, but consider it necessary for a sound understanding of the phenomenological movement with all its consequences.

3 *Pure phenomenology and phenomenological psychology*

The main problem, however, is that of the significance of *pure phenomenology*, understood after Husserl himself as a radical philosophy, for the actual building up of a *phenomenological psychology*. From the very beginning phenomenology has undoubtedly been psychologically oriented. The problems raised by Brentano about consciousness and perception and, similarly, those on which the early Husserl focused his interests (in particular the nature of multiplicity, as it is treated in the *Philosophy of Arithmetic*) were, at the same time, fundamental psychological issues. None the less, we will try to show that the actual practice of phenomenological psychology does not require a thorough philosophical study of the works of these authors. The experimentalist who would be reluctant to accept this starting-point and who would claim that reference to phenomenology is always historical, should remember that no experimentalist ever refers today to Fechner or to Wundt. Once and for all, one must abandon the idea that phenomenological psychology (which is still nowadays largely in the making) has declared war on scientific psychology by virtue of an anachronistic obedience to a historical method of philosophy – a method which is equally rejected today by the great majority of technically-minded philosophers. It will be a good opportunity to stress the spirit of renewal which characterises phenomenological psychology in its tentative criticisms of outdated mechanistic causality. This, of course, calls for positive propositions at least as convincing as the classical reductionist procedures currently used in psychological research. As Strasser writes,

> According to the 'scientists', the object determines the subject's act of knowing, but in the view of 'existentialists' the conscious subject posits a world of objects . . . Both views lead to impossible consequences. We want therefore to oppose to these views a position that deviates fundamentally from both and claim that *'the object' is a discovery made by human subjects and that objectivity is the result of a certain subjective approach.*[1]

Historically speaking, such a theoretical starting-point would never have been asserted without the actual emergence of phenomenological criticisms in the development of psychological systems. To be sure, it is through these critical analyses that a number of epistemological issues were drawn to the attention of scientific psychologists – without succeeding, as a rule, in evoking any sympathy, or at least receiving only a minimum of 'objective' consideration. Among these issues, some became topics in the philosophy of the human sciences and were extensively treated in a series of basic texts, particularly since the appearance of Merleau-Ponty's *Structure of Behaviour* (1942; English translation 1963) and principally since the publication of his *The Phenomenology of Perception* (1945; English translation 1962).

---

[1]S. Strasser, *Phenomenology and the human sciences*. Pittsburgh, Duquesne University Press, 1963, p. 60 (original author's italics).

4   *Some basic propositions*

These topics may be conveniently summarised under the following head-ings:

(1)   The subject-matter of psychology differs fundamentally from that of the traditional scientific disciplines: it is the human subject in his situation and not the subject as defined by laboratory experiments.

(2)   The privileged nature of this subject as an object of investigation does not amount to making psychological science impossible, but it calls for a type of approach essentially different from classical objectivistic procedures.

(3)   Hence, a completely new conceptual framework has to be built in order to establish true psychological facts.

(4)   The behaviour of the psychological subject is neither the sum nor the combination of space-time determinants as deduced from physical experiments.

(5)   The subject is a living body in a world of intentional significance. It is not a pure reactive system as imagined by Behaviourism.

(6)   Psychological theories cannot, by themselves, lay down the necessary foundation defining the limits of legitimacy of their own propositions.

(7)   The principle of causality of the natural sciences can be transferred to psychology by an arbitrary decision but not by virtue of any inherent epistemological property of the sciences dealing with man.

These propositions, whose validity this book will try to discuss, have been thoroughly analysed, in the light of a wealth of concrete instances, by E. Straus in his book *The Primary World of Senses* (published in German in 1935 and translated into English in 1963). Some comments must be made about the actual influence of this basic text, as well as that of other critical studies dealing with the foundations of psychology. One is struck by the fact that studies, which raised fundamental issues about the scientific value of psychology, only reached a rather limited circle of scientists and were almost never quoted in general textbooks. In most cases, until recently, textbooks written in English opened with an introductory chapter whose epistemological content was elementary and which consisted of common-sense generalities on objectivity and control. The reading of such introductory remarks made it obvious that the authors were not aware of the existence of an important literature dealing with the foundations of their own science. This is to be ascribed, in our opinion, to the fact that most basic texts in this field – at least those directly inspired by phenomenology – were originally published in German or in French. English translations of some of these works only appeared twenty or thirty years later, most of them in the 1960s. This could easily convey to the English-speaking reader the impression that these texts were dealing with topics which, he might argue, had not in the meantime given rise to any important controversy.

Another aspect of the question which should not be disregarded is the fact that the first practical effects of phenomenological concepts made their appearance in psychopathology and, as a result, in clinical psychology. The latter being often considered by experimentalists as a field where personal contacts and non-scientific approaches play a decisive role, it is not surprising that phenomenology should often have been accused by scientists of promoting a kind of psychology practically devoid of rigorous control. True enough, the kind of psychology towards which phenomenology is striving aims fundamentally at a reconsideration of the main problems dealt with by scientific psychology in the perspective of the subject as being-in-the-world. Nevertheless, such an attempt is actually opposed to the naïve reductionism of positivism as well as the purely subjective constructs of rationalism. It is in that opposition that the deep meaning of an existentially founded psychology must be sought. And, obviously, so-called existential problems were more readily available in the psychopathological and clinical fields than anywhere else. But it will become clear in the course of our exposition that the requirements of a truly subject-centred psychology are basically the same for experimental research.

5   *Misinterpretations of phenomenology*

In expounding the main features of pure phenomenology in relation to psychological thinking, care will be taken to shed light on the similarities and differences between phenomenology in the technical sense, and existentialism; the latter has been used in such a variety of contexts that it needs careful definition before being introduced into a study like this. Existentialism refers to one of the major philosophical revolutions of our century. If one places it in its historical context and follows the evolution of its meaning from Kierkegaard to Heidegger and to its later developments in France with Sartre and Merleau-Ponty, one will easily be convinced that contemporary scientific psychology cannot any longer submit to existentialists' criticisms without analysing their technical value if any. The main point in this respect is that phenomenological and existential modes of thought have already brought about deep changes in the way in which psychologists of empirical persuasion conceive their own task. The trouble is that as these influences have made their way through scientific traditions by their own force, the role ascribed to them is generally the opposite of their epistemological requirements.[1]

Due to the widespread idea that the phenomenological method attempts to exclude the study of controlled parameters in favour of purely descriptive

---

[1] Merleau-Ponty's *Structure of Behaviour*, for instance, inspired various scientific hypotheses in psychological research. The same cannot be said of Sartre's phenomenological work on imagination.

procedures, some scientific psychologists have either confounded phenomenology with a kind of personal or cultural humanism, or have indulged in theoretical considerations which were considered as a *complementary reflection* on their experimentally based interpretations. In this way, they hoped more or less to legitimise some particular *qualitative aspects* of their work which had escaped parametric reduction. Needless to say, phenomenological psychology has nothing to do with a subsidiary filling-in procedure of this kind. As far as humanistic views are concerned, it must be borne in mind that humanistic psychology is, as such, distinct from phenomenological psychology, though both fields have important points in common. Reference should be made here to Husserl himself. In his *Philosophie als strenge Wissenschaft* (1911 – *Philosophy as a Strict Science*), Husserl already warned cultural philosophers and historians against a confusion tending to assimilate phenomenology to philosophical aspirations devoid of scientific rigour.

As a basis for psychology, phenomenology is characterised by its epistemological radicalism, its opposition to a mere imitation of exact science in the study of man, and its determination to place experimental research in the realm of a completely new conceptual framework. The status of theoretical constructs must therefore be appreciated on a level which excludes both naïvety and abstract developments dissociated from the meaningful relation of the subject to the world of his lived behaviour.

6   *Main topics of this book*

The effects of culturalism, as quoted above after Husserl, will be considered in Chapter 1 in relation to the early conception of scientific psychology. Much confusion seems indeed to have arisen in the definition of psychological science, because the description and the attempt at quantification of psychic phenomena relied on concepts whose scientific or cultural origin was not clearly established, thus allowing a great deal of ambiguity in the treatment of phenomena and in the elaboration of explanatory systems. Chapter 2 will be devoted to Brentano and his followers and to the gradual evolution of the teachings of the Graz school, already mentioned, towards Husserlian phenomenology and Gestalt theory. Considering further the implications of these systems for the theory of the subject, it was thought necessary to study this latter topic from the physiological point of view too. The main references here are to the work of Sherrington and that of Buytendijk, since they furnish an exceptionally firm foundation for a description of subjectivity in terms of organic structure, in contradistinction to the reductive conceptions of early experimental psychologists in this matter (Chapters 3 and 6).

Chapter 4 gives an illustration of the difficulties met by attempts at psychological renewal, when exclusively inspired by philosophical conceptualisation. The critical analysis of Politzer – a French theoretical psychologist mostly unknown in Anglo-Saxon psychology – was selected as the most illuminating instance in this respect. It is hoped that it will be shown that, in spite of the legitimacy of his criticisms, Politzer lacked the biological frame of reference which would have guaranteed him scientific effectiveness.

These historical and altogether epistemological analyses will be synthesised in the last chapter, where we shall examine the possible contribution of phenomenological psychology towards a science of subjectivity relying on biological facts. The main endeavour of the author has been to examine whether the concepts of phenomenology and those of biology may converge in some respects immediately one admits that psychology should study the living subject in the first place. It may help to dissipate some misunderstandings which have all too often prevented fruitful dialogue between experimentalists and phenomenologists.

Contents

Introduction

1 Technical knowledge v. individual experience

The evolution of modern thinking since the great scientific impetus of the sixteenth century has progressively resulted in an intellectual attitude in which the ideas of rigour and effectiveness have been more and more difficult to dissociate. Considering the successful practical developments of discoveries which seemed, at first glance, to be sheer curiosities, one wonders whether the main aspect of Western genius should not be defined as a capacity to evaluate disproportions between causes and effects. Most of the fundamental scientific discoveries, from the law of gravity to radioactivity, have been initiated by observations that could have been considered as unimportant by an ordinary observer.

This amounts to saying that physical principles, as they are discovered and applied by physicists and engineers, have no direct bearing on the life of the human person. Such a statement does not deny the actual influences exerted on man's life by the work of exact science; progress in scientific knowledge is, on the contrary, the basic cause of the improvement of practical life in our civilised world; in saying that the physical discoveries have no direct bearing on the life of the individual, we mean that they cannot be personally experienced in the same way as ordinary events. This is all the more puzzling, since physical knowledge can only become systematised from direct life experience (the physiological and psychological experience of effort being, for instance, the remote origin of the concept of mass and weight, etc.). It may be that the discovery of a physical law is precisely due to men who are apparently endowed with the capacity of grasping (in some obscure way described as due to 'genius') the universal significance of current happenings. It is the ordinary event which leads to the scientific phenomenon, but the process is only potential in the behaviour of the ordinary man facing the everyday world.

This leads us to consider the status of scientific knowledge when it becomes an object of public information. Once established, a scientific truth will reach the ordinary man through a number of communication channels. The content of such popularised knowledge is then ready to become part of current life-experience. Innumerable proofs of it can be found in the enthusiastic reactions at all levels of opinion before the spectacular achievements of present-day technology. They gain acceptance not because they are technically understood, but because they give to every private person a means of renewing his self-image in the world; in other words, they contribute to enriching our emotional experience without calling for any kind of serious intellectual effort.

What is true of exact science and technology is all the more true of the human sciences. Problems of sociology, psychology, politics, economics, etc. are discussed by the man-in-the-street with a tone of assertion and in a spirit of critical appreciation which conveys the impression of competence. No one would hesitate to pronounce judgements and make predictions on questions like child education, on the status of women in the organisation of work, while very few would venture to give their opinion on electrical circuits, nuclear fission or colour measurement. An important consequence of this attitude is that the human sciences are permanently threatened by their non-technical appearance. The main reason must be found in the fact that these fields of knowledge express their propositions in ordinary language. As Wittgenstein puts it, 'In the language of everyday life it very often happens that the same word signifies in two different ways – and therefore belongs to two different symbols – or that two words, which signify in different ways, are apparently applied in the same way in the proposition'.[1] Therefore, if a science, in the true sense of the word, has to be built with the aid of semantic tools of this kind, the result is bound to be ambiguous. Man lives in a basic ambiguity and refers to facts of everyday existence in a necessarily ambiguous manner. I can feel my headache, but I am unable to express it formally in terms of quality and intensity. My private estimate of light-intensity in my dining-room is totally foreign to the photometric measurement of it. Meanwhile, I am conscious of the fact that my body is a physical system. But when I utter the proposition 'My body is a physical system', I do not refer to any precise physical knowledge of it. I only express the general situation of my body as a material reality among other material realities. In doing so, however, I feel and I know that the materiality of my body is given to me basically, not as the result of systematic comparisons between external objects (animate and inanimate) and myself, but as a subjective experience of *my* embodiment.[2]

2   The embodiment

Because of the experienced character of my bodily situation, my physical existence will always remain for me a confused one. The physical 'proximity' of my body is a condition of survival which forbids any anatomo-physiological analysis of my own physical organisation. Moreover, the perception of my external bodily structure (which is only possible for some parts offered to direct examination), is itself confused and devoid of any systematic criterion.

Subjective experiences are therefore continually based on a double ambiguity:

[1] L. Wittgenstein, *Tractatus Logico-Philosophicus*, London, Routledge & Kegan Paul, 7th edn, 1958, 3.323, p. 55.
[2] Cf. on this topic R. M. Zaner, *The problem of embodiment. Some contributions to a phenomenology of the body*, The Hague, Nijhoff, 1964, p. 136, note 3.

(1) The peculiar inaccessibility of internal constituents of the body in everyday behaviour.
(2) The basically confused experience of the external body as it is perceived or felt in everyday experience.

The analysis of the body as an object is the task of the anatomist and the physiologist. Their work can only take place if the body is considered outside private experience. It cannot teach us anything of the way the body acts in the realm of subjective life. The body of a living subject can be experienced or observed; these two situations are mutually exclusive. This explains why psychology has been ruled since its Cartesian origins by a fundamental dualism which has taken different forms in the course of history: the dichotomy 'body–soul' has been followed by the dichotomy 'body–consciousness' and has led finally to psychophysics and psychophysical parallelism.

Classical psychology only makes sense if one admits from the start that man is constitutionally made of two distinct 'substances'.

3 Dualism and its consequences

It is essential to inquire whether the only effect of Cartesian dualism has been to focus later scientific psychology on problems of consciousness. Turning to the insistence of Descartes and his followers on scientific methodology, it is important to establish whether the dualism did not determine in a particular way the tendency to apply classical methodological principles to non-physical realities as they were defined under the general heading of *pensée* (which, in the vocabulary of Descartes, encompasses all aspects of subjective life described later as 'consciousness'). The main point here is that the idea of a science of consciousness appeared early in the history of modern European thinking. Its importance does not lie only in the historical development of a psychology of the psychophysical type, but first of all in the inexorable evolution resulting from the assumption that the subject had to be studied in terms of natural science (in the particular meaning of the German *Naturwissenschaften*).

It is remarkable, in this respect, that psychology was continually related by Wundt (1873) *to physiology and not to biology*. In present-day science the distinction may appear irrelevant, because the various branches of the biological sciences are increasingly becoming integrated. Physiology, biochemistry, genetics, ecology, ethology, and many other specialised fields of biological research all converge in the study of the same fundamental adaptation mechanisms. In the days of Wundt, no such ties existed, mainly because the majority of the above-mentioned sciences had not yet developed. The Darwinian theory of evolution (1859) indeed offered a comprehensive conceptual scheme capable of serving as a frame of reference for the new psychology. It actually became a foundation of the Galtonian school and of later biometrics and psychometrics, on the one hand, and of analogical conceptions in animal psychology, on the other: this, in spite of the fact that Darwin had paved the way for comparative ethology as early as 1873 (the very year of publication of the first part of Wundt's *Grundzüge der Physiologischen Psychologie*) with the publication of his *The Expression of the Emotions in Man and Animals*. Whatever may be the case, there is no doubt that the early relation of scientific psychology to physiology was not truly biological. Rather it was a mental model abstracted from some basic physiological discoveries in the nervous system and the sense organs made during the course of the nineteenth century. Apart from their purely physiological significance, some of these phenomena were particularly apt to be interpreted in terms of mental structure and to allow a reconstruction of 'consciousness' in terms fitting very well with the all-pervading dualistic teachings.

In 1811, Charles Bell performed an experiment which furnished experimental support for a very ancient idea. Stimulation of the anterior nerve-root of the spinal cord provoked muscular movement even when the posterior root had been previously cut, whereas stimulation of the latter did not cause any kind of motor reaction. Bell's conclusion was that the posterior root played a purely sensory role and that the anterior root had an exclusively motor function. In 1822, François Magendie, unaware of the publication of his predecessor, independently rediscovered the same phenomenon in a different experiment.[1] For the physiologist, the Bell–Magendie law established the anatomical distinction between sensory and motor nerve fibres. For the experimental psychologists to come, it seemed to indicate that the mechanisms governing mental life were distinct entities. The idea that different nerves are at work for sensations and movements is to be found in the writings of Descartes and even earlier. The coupling of Descartes' teachings about thought and extension with anatomical discoveries such as those just described, had a deep influence on the spirit in which the first scientific psychology was conceived. In order to emerge from radical doubt, Descartes finds no other recourse than the quasi-introspective statement of the fact that he thinks. The experience of thought being the sole indisputable *fact*, anything else may be considered as doubtful and therefore liable to be the result of an 'illusion'. This resort is an existential one, from which every reality will have to be reconstructed according to a limited number of methodological principles. The main principle holds that the ultimate criterion is the 'clear and distinct' idea. The nature of the physical world around us, physical objects, the body included, must be understood in this way. The analysis of the physical will have to proceed step by step from the simple to the complex as in mathematical procedures. As far as mental events are concerned, Descartes experienced enormous difficulties in explaining how thinking processes (and mental events in general) actually do take place within the physical body, and

[1] More historical details on this problem will be found in J. Cohen, 'Charles Bell and the roots of physiology', *New Scientist* (1974), p. 498.

he proposed, as is well-known, his hybrid theory of animal spirits (i.e. a mental reality which is simultaneously physical), which finally resulted in psychophysical parallelism.

Parallelism is the solution which allows one to conclude that no solution is to be found and that the processes compared are fundamentally foreign to each other. Any anatomo-physiological data capable of bridging the gap between the physical and the mental will therefore be accepted because parallelism precludes any genuine explanation. Hence the above-mentioned interpretation of the Bell–Magendie law, an interpretation which has never been explicitly stated in later psychological work. A similar fate was reserved for the theory of Johannes Müller on the theory of specific nerve energies (1888), the doctrine of localisation of functions in the brain, and in general for all anatomo-physiological findings giving the impression that mental processes could be ascribed reference-points in the body of the subject. At this point, an important conclusion may be drawn: *Dualism evolves necessarily into mental atomism.* An additional remark is, however, necessary: the dualistic conception that originated from Descartes' *Cogito* is linked with the scientific principles he held to be valid for physical reality extended in space. Scientific psychology, for this reason, has found an exceptionally favourable settling-ground in the Cartesian application of these principles to the particular physical reality of the body. The first historical age of scientific psychology is therefore characterised by a bodily approach to 'mental' problems. The question which is then raised is the following: how is it possible to ascertain that processes actually observed at the physiological level do correspond to particular mental events? And, if the required proofs are lacking, is it legitimate to use the same methods for the mental as for the physical? The answer to this problem was, for many decades, *introspection*.

Introspection is an outdated concept in today's psychology, at least in principle. It presupposes not only that physical events of the body and mental events are ruled by an unequivocal correspondence, but that the mental can also be unequivocally explored by language, more precisely by *ordinary* language. We have already mentioned the basic shortcomings of ordinary language for the building up of a strict scientific conceptualisation. We must now add that the unavoidable intervention of language in introspection obliges the scientific psychologist to accept a non-controllable description as the basis of his abstract constructs. The Behaviouristic reaction has excluded introspection, but not language as a form of behaviour. What is it then that differentiates *uttered* language and *observed* language? Does Behaviourism possess the necessary scientific qualification that puts it in a position to grasp the sense of language outside the relations between the speaker and the listener, viz. between the subject and the observer? Introspective psychology and Behaviourism are only mentioned here to describe in a concise manner the permanent division of psychology since its scientific infancy. In fact there is no basic need to refer to particular schools in order to understand the theoretical and practical results of the originally assumed dualism. The specific problems raised accordingly by the emergence of Gestaltism and Phenomenology will be treated in the course of Chapter 2.

Keeping to the fundamental teachings of the dualistic doctrine, there is no doubt that it has been and still is the implicit basis of every scientific tendency in psychology. We hope to show that important developments which took place in the thirties and the forties have come today to a point where it is practically possible to foresee the end of the dualistic period. Similar views have been developed by the author in previous publications.[1] They will be outlined more specifically in the present book.

As has already been pointed out, the assumption of the dualistic character of the subject has prevented a sound biological treatment of psychological problems. We may say, in a rather crude manner, that objective psychology has always been sufficiently loose to allow pseudophilosophical discourses on subjective matters on the one hand, and pseudoscientific formalisations of external behaviour on the other. Such an ambiguous state of affairs could only result from the lack of a sound epistemology. In current practice, it has all too often popularised the idea that the psychologist is either a sort of non-medical healer dealing with private problems not truly pathological, or a laboratory research-worker distinct from the recognised life-scientist. In this connection, it is not quite legitimate to refer to the so-called multidisciplinary character of psychological science in order to account for its lack of precise goals, not because one would dream of transforming a probabilistic discipline into an exact one, but because such a statement amounts to defining psychology as *necessarily* dualistic.

4   *The* a priori *in the epistemological framework*

The reasons for rejecting dualistic views should be well understood. There is, of course, no philosophical argument which is strong enough to be compelling in this respect, as far as *conceptions* of the subject, whether human or animal, are concerned. If this were the case, one would have to argue on the sole basis of philosophical considerations, and the final choice would be arbitrary. At this level of reflection, any argument in favour of dualism could be turned against it from the opposing point of view (i.e. the holistic), and the holist would have, in his turn, to supply proofs similar to those offered by the dualist. This leads inevitably to an endless circular dialectic making it impossible to reach a firm conclusion. The weak point in all this is that we admit from the start that *conceptions* of the subject have a role to play, which condemns us to treating the subject philosophically whatever may be the starting-point of our analysis. We should therefore conclude in principle that

[1] G. Thinès, 'Le langage de l'expérience et le langage de la théorie en psychologie', in *Hommage à André Rey*, Brussels, Dessart, 1967, pp. 199–221; *La Problématique de la Psychologie*, La Haye, Nijhoff, 1968; 'The phenomenological approach in comparative psychology', *J. Phenom. Psychol.*, 1970, I, 1, pp. 63–74.

a radical treatment of the problem excludes *a priori* any kind of philosophical analysis. This problem is a difficult one, since it is not easy to draw distinctions within the philosophical approaches themselves, in order to show that, beyond sheer school-oppositions, there is a single philosophical basis for every psychological question. The important distinction is not between philosophical views as such, but between the inclusion or exclusion of philosophical analyses at a given moment in a psychological theory capable of leading to valid investigations. In other words, there is an epistemology to be found in the absence of which psychological work loses its significance. The task which remains finally is to define the main characteristics of such an epistemology. This supposes that the conceptions – or misconceptions – about the subject are unacceptable in a certain number of instances, not only because they are rooted in *a priori* ideas, but because they are false from the epistemological point of view. As there is no pure approach to the subject because no psychological analysis can pretend to begin at an 'absolute' origin, it must be borne in mind that the *a priori* is not a condition of philosophical thinking alone. Neither in historical time, nor in the actual time of the private observer, does the possibility exist of setting oneself in an ahistorical position to collect data and pronounce judgements on experienced reality. Realism itself as a system is an *a priori* and so is any kind of organised or organising knowledge. The very intention of knowing has to secure firm grounds from which to proceed, the search for such 'absolute' bases being, in itself, foreign to objectivity. This can be formulated in a different and altogether more particular manner by saying that objectivity is, in itself, a special form of the *a priori* which has gained acceptance in the Cartesian history of Western thinking and our accepted modes of scientific investigation. To be sure, the objective *a priori* appears as a kind of unrealism aimed at founding scientific realism by escaping first from the real world of life. Erwin Straus, by far the deepest analyst of the Cartesian nature of objective psychology, writes as follows:[1]

> Descartes thought that he had succeeded in finding an Archimedian point outside the world of man. He assumed that the method of radical doubt made it possible for him to set himself apart from that world to the extent that he could construe and comprehend the material world through exclusively mathematical deductions. Into this realm of *res extensa*, he exiled the bodies of man and animal, including that body he knew as most closely related to himself: his own. In this leap, Descartes, the man, transformed himself into a *res cogitans*.

It is a constant objection of philosophers of science (and concerning human science in particular) that the very exercise of scientific activity in a given field does not produce and does not even promote the epistemological problems

[1] E. Straus, *Vom Sinn der Sinne*, Berlin, Springer, 1935 (2nd Edn. 1956). English translation by J. Needleman, *The Primary World of Senses: a Vindication of Sensury Experience*, New York, Free Press of Glencoe, 1963.

raised by its own activity. Fundamental problems arise in relation to the significant questions implied by a permanent trend of theoretical (and partly practical) effectiveness, but, as such, these problems can only be properly approached from a point of view which is not that of the specialised field concerned, the main reasons for this being that the basic implications become unfolded with a certain delay and that the means of investigation do not allow, by themselves, any questioning of their actual use.

Turning back to dualism, we may now understand in a more concrete fashion why we have to consider it as an insufficient foundation for a general epistemology of the subject. The position of psychology as a science having emerged from Cartesianism is that of a human science founded on the deductive powers of a mythical non-worldly observer. Our thesis is that the epistemological process has missed its goal in this instance because the starting-point of Descartes is that of a mathematician unsatisfied with the relativism of sensory activity. As a consequence, the difficulties of a return from the model of the lifeless Cartesian machinery to the experienced body of the living observer and to the living organism (human and animal) acting on its actual behaviour, has resulted in an essentially compensatory approach in which the living had constantly to be *recovered* from the abstract. This explains, in our opinion, why, in psychology, the great majority of concepts used in different areas belong to a peculiar kind of face-operationalism. We may therefore characterise scientific psychology as a sort of *intuitive biology*. It is a biology in which, curiously enough, the observer ignores the living as such and performs experiments whose results are interpreted as a function of an abstract model.

Chapter 1

Biology and Culture
in Objective Psychology

1   *The historical perspective and the* a priori

In order to attain objectivity, scientific psychology had to free itself from philosophical interpretations of man and was led to consider man as the object of controlled experiments. The brief outline of this historical process has shown us that, in order to achieve this aim, the psychological subject as an individual being had to be transformed into an abstract entity. The meaning of this transformation should be examined carefully. One may object that the philosophical interpretation of man was itself dealing with an abstract image and that the scientific outlook was precisely the historical result of it. Philosophical abstractions and scientific abstractions are nevertheless different. The former are built up by pure deductive reasoning and may be influenced to a great extent by historical factors such as beliefs and patterns of conformity. The latter are the result of inductive procedures and are therefore more schematic, since scientific control requires that the individual should be reduced to a set of relations which may be considered apart from its roots in actual life and from the reality of expressive behaviour. But in spite of their fundamental differences, deductive and inductive approaches to the individual testify to the *a priori* in every attempt at gaining knowledge about any possible object of investigation. As in any other field, psychological problems can only be tackled by accepting at the outset a certain kind of *a priori*; thus, the issue is not whether it will be accepted or rejected, but whether *this* or *that a priori* will be considered adequate. No such choice can be made without referring to epistemology, i.e. to a realm of concepts establishing some sufficient foundation for further analyses.

In this respect, much has been said on the methodological side regarding the necessity of systematic planning before embarking on an experiment. This constant reminder of the preparatory constructs in scientific work is only a way of stressing the *a priori* character of experimental thinking (a character which it shares with any sort of productive effort), and the relations of logical necessity existing between the hypothesis and the theory. The existence of an *a priori* step at the outset of every piece of research has often been ignored by scientists, though it has been widely discussed by epistemologists.[1] Once again, the implicit assumptions made by the scientific psychologist at the moment he sets to work appear to him to be devoid of importance in comparison with the facts he begins to collect. In fact, the experimentalist considers himself as an observer only when he has already taken the necessary step of defining the observable. This is the psychological origin of his regarding himself as acting *objectively*, a thing he could never achieve if he did not proceed on the firm grounds of that particular *a priori* named the scientific or objective attitude.

2 *Objectivity as a construct*

When the scientist decides to start an experiment, he does not evaluate the significance of his decision's having originated at a particular stage of the evolution of the science in which he happens to be a specialist, nor does he evaluate the degree of his specialisation in relation to the total population of existing specialists in the field under consideration. Leaving aside the rather crude ignorance of published facts on the problem with which he wants to deal, the possibility of his not being aware of certain classical or recent techniques, etc., his decision to tackle this or that problem in one or another way is entirely spontaneous. The scientific approach seems at first glance to be *the* natural approach since its scope is to study natural phenomena. It possesses the characteristic of coming under the immediate control of sense-data, a control which is assumed not to be at variance with the observer's logical capacities. What I am doing can be called an experiment in the proper sense of the word, precisely because I have taken all the necessary measures in order to be able to proceed without ever experiencing that kind of discrepancy. But, in spite of all these systematic decisions – which amount to a definition of and subsequent methodological construction of categories of scientific phenomena – the scientific act appears very close to, and even confounded with, the ways of dealing with everyday facts and events. There seems to be a striking similarity and, according to non-critical views, a fundamental identity between the act of perceiving and the act of measuring, between estimating the number of people in a crowd and counting them accurately one by one, between setting the distance of the lamp on my desk in order to have enough light and measuring with precision the illumination level with the help of a photometer, etc. *The scientific act is all too often interpreted as a perceptual act because of its constant reference to sensory data.* But this reference is remote and its essential role is to make possible indirect methods whose results are artificial constructs subject to control. To summarise:

---

[1]The problem of the *a priori* as the unavoidable primary foundation of every system of knowledge is foreshadowed in Mach's theory of founding sensations (see Chapter 2) and is a fundamental theme of Husserl's transcendental phenomenology (see Chapter 5) in relation to his discussions of the epistemological value of natural science.

scientific facts exist at the natural level but never occur *as such* in nature, insofar as the latter word refers to the phenomenal reality of everyday life. Phenomenal reality is claimed to be the subject-matter of psychology. It ranges from mere perceptual awareness to the most elaborated representations and phantasms. Thus scientific facts in psychology do not exist at the level of ordinary experience: they have to be elaborated in some particular fashion. They are abstract constructs intended to fit 'reality', but the latter may be at variance with phenomenal or experienced reality.

The point of importance in this respect is that the *a priori* elaboration of objectivity must eliminate the time-perspective of the living subject in order to proceed efficiently. What happens in a psychological experiment cannot be registered accurately and worked out rigorously if the experimenter is reminded all the time of the subjective phenomena continuously experienced by his subject as the experiment goes on. No experiment whatsoever could be performed if subjects did not at least agree to listen to instructions, or if, having done so, they interrupted the psychologist now and then to tell him what they felt about the situation they had been put in, whether they liked it or not, etc. Supposing that the experimenter would be willing to take into account such non-programmed data and to devise his experiment so as to include them in it, he would still have to plan these according to various 'sub-programmes' which in turn would have to comply with the general requirements of his procedure – an endless process. The problem of time-perspective will be treated in detail in the last section of this chapter. We may note in passing that in some kinds of psychological investigation the experimenter explicitly states that he will consider the attitudes and responses of his subjects to the situation itself as data belonging to his programme. This is especially the case in social psychology. But here again, the decision to pay attention to such aspects of the subject's behaviour (verbal or not) can never be fully carried out, since it just aims at collecting scientific data of a particular kind without questioning the fundamental meaning of a controlled experiment of such a nature. In other words, the issue here amounts to asking to what extent the facts observed are actually social ones as, for instance, in the case of those that are observed by an ethologist watching a group of monkeys or by a child psychologist watching infants playing. In animal and child studies, spontaneous behaviour can be observed and described and any experiment which makes sense is devised on this preliminary basis. I do not know of any psychologist who observes adults in the same fashion before turning to hypotheses and methodological design.

The difference is obvious: in order to leave spontaneity untouched, the naturalistic observer takes into account the perspective of expressed behaviour as it manifests itself in ontogenetically regulated acts. This he can do because he is coping with non-cultural subjects. The experimenter, on the other hand, cannot but exclude this approach, because it is incompatible with scientific accuracy. Experimenting on spontaneity is a self-contradictory enterprise. The experimenter is studying cultural beings and he must extirpate cultural biases if he wants to reach what he supposes to be the true deterministic realm of behavioural facts. He expects to find them in physiology, not in ontogenetic time; in timeless realities, not in history; in the behaviour of an abstract subject, not in the historical subject. But we immediately notice that historical facts cannot be objects of experience in the same direct sense as sense data. They are only known to us in the form of language or documents which are interpreted and verbalised. Historical facts are expressed by words whose relative position on the time-scale is determined by various critical procedures. Only the material documents establishing the validity of a proposition expressing the position of an event in time can give rise to direct sensory experience. At first glance, however, there would seem to be no characteristics common to history defined as cultural dimension and to history considered as an essential dimension of the living subject.[1] The common ground, as we shall see, must be sought in a biologically-based analysis of subjectivity, i.e. an analysis relying on the characteristics of the subject, as it actually expresses itself in its own ontogenetic time-dimension, i.e. as an active organism coping with its environment and not an abstract point of reference tentatively conceived as a physical timeless entity. The role of phenomenology in this perspective will be discussed in its turn.

3 *The abandonment of subjectivity*

Strangely enough, the elimination of the time-perspective from the scientific approach to the subject has resulted in the actual manifestations of subjectivity having been lost sight of. One might indeed have expected that the depersonalised subject of objective psychology would have lent itself more readily to factual determinations because it was always studied in experimental situations, whereas the subject as it appeared in purely reflective contexts could only exist as an abstract entity.

In fact, the subject is reduced to an abstract entity both in deductive and in inductive psychology, but for different and even opposite reasons: in the former case because speculative systems are entirely and sufficiently defined by a conceptual organisation, of which the notion of subject is a part; in the latter case, because the technical setting up of experiments and the mathematical treatment of data collected on the psychological subject cannot be achieved unless it is reduced to a system of immediate causes, i.e. to the actual source of the data, and ceases therefore to be the living organism endowed with life-experience. Factual determinations were foreign to philosophical theories on the subject; they remain limited to a timeless

---

[1]Cf. on this distinction, H. Spiegelberg, *The Phenomenological Movement*, The Hague, Nijhoff, 1960, Vol. I, pp. 337f. It is fashionable, however, in many phenomenological texts, to refer to the subject as a 'historical' being in a sense akin to Heidegger's definition of the 'historical', which need not be analysed in detail in the context of this book.

pinpointing of discrete atomistic facts in experiments based on physical measurements. We may conclude from this that the abandonment of the historical approach which occurred as a consequence of experimental development in psychology was foreign to deductive psychology as such. It appears rather that when philosophers left the psychological scene, the idea of the individual as *becoming* was gradually dropped in favour of a punctate concept (and later of an operational concept) of subjectivity. It was the end of a mode of thought which had itself no essential roots in a subject-centred time-perspective.

But, one may ask, is a time-centred approach important in psychology? How does it happen that all epistemological critiques of the value of scientific psychology have consistently contrasted the historical subject with the purely spatially-determined scientific data obtained on the abstract timeless subject used in experiments? Why do phenomenologically-minded psychologists consider that controlled replications of an experiment in time (as, for instance, in longitudinal studies) do not in fact truly comply with the basic requirements of subjective time-perspective? Is such an expression not just a word that conveys some kind of regret on the part of clinical practitioners who have necessarily to cope with case histories and who consequently do not see any useful purpose in measurements pertaining to a particular moment in time because they feel or know by experience that tomorrow's data may contradict today's? And why then should philosophical reflections be invoked as an aid when scientific data appear irrelevant or useless? Are problems not being mixed up and would it not be worth trying to adjust accurate procedures for basically inaccurate situations? Finally, is the time-centred subject not just another definition and will not science progress efficiently in spite of all definitions whatsoever?

All these questions amount to asking: what is the essential meaning of the time-dimension in psychology? If our analysis is to achieve its aim, we should consider time-perspective neither from the point of view of time-psycho-physics, nor from the point of view of individual history. Our hypothesis must be a scientific one, more precisely a *biological* one, as we said before.

We hope to show that there exists a third solution in that direction and that this may help to eliminate the classical and mostly useless dichotomies of psychological systems and contribute ultimately to a better understanding of what the living subject really is. It is a hopeless attempt to try to reconcile philosophers with one another, a not less dramatic enterprise to bring scientific psychologists to agree on psychological laws which they would consider as having the universal meaning of physical laws, and it is often an impossible task to try to bring philosophers and scientists to use the same language though it is the only way to determine whether there may be some common ground of discussion. Whatever may be the case, the abandonment of subjectivity in favour of a schematic timeless representation of the individual did not allow psychology to realise its scientific ideal. In spite of the methodological one-sidedness which resulted from copying naturalistic procedures in the positivist age, experimental psychology in the strict sense remained, up to the present day, a field of ever-changing interpretations and of much inconsistent theorising. For nearly a century, the stress was laid on method refinement without questioning – except precisely in the phenomenological trend – the adequacy of the point of view (or *a priori*) implied by the so-called positive approach.

Let it be clear that the various methods devised or borrowed since the epoch of psychophysics can be justified as long as one keeps to their *internal* coherence. The debatable point is not their actual consistency or effectiveness in producing results considered as quantitative data apart from any particular context; it is their fitness for generating interpretations relevant to the active subject, in other words their *external* coherence.

Abandoning subjectivity amounts to overlooking the latter in favour of the former.

In the course of this process, different images of man as the subject-matter of psychology have been shaped. They range from the 'conscious' programmed subject as imagined by Behaviourists and model-espousing theorists to the 'unconscious' subject described by the various psychoanalytical schools, with a number of intermediate pictures corresponding to the beliefs or the various *a priori* of the systems which appeared in the history of psychology. Defining the latter as the science of behaviour does not solve the problem, since behaviour can be defined in many ways according to the point of view adopted. Behaviourists claim to be the only ones to study behaviour in a factual manner. But what argument can they put to the psychoanalyst who claims to be studying neurotic disturbances or adjustment imbalances? Is he not studying behaviour just because he refuses the behaviouristic image of man? Where, then, are the facts of behaviour? Who is objective and who is not?

This shows clearly, in our opinion, that the 'objectivistic' and 'subjectivistic' psychologists both philosophise about the psychological subject. Psychologists may be classified as philosophers who replaced old philosophical images of man by other images modelled on natural science. Their methodological efforts will not bring about any change in this situation unless they are ready to question their beliefs. Classical experimental psychology, Functionalism, Behaviourism, Gestaltism, Psychoanalysis, etc. were beliefs, and so are all recent trends insofar as they select an image of the subject without justifying their choice epistemologically.

This peculiar characteristic of psychological systems shows that they are cultural movements rather than true scientific systems, i.e. systems of ideas which borrow concepts from positive sciences and transform them according to current opinions about man and the world, thus leading to theories using a scientific vocabulary which does not necessarily refer, as such, to scientific facts.

For the sake of brevity, we shall refer to this phenomenon as 'culturalism' in the following sections of this book.

4   *The cultural origin of psychological concepts*

To what extent has scientific psychology been related to fundamental biological teachings during the course of its history? Since the very first moments of its official existence, experimental psychology was bound up with physiology in a very explicit manner. The meaning of this relation is to be found in the conviction that the origin of subjective phenomena was the activity of the sense organs. Comparative and animal psychology originated from the work of Darwin, who for the first time defended a general theory in which all living organisms, including man, were linked with each other on a zoological continuum. In addition to this, the psychometric trend resulting from Galton's investigations can also have ascribed to it an authentic biological origin, because it was founded on biometrical measurements and aimed at an improvement of the species through eugenics. How can it be understood that psychology gradually evolved apart from biology and even came to be at variance with biological teaching, given the fact that its foundations were sensory processes, evolutionary continuity and bodily measurements? The answer suggested in the previous section is that the first scientific psychologists, though unceasingly reasserting the biological or physiological origin of their newly-born discipline, *transformed it unawares into a cultural system.*

Wundt, for instance, uses physiological concepts like 'sensation' in order to promote the introspective search for elements of consciousness. But such an act, insofar as it proves possible, has more to do with the romantic discovery of the individual self than with laboratory measurements of peripheral functions. His tenet that the so-called higher functions can only be studied in a psychology of peoples (*Völkerpsychologie*) amounts to diluting objective psychological approaches in a vague sociological culturalism. Fechner's earlier psychophysical work originated, as is well known, from an animistic mysticism dealing with the relations between the material and the spiritual. Thirty years later, Loeb was to try to establish universal mechanicism and to find in his tropisms a sufficient experimental basis for philosophising on human liberty. Watson was for a time a very technical experimenter and methodologist, but he turned finally to Behaviouristic propaganda, being similar, in this respect, to Pavlov who spent a great deal of time delivering lectures all over Russia to spread the reflexological faith. To those tempted to consider this curious scientific proselytism as belonging to the heroic epoch, the way Skinner jumps from operant conditioning to education and social happiness should demonstrate that scientific psychology still indulges in culturalism.

One may wonder, however, whether these cultural alterations and misuse of scientific concepts would have been possible if the concepts themselves had been authentically scientific. Only pseudo-biological concepts can evolve into the rudimentary and altogether misleading philosophy of life that still pervades a great deal of psychological work. In other words, the concepts borrowed from biology may be precisely the ones which biologists themselves would already consider in many instances as uncritical or controversial. Mechanistic and vitalistic concepts, for instance, belonged readily, in biology itself, to controversial issues. They were more likely to be interpreted 'psychologically' than concepts endowed with a technical meaning, such as 'metabolic rate' or 'action potential'. In such cases, however, psychologists are tempted to use them as indices of subjective experience without boldly adopting them. Today's physiological psychologists are aware of the dangers of hasty interpretations in this field.

To summarise, there is a double movement in the alienating evolution of objective psychology: firstly, an extension of biological concepts to so-called subjective phenomena which, as such, are supposed to exist exclusively at the level of private consciousness; secondly, a transformation of these subjective phenomena into a cultural system of concepts simply replicating the current life situation.

A cross-examination of the comparative vocabularies of biology, psychology and current culture would show that in many cases some words are missing and that there exists a list of biological terms without psycho-cultural equivalents and vice versa. What psychological term could be found that might correspond to 'efference' or 'blood irrigation of the cortex'? Conversely, which biological terms will translate psychological concepts like 'fear' or 'disgust', not to mention 'emotion' or 'feeling of security'? There is, of course, much scope for discussion and interpretation of a great number of words at present used in the psychological and cultural vocabularies. Let us just remark in passing that the most misleading words are, as would be expected, those which refer to dissimilar phenomena under an identical form: 'fatigue', 'adaptation', 'activity', etc. do have precise meanings in physiology and biology. Psychologists do use them very frequently, but one may wonder whether they could furnish anything but a vague description, if they were required to define the words in question.

In all cases where a meaning is generally accepted, the concepts refer to facts and events that clearly belong to biology, as in neuropsychology, objective animal behaviour studies, biocybernetics and bio-communication studies.

5   *Reductionism and intuitive biology*

Psychological culturalism appears to distort biological teaching unavoidably because of the illegitimate extension of operationally defined scientific concepts to the human action of the subject. Thus objective psychology was at first a composite of positivism and nineteenth-century individualism. Its later developments can be related in the same manner to important social and ideological changes, to basic discoveries in other fields of knowledge, etc. Behaviourism and Functionalism find their conceptual origin in American liberalism and industrialism, in the sense that a model of efficiency in competition was a natural demand of such a social system. There is no need to add that the enslavement of psychological theories to philosophical creeds has followed similar lines of emergence. Gestalt psychology, for instance, may be considered as the final product of Kantian phenomenalism, or, more precisely, as an attempt to establish a kind of perceptual realism set free from doctrinal positivism, and from the sensation-cognition dilemmas of the Graz school. Many more instances of this conceptual evolution could be quoted.

The main point remains, however, that authentic scientific concepts cannot, in virtue of their very nature, undergo degenerative processes of this kind. The notions of mass and energy are not subject to opinion changes and will never become cultural topics. As Drüe (1963) rightly remarks, Relativity Theory did not destroy Newtonian physics. It actually enlarged the scope of classical physics by considering phenomena at a different order of velocity, this transformation having had as an indirect consequence that the status of the observer in physics became an object of epistemological inquiry.[1]

Psychological culturalism, on the other hand, does not succeed in completely eliminating subjective experience and even helps to bring back the subject to concrete situations from which he was excluded by the scientific approach. In the latter perspective, his fundamental time-dimension, for instance, which corresponds to experienced time as opposed to measured or objective time, fades away because every objective determination occurs as an event occupying a particular position in a succession of discrete moments. Should this process be fully completed in any psychological experiment, there would be no means of distinguishing between a psychological experiment and a purely physiological one. But it never happens, because the cultural transformation of borrowed biological concepts place both the subject and the investigation in an extended frame of time. The subject is never reduced to the absolute crossing-*point* of a given set of variables. The dimensions of the psychological experiment are described and tentatively transformed into parameters in an incomplete fashion. They belong *in principle* to the impersonal order of numerical data and mathematical functions and *theoretically* reduce the subject to a limited number of operational

[1]H. Drüe, *Husserls system der phaenomenologischen Psychologie*, Berlin, De Gruyter, 1963, p. 7. It is noteworthy that the problem of the observer arose in physics as a consequence of relativity, though actual relativistic effects cannot be observed at the orders of velocity of subjective time. On the contrary, the time framework of classical physics is, in many instances, of the same order of magnitude as the observer's subjective time. This explains why physicalist reductionism necessarily refers to Galilean and Newtonian models as a matter of course. It also shows that relativistic concepts cannot give rise to a new type of physicalism in psychology. They lend themselves, however, to cultural assimilation. Cf. in this, respect J. Ortega y Gasset, *The Modern Theme*, London, Daniel, 1931, pp. 135f.

probabilities. But, *in fact*, this reduction process is never completed because the subject is an organism who spontaneously inserts himself in the experiment as in any other current life-situation, who speaks to the experimenter in his own language, who accepts the experiment as something ordinary or pleasant, or rejects it in the same manner as he endures a boring visit, etc.[1] But in these conditions, the experiment has become unscientific at the beginning of the very first operation of the experimenter's programme.

Something should therefore be added to the analyses which Straus[2] and von Weizsäcker[3] in particular have devoted to this topic. These authors have stressed very clearly the shortcomings of physicalist procedures in human (and comparative) psychology. They have shown convincingly that dealing with a human individual means dealing with an organism, not with an entity. However, critical views entirely based on the contrast between what is experimentally formalised and what is subjectively experienced have little chance, in our opinion, in resulting in effectively constructive and heuristic propositions. The strong point of such analyses is the manner in which they throw light on the limits of the implicit epistemology of classical objective psychology. Their weak point is to accord a true scientific status to concepts and procedures which, in fact, do not deserve such a characterisation. A great many experiments performed on the human subject are not rigorous ones according to the standards of the exact sciences psychology tends to imitate. Therefore, every criticism directed at the negative effects of physicalism in psychology should first establish that the latter can really be considered on a par with the natural sciences. We do not see how such equivalence could be proved. This being the case, one is bound to conclude that the charge of neglecting subjective experience is not sufficient to condemn objective psychology as a whole. A much heavier charge involves stressing the basically cultural nature of apparently scientific concepts. In other words, the main fault of objective psychology is the building up of a science with face-validity.

---

[1] An important theoretical clarification of this problem can be found in A. Giorgi, 'Phenomenology and Experimental Psychology, I', *Rev. of Exist. Psychol. and Psychiatr.*, 1965, 5, pp. 228–38, and 'II', *Ibid.*, 1966, 6, pp. 37–50. The fruitfulness of the phenomenological approach in actual experimental work is illustrated by the same author's study: 'A phenomenological approach to the problem of meaning and serial learning', *Rev. of Exist. Psychol. and Psychiatr.* 1967, 7, pp. 106–18. In this experiment, subjects had to learn words or letters using the method of serial anticipation. At the end of the performance, they were asked to state which of the two lists was easier to learn. In doing so, they were in a position to consider 'the dialectical relationship between the already-constituted meanings of the *items* and the act of constituting a meaning in the *situation*' (*Ibid.*, p. 117). The author stresses the fact that the use of such a phenomenological approach modified the meaning of the experimental results. This example shows that the combined use of experimental methods and a phenomenological analysis of the experimental situation itself is significantly enlarging the psychological scope of classical experiments.

[2] E. Straus, *Vom Sinn der Sinne*, Berlin, Springer, 1935 (2nd edn. 1956). English translation by J. Needleman, *The Primary World of Senses: a Vindication of Sensory Experience*, New York, Free Press of Glencoe, 1963.

[3] V. von Weizsäcker, *Der Gestaltkreis*, Stuttgart, G. Thieme, 1939.

Considered in this way, psychology often appears as a kind of intuitive biology.[1]

The elimination of subjectivity in favour of objective reductionism appears, however, less complete than it would seem to be at first glance. The reason for this is that the typical culturalism of psychology still allows for subjective experience, but within a horizon of time which never transcends enthusiasm, irrational assent, fashion or ephemeral social demands. As long as pure phenomenology will not consider such a problem worthy of its attention, its role in phenomenological psychology will remain limited to that of being its historical roots. The motivating forces of today's psychology are as radical as those of phenomenology itself when Husserl raised his claims against psychologism, logicism, historicism and sheer philosophies of culture. The psychology in the making can become an authentic science given that it will evolve from the stage of intuitive biology to that of biology in the true sense of the word. We mean *biology*, not *biologism*.[2] Such an achievement can only be thought of if culturalism leaves the scene and opens the way to the broader perspectives of ontogenetic and phylogenetic time.

The requirement that the time-dimension of the subject should be the proper reference-point of a biologically oriented psychology raises in its turn a number of crucial issues. It may be argued, for instance, that the ontogenic aspects of man must have been thoroughly studied in developmental psychology, and that a wealth of biologically well-based data has been collected in observations and experiments on children of various ages. It is a fact that genetic psychology is very close to an authentic biology of behaviour. A significant proof of it can be found in the comparative developmental studies of the young child and the young chimpanzee, not to mention recent studies on facial expression and non-verbal behaviour in children and monkeys.[3] These approaches are truly biological because they are outside the realm of language. But as soon as the child has mastered his mother tongue well enough to cope with current situations, he becomes an object of study for psychometry. From this moment on, behaviour-observations are replaced by tests and the psychologist looks for aptitudes and skill. It had been known for

[1] The extension of neurophysiological concepts like 'reflex' or 'inhibition' to broad behavioural patterns and to psychotic states, for instance, appears in many cases as an arbitrary semantic shift. On the other hand, there have been many 'good guesses' in psychological theory. Psychoanalytical notions relating to the neurogenic effects of early experience, for instance, found their biological counterpart in the phenomena of imprinting as observed by ethologists.

[2] Biologism understood as a reductionist epistemological standpoint can be criticised on the same grounds as psychologism, though the idea that biology is the fundamental science of man has gained wide acceptance today, albeit in a different sense, under the influence of comparative ethology.

[3] J.A.R.A.M. Van Hooff, *Aspecten van het sociale gedrag en de communicatie bij Humane en hogere niet-Humane Primaten* (Aspects of the social behaviour and communication in human and higher non-human primates), Rotterdam, Bronder, 1971; *Idem*, 'A comparative approach to the phylogeny of laughter and smiling', in R. A. Hinde (ed.), *Non-verbal Communication*, Cambridge University Press, 1972, pp. 209–41.

decades that the vast majority of tests are culture-bound and that they cannot pretend to yield evidence on any true biological element in a child's action patterns.[1] This is not surprising since the demands of society can only be fulfilled in terms of acquired behaviour. In civilised communities, the 'natural man' does not exist and there is no room for individuals who do not comply with socially established learning requirements. The only categories of behaviour that are proper to the species and are directly enhanced by the cultural milieu are either primary bodily functions like walking, or instincts underlying sexual behaviour. A more detailed analysis of this question will be given in Chapter 5.

6   Clinical cases and scientific phenomena

Let us now consider a completely different domain, where psychological culturalism has exerted a considerable influence, viz. clinical psychology in the broad sense. According to a well-established tradition, clinical psychology investigates the assets and liabilities of the individual with a view to finding, in each particular instance, optimal lines of development, and to facilitating adjustment to ordinary life. Harriman (1947), from whom this tentative definition is partly quoted, adds that 'tests and measures are used as helpful tools in gathering data, but much of the benefit comes from the practical experience of the clinical psychologist'. A survey of other current definitions given by textbooks shows that most authors consider clinical psychology as a field in which scientific laws are applied to reach a solution in individual instances, so that it is finally considered as an area of the 'science of human behaviour' aiming at a global understanding of the individual.

One may ask, however, how scientific inquiry can have anything to do with the treatment of individual cases. It might of course be argued that clinical work – psychological or medical – may become scientific by virtue of repeated success: initially non-scientific procedures that 'work' in a great number of successive 'cases' should be considered as approaching the status of an inductive truth. At first sight, such an assimilation seems legitimate. In fact, it is misleading for the following reasons: firstly, the criterion of repeated success is, in itself, purely pragmatic. It is never possible to determine whether similar positive outcomes are due to identical causes if comparability between different instances has not been previously established. Secondly, the successes obtained with different individuals vary in meaning according to the private history of each single individual.

The *private case* cannot be considered the equivalent of a *single case* occurring in a series of reproducible events. Indeed, if they were to be so

---

[1]Cf. A. Gobar, *Philosophic Foundations of Genetic Psychology and Gestalt Psychology*, The Hague, Nijhoff, 1968. This work analyses several basic aspects of the relations between psychology and biology, and gives a critical account of Piaget's genetic epistemology from the point of view of the philosophy of science.

considered, it would be hard to understand why the personal experience of the clinical psychologist is so important in securing success in therapy. Having regard to the wide range of clinical methods and to the endless controversies between them, one may suspect that the theoretical views that are put forward to justify them are very far from expressing fundamental laws of human behaviour.

But, once again, this cannot be held to be a basic objection against clinical psychology as such. For one thing, in spite of their theoretical disagreements, all clinical approaches emphasise, in one way or another, the need for reconstructing the history of the individual in order to unravel the particular events that may be responsible for his present state. Much confusion has arisen from the conviction that such particular events may be termed 'causes' in the scientific sense of the word. A true causal event results from a controlled situation in which the so-called causal factor has been singled out and varied in isolation. Because of the impossibility of tracing back true causes in an individual history by applying strict deterministic procedures, some clinical schools – existential psychopathology and phenomenological psychiatry in particular – have rejected every form of causal analysis. They consider that causal thinking as such is unfitted for any kind of psychological work. This has led them logically to condemn experimental psychology *in toto*, and even every reference to physiology and to biology in their own field in favour of 'understanding'.[1] The important point for our purpose at this stage of our analysis is the bearing of this anti-scientific attitude on the time-dimension of the individual. It may seem, on superficial examination, that the centring of clinical approaches on the private history of an individual is an exceptionally good way of introducing and preserving his temporal status in psychological work.

But how does the psychologist actually establish individual history? He will first claim that he is respecting subjective motives by insisting that the patient should collaborate with him in looking into his personal past life in order to extract from himself the salient features of his development that may contribute to a deeper understanding of his present maladjustment. This the person under treatment does by telling the therapist of such and such events of his life that he remembers in a more or less precise manner. By talking with the therapist, the patient will progressively find that he can remember things which had fully disappeared from his consciousness. The emergence of such events at the conscious level is achieved – in psychoanalysis and in other kinds of clinical approach – by formulating past experiences in the actual language of the therapeutic dialogue. In other words, the individual past history is being

[1]On the philosophical origins of the opposition between *causalism* and *understanding* in psychology, cf. A. Giorgi, *Psychology as a Human Science*, New York, Harper and Row, 1970, pp. 21f. Giorgi's analysis gives an excellent account of Dilthey's original part in shaping the thesis of his book. In a further section, Merleau-Ponty's critique of causal relations is discussed (pp. 199f.).

reintroduced into the lived present through language. No such operation can be endowed with the authenticity of a *fact*, unless the actual wording of events refers to a previous wording of the same by the subject. This previous wording may have occurred in completely different terms and even in a very imperfect form – but it *must* have happened. I cannot possibly refer to any object or living being of my early individual history if I did not *name* them in one way or another at the precise moment of my past at which I was actually confronted with them. If this guarantee fails, I am talking of something that lies outside my own history because the first moment of *my* history coincides with the memory of the first sentence I ever uttered.

This means that my individual history has begun when my ontogenetic development has been already on the way for some time. Such a statement may sound rather trite, but it stresses a fundamental difficulty which arises as soon as one is tempted to confuse history and ontogeny. The development of language is a biological fact that may be compared, so far as its organic mechanisms are concerned, with the development of any other communication system in animal species. But because of its characteristic algorithmic transformations,[1] it represents a unique evolutionary feature, whose effects have been the emergence of a human world essentially different from the world of all other beings. Therefore, the basic differences between animals and man, from the point of view of organism–environment relations, is that the animal's ontogenetic development proceeds, so to speak, on a continuum of events, all of which remain comparable at all moments of its life, whereas man transcends his ontogeny by symbolic language, and starts exerting a distinctively human influence on his surroundings, as soon as he begins to use speech.

Consequently, adhering to a historical perspective proper to the human individual does not lead to the objective consideration of his situation as an organism endowed with certain particular potentialities which should be approached biologically. This is a specific problem encountered by students of human ethology.[2]

Considering now the way in which clinical psychologists try to theorise on the basis of their relation with their patient, it appears clearly that the major obstacles they meet result from their obligation to reconstruct ontogeny from individual history. More precisely, they seek to go back to the biological foundations of behaviour from the sequence of individual experiences, as told by the patient while recapitulating his own history in the course of the clinical dialogues. This explains, in our opinion, why clinicians with an excellent

---

[1]N. I. Zhinkin, 'An Application of the Theory of Algorithms to the Study of Animal Speech: Methods of Vocal Intercommunication between Monkeys', in R. G. Busnel (ed.), *Acoustic Behaviour of Animals*, Amsterdam, Elsevier, 1963, pp. 132–83.

[2]Cf. on this point R. A. Hinde (ed.), *Non-verbal Communication*, Cambridge University Press, 1972; J. Illies, *Zoologie des Menschen*, Munich, Piper, 1971; K. Lorenz, *Die Rückseite des Spiegels*, Munich, Piper, 1974. For a general introduction to human ethology, 1 cf. I. Eibl-Eibesfeldt, *Ethology, the Biology of Behaviour*, New York, Holt, Rinehart & Winston, 1970, pp. 248f.

training in physiology and neuropathology have often indulged in hypotheses and theories that make little or no sense to the biologist. Freudian concepts like the Oedipus complex, the 'murder of the father', the 'death instinct', etc. – not to mention more refined concepts put forward by various psychoanalytical sub-groups – are totally devoid of meaning if they are presented as expressing biological realities of the organism as an adaptive system. Oddly enough, psychoanalytical concepts that prove biologically acceptable are precisely those that are based on behaviour patterns observed during phases of development before the appearance of language. The typical relations between the mother and the newborn child, for instance, can easily be translated into ethological terms. Nevertheless, psychoanalytical theory has endowed these relations with symbolic meanings that are evidently cultural and mythical.

7 Subjectivity v. subjectivism

Many critical views on the value of psychology as a science have one point in common, viz. the accusation of subjectivism as opposed to the rigorous objectivism of positive scientific knowledge. However, the mere use of such a word does not clarify the epistemological difficulties encountered by psychology in elaborating its concepts and systems of reference. In many instances, *subjectivism* has been grossly confused with *subjectivity*, which amounts to a condemnation of psychology as a whole because its subject-matter is the human subject.

Sinha (1969) remarks that 'subjectivism' may have different meanings. According to him, it may be considered as describing everything that is psychologically determined. *Subjectivism* in this sense is equivalent to *psychologism* and can be contrasted with *objectivism*, the latter defining the point of view of positive science. But the term is also used to designate the 'merely personal'. Sinha adds: 'this meaning, it is obvious, is closely analagous to the first one, and the two ... may almost be regarded as emphasising respectively the two aspects of the same truth – what is personal is empirically a psychological entity, and what is psychological is at the same time personal'.[1]

Two more interpretations of 'subjectivism' are further discussed by Sinha: they express the subject-relatedness of phenomena and the constitutive character of the perceiver. In our opinion, a still more profound definition of subjectivism may be tentatively given. From the epistemological point of view, it is the subject-related character of any phenomenon that should receive the most careful consideration because it is from that point of view that the time-dimension of the subject can be properly analysed. But, if one keeps in mind the distinction drawn above between *ontogenetic* and *historical* perspectives, it

---

[1] D. Sinha, *Studies in Phenomenology*, The Hague, Nijhoff, 1969, pp. 51–2.

appears that the difference stressed by Sinha between what is subjective and what is private can be interpreted in a more fundamental manner. Subjectivity, seen from the point of view of constitution, has an unequivocal meaning if it is related to ontogeny. Subjectivism, on the contrary, appears as soon as ontogeny and history are being confused since history presupposes language, as we have already said. It is by virtue of this surreptitious confusion that subjectivism readily refers to a distortion of subjectivity in its constitutive sense.[1]

This may help us to understand why many concepts of psychology have been borrowed from biology and transformed into cultural entities. It helps, moreover, to understand why the objective scientist rejects these concepts as 'subjective'. His rejection is based on the fact that he perceives the non-constitutive character of cultural modes of speaking insofar as the latter are expressed in terms which only make sense in a biological vocabulary.

Two conclusions may be drawn from the preceding analysis. The transformation of biological concepts into cultural entities has led psychology to extrapolate its theoretical constructs, so that it pronounces on problems which are basically foreign to its subject-matter. This explains, at least partly, why psychological research of the experimental type has always encountered major difficulties in trying to relate behavioural facts to so-called underlying mechanisms: these mechanisms can only be traced in authentic biological experiments allowing, as in animal behaviour, work on an ontogenetic continuum. The fact that scientific psychology is unawares cultural in its nature raises the problem of its value as a general anthropology. It may indeed be argued that the cultural value of psychology and its purely historically-based nature make it more liable to become a truly human science than a biologically oriented one. Such an argument can only be properly discussed in the light of the possible relations between phenomenology and ethology. This topic will be considered in Chapter 5.

8   *The time-perspective in psychology*

In the course of this chapter, we have referred repeatedly to the time-dimension of subjectivity and stressed its theoretical importance in the epistemological analysis of psychology. This point must be treated now in a more detailed manner.

The reason for considering the time-perspective as a basic issue in psychological epistemology is the very nature of the subject's temporality. The main trend of analyses in this field has been mostly a negative one; it has

[1] The phenomenological theory of constitution refers to the progressive structuring of the world by consciousness. It is linked in some way with the organising power of perception as expounded in Gestalt theory and can be analysed in its passive and active aspects. Suffice it to say here that it is one of the phenomenological themes which has the most obvious relations with the theory of the organisms' own worlds as outlined by J. von Uexküll and the biologists who followed his teachings, among whom early ethologists should be quoted in the first instance.

resulted in a sheer opposition between physical time and subjective time. This dichotomy corresponds to a factual difference between physical and psychological phenomena, but it would be of little use to underline it without trying to draw the consequences of it for the building up of an adequate *a priori* conception of the psychological subject. Once again, the use of the expression *a priori* should not convey the idea that we must rely at the outset on an arbitrary definition of the subject in order to proceed further; it should be understood once and for all that we are *bound* to adopt a point of departure to characterise the realm of phenomena we call psychological and that this obligation leads us, by its very existence, to remark that the classical idea that the subject is a physical system among others (Reductionism) is devoid of meaning both in psychology and in biology.

The peculiar nature of subjective time was first stressed in an explicit manner by Bergson; it was not primarily a phenomenological issue. However, in contrasting the continuous time-flow of consciousness with the discontinuity of measurable physical time, Bergson inaugurated, concurrently with William James, a new approach to the nature of consciousness which had major consequences in phenomenology and in psychology. His interpretation of physical time (the 'time of clocks') as being the result of dividing the subjective continuum by geometrically-inspired intellect need not concern us here, nor his theory of the *élan vital* and his doubtful interpretation of evolutionary processes. Nevertheless, Bergson deeply influenced Minkowski's phenomenology of 'lived time'.[1]

Though Bergson himself never referred to 'lived time' as such, his conviction that intuition could grasp the continuous flow of consciousness contributed to drawing the attention of psychologists to qualities peculiar to subjective life. In the phenomenological movement itself, the founding systematic study is due to Husserl himself whose researches on the phenomenology of the consciousness of time were carried out between 1905 and 1917 and published by Heidegger in 1928.[2] Among later analyses of subjective time inspired by phenomenology, the various contributions of Binswanger and Straus deserve special mention.[3]

Phenomenological analyses of 'lived time' do not specifically focus on the 'lived' understood as the impression of duration or time-span, or interval, etc. as experienced by this or that individual in particular conditions. This topic is that of the subjective time-content and has been widely treated in experimental psychology. However, the point under discussion transcends the problems of reaction time, decision processes, time estimations and the like, which all suppose that subjective time can find an adequate expression in

[1] E. Minkowski, *Le temps vécu: Etudes phénoménologiques et psychopathologiques*, Paris, D'Artrey, 1933. English translation, *Lived time*, Evanston, Northwestern University Press, 1970.
[2] E. Husserl, *Vorlesungen zur Phënomenologie des inneren Zeitbewusstseins*, Halle, Niemeyer, 1928.
[3] L. Binswanger, *Grundformen und Erkenntnis menschlichen Daseins*, Zürich, Niehans, 1942; E. Straus, *Vom Sinn der Sinne*, Berlin, Springer, 1935.

corresponding values of physical time. Here more than anywhere else, the psychophysical approach remains prevalent. Besides, the problem of psychological time was raised indirectly in new terms in relation to the design of 'purposive machines', which were, for a time, rather hastily endowed with temporal characteristics similar to those of the living subject.

Referring to this transposition (as expressed by Wiener in his seminal work on cybernetics published in 1948), Buytendijk writes: 'Thus the modern automaton exists in the same sort of Bergsonian time as the living organism. This is only *apparently* the case. The automaton does show quasi-living forms of time; duration (*durée*-Bergson), prolepsis, "tentative and retrograde purpose" (Auersperg), a memory (knowledge of the past); but it is impossible to take these properties into consideration *in* themselves, i.e. without the designer who has included all this in his programming. The machine is only a "reality", that is to say, a perceptible and thinkable phenomenon in our human world, together with the designer; this is also the case when an automaton can *itself* program *on the basis of* a programme.' He concludes: 'A subjectively determined performance cannot be described as a series of processes which take place in physical time, because each performance develops *itself*. The concept of *genesis* can only be used in the organic world.'[1]

This summarises the reasons which force us to give up every hope that any kind of psychophysical approach to subjective time, however refined it may be, may tackle the problem of subjective time-constitution as such. Moreover, as Buytendijk's text suggests, the biological outlook is, *as a scientific mode of analysis*, entirely different from a psychological approach borrowing physical concepts to apply them to the conscious organism and from any attempt at devising machines or models supposedly endowed with the time-features of the living subject.

If the claim of phenomenology is that 'lived' time should neither become some private dimension of life – which would bring us back to the introspective point of view – nor a pure object of quantitative subjective determination – as in current experimental psychology – what is the meaning of its stressing the basic significance of the time-perspective for an adequate study of the subject?

First, from a general epistemological point of view, the time-perspective appears as the basic aspect of psychological phenomena which allows definition of them at a level of *a priori* which places them in their own realm and therefore dispenses with any reductive procedure. Seen from this angle, phenomenology appears as the sole basic discipline liable to guarantee psychology a true autonomy of standpoint. The spontaneity of behaviour, which is also stressed in ethology, can only be fully recognised and taken into account in working hypotheses, if the special nature – or 'essence' in the

[1]F. J. J. Buytendijk, *Prolegomena to an Anthropological Physiology*, Pittsburgh, Duquesne University Press, 1974, pp. 223–4.

phenomenological sense – of subjectivity is properly acknowledged in its *factual* existence.

It is therefore in the facts themselves that a justification of this point of view must be found. In the traditional outlook, the design of experiments on perceptual or cognitive phenomena is based on a preconception according to which sensory information necessarily precedes responses in time and may therefore be readily considered as their cause. This postulate has been universally accepted since the early days of psychophysics and of sensory psychology. However, as Buytendijk puts it, 'we note that each performance proceeds in such a way that it has reference from the beginning to what still has to come and to what has already occurred. Moreover, V. von Weizsäcker in his theory of the 'Gestalt circle' has claimed: 'that no causal relation between sensation and movement exists in a performance . . . The "Gestalt circle" is, therefore, an absolutely different concept from a cybernetic circuit, for subjective self-regulation has a *time structure of its own*'.[1]

It is this structure which is overlooked in all cases where experimentation is carried out within the atomistic framework of conceptual physical time. The succession of separate events reducible to dimensionless points is no adequate model for the actions of an organism. No goal-directed behaviour, for instance, can be properly analysed without considering expectation, anticipation and remodelling of the teleological processes when they are already in the stage of realisation. The analysis of the phenomenon of 'emptiness' is a good illustration of what is meant here.[2]

Keeping in mind the requirements of scientific method and of scientific explanation themselves, the fundamental issue in the criticisms of Buytendijk, von Weizsäcker and Straus is that extrapolating the theoretical model of physical time to the study of the behaviour of organisms leads to conclusions

---

[1]Buytendijk, *op. cit.*, p. 222.

[2]'Silence and not speaking are not one and the same thing, except from a physical standpoint. Nor is silence and the lack of sound waves one and the same thing. Silence is experienced as emptiness because, within the context of our primary relationship to the world, we ask questions which remain unanswered. All sensory impressions are answers to questions; they are not simply there in the way in which the physiological processes underlying them are. We receive sensory impressions insofar as we orient ourselves within our primary relationship with the world by questing, seeking, expecting. Here too, we may be left without answers. We then experience silence, or any of the other manifestations of emptiness. We have learned from Pavlov's experiments that animals also respond to emptiness. We must conclude from this that they sense the world about them, to which – anticipating a response – they are directed in searching. If this is so, we must further conclude that the phenomena which Pavlov called conditioned reflexes cannot really be reflexes at all. It does not explain phenomena to speak of them as the supposed epiphenomena of hypostatised physiological processes. And it adds to the confusion to resort to a theory of isomorphism in order to account for the relationship between experience and physiological processes. We do not reject such a theory because it has not yet been proven but because we consider it basically impossible . . . Pavlov's basic mistake, which he inherited from Cartesian philosophy by way of natural science, is the view that it is possible to explain any relationship to the world as a process in the organism, that a situation can be explained as a situs, and that the process of becoming can be understood as an objective time sequence.' (E. Straus, *The Primary World of Senses*, New York, Free Press of Glencoe, 1963, pp. 101–2)

which do violence to what observation reveals. More will be said on this in the course of Chapter 3 when we shall consider the meaning of Sherrington's physiological teachings for the objective study of behavioural phenomena. But we must already note that the acceptance of the phenomenological perspective as the foundation of psychology shows a striking convergence with the point of view of biologists and physiologists concerned with an approach to behaviour and functions linked with the basic potentialities of the living organism. And it is not mere chance if the subjective time-dimension emerges in both fields as the main aspect of the organism's behavioural constitution.[1]

A last problem must be considered. Leaving aside the classical dualistic views which confused subjectivity with private consciousness, we came progressively to the conclusion that subjectivity is, in its positive meaning, an essential feature of the behaving organism. Hence the adequacy in principle of a biology of behaviour in the epistemological context of phenomenology.

As far as subjective time as a constitutional aspect of the living organism is concerned, we shall see later that in Sherrington's description of the structure of behaviour, space and time cannot be dissociated from each other.[2] The primary nature of time which we underlined in this paragraph must therefore be further justified.

In the structure of the organism's subjective field, space can be extended or contracted. It is endowed with reversibility. But the 'far' and the 'near' can give rise to equally meaningful relations when the organism actively explores his surroundings. Subjective time, on the contrary, is irreversible and does not allow for any kind of symmetrical variation. It is this irreversible course of actualisation which makes time the primary dimension of behavioural expression. Only in theoretical physics can time be reversed and contracted. But these transformations are beyond subjective awareness by virtue of their representational essence.[3] And so is the historical time of culture, which is

[1] It may be argued that physiologists, psychologists and psychiatrists who developed these views did so precisely because they fell under the influence of pre-existing phenomenology, so that invoking the convergence of their theories with phenomenological teachings is a vicious circle. The important issue, however, is not primarily historical. Whatever the priorities in time may be, it remains true that interpretations which originated from different fields of analysis actually fitted together and led, in one way or another, to the rejection of objectivistic postulates in psychology.

[2] Cf. Chapter 3, p. 88.

[3] The problem of representation in physics and in psychology is not entirely solved, however, by simply opposing physical time as an abstract frame of reference to subjective time as a lived experience. The theoretical limits of this opposition can be understood more clearly if one refers to Relativity Theory in the technically accessible presentations of it given by Einstein himself (A. Einstein, *Relativity, the special and the general Theory*, London, Methuen, 14th edn, 1946). In this text and in similar ones (cf. for instance J. H. Smith, *Introduction to special Relativity*, New York, Benjamin, 1965), an attempt is made to convey an idea of the basic phenomena of Relativity by referring to examples taken from current situations of observation. The contraction or dilatation of time is illustrated by the well-known example of the two observers, one reading the time on a clock in a moving train, the other on a stationary clock on a station platform. The issue is that the two observers will read different times on their respective clocks, although an *actual* difference in readings would require that this comparative experiment should be performed at the velocity of

only conveyed to us by knowledge and which can only be present in our actual behaviour under the form of symbolic representation. In the latter, we have to do with abstract time, whose image is, as in physical diagrams, a line on which we can locate discrete points.

Referring to what we said before of 'culturalism' in psychology, we may now understand better why psychological concepts based on such foundations do not fit actual facts of behaviour and lead to experiments and theories which are not relevant to the subject's own phenomena. This process, as we noted before, is one which develops in two steps: natural science is the basic model that is tentatively imitated, but it appears after a time that this can only be successful in devising some particular methods. In a later phase, as hypotheses and theories prove unable to assimilate physical concepts – a process in which neither their contents nor possible translation rules are considered – psychology turns unawares to opinions, but still tends to use the vocabulary of its initial model.

Contrary to well-received ideas, the attempt to copy physical models not only deprives psychology of the means needed to adequately achieve its purpose – studying the behaviour of the organism – but also reduces its accuracy. Again, the explanation of this is to be found in the fact that what is imitated or copied is not authentic natural science, but its cultural surrogate. Abstract pigeon-holing of 'stimulations', 'functions', 'motivations' and the like is effected in a historical perspective which is devoid of the exactness of physical time-determination but sufficiently remote from the actual time-dimension of the subject to allow for the elaboration of psychological systems endowed with a minimum of internal coherence.

Neglecting the expressive dimension of behavioural acts as it can be observed at any moment of ontogenetic time condemns objectivistic psychology – and the human sciences in general – to using a great deal of sound methodology to investigate ill-defined objects.

---

light. The difficulty in grasping the point of this example is due to the fact that it is imagined in the framework of classical physics, where time is a universal invariant. In Newtonian mechanics, the invariance of time is an easily accepted postulate because it corresponds more closely to the abstract ideas of uniform or accelerated motion, in which space alone is changing. Both Newtonian and relativistic times are representations but the former *seems* less foreign to experienced time than the latter, because behaviour phenomena occur at the same order of velocity as the motions of inanimate bodies which we currently observe. The error of objectivistic psychology is to deduce from this that Newtonian time and subjective time are essentially one and the same thing. In fact, subjective time as such corresponds neither to Newtonian nor to relativistic time-constructs, although they are both *objective* at their respective orders of velocity. To summarise: subjective time exists at the same order of magnitude as Newtonian physical time but, as a biological self-constitutive phenomenon, it cannot be expressed adequately in terms which only make sense for events occurring in pure inertial systems. Hence the necessity to accept the principle of a time *a priori* specific to the *objectively observed* behavioural systems.

Chapter 2

The Development of Phenomenology

In the preceding chapter we tentatively outlined the epistemological problems raised by the points of view currently adopted in psychology. We have stressed the fact that the basic criticisms directed against them originated in phenomenology. We noted further that some life-scientists influenced by phenomenological teachings had paved the way to a new biology of behaviour stressing the constitutive aspects of organic subjectivity. Finally, we discussed the nature of subjective time as opposed to physical time.

In order to understand more fully the origin and meaning of these problems, we must consider now the historical development of phenomenology.

1 *Empirical and experimental psychology*

It is customary to quote Wundt as the founder of scientific psychology without referring to the contribution of Brentano, his contemporary. The purely scientific tendency of Wundt stands at the beginning of laboratory psychology and is closely related to the psychophysical movement, which begins with Fechner who published his *Elemente der Psychophysik* in 1860. The reason why Brentano's work is mostly disregarded by psychologists is to be found in the fact that his *Act psychology* determined the later development of fundamental phenomenology. We shall see that Brentano's influence on Gestalt psychology has also been very strong, through the Graz school, and that phenomenology has taken two directions, one linked with experimental research (Stumpf) and one purely philosophical (Husserl).

In spite of the fact that Brentano called his psychology an *empirical* one, psychologists did not recognise him as one of their main ancestors because they always associated his name with phenomenology in the Husserlian sense, while ignoring the fact that Brentano published in the field of experimental psychology and had several followers who were true experimentalists. Among the latter, von Ehrenfels is often cited in connection with the theory of form-qualities, which is generally considered to be the corner-stone of Gestalt principles. This is only partly true, since the concept of Gestalt can be traced back with equal legitimacy to the theory of the 'figural moment' developed by Husserl in his *Philosophy of Arithmetic* (1891). To these names, those of Meinong, Cornelius, Witasek and Benussi should be added. Meinong appears as the leading figure in the Graz school. He founded the laboratory of experimental psychology in Graz in 1894 and favoured experimental work, particularly in the field of perception.

Perception was, indeed, the main topic of Austrian psychology at the end of the nineteenth century. But, unlike the elementarist school of Leipzig, the disciples of Brentano never attempted to study perceptual phenomena by assuming that every perception should be analysed in terms of aggregates of sensations, governed primarily by associative processes. The absence of associationism that characterises the Graz school enables one to understand that the main influence exerted by it on later developments in psychological theory – and on Gestalt views in particular – was an unravelling of the phenomenal aspects of perception, a direction basically foreign to the introspective reconstruction of the 'content of consciousness'.

Both Wundt and Brentano erected their psychologies on philosophical principles, but it is clear that Brentano's system was, from the start, oriented towards explanations allowing for a more 'subjective' kind of interpretation. If the intentional act is the leading concept, and not the analysis of consciousness (considered as a mere object of investigation), it is not surprising that a psychology developed on such a postulate should evolve into a phenomenology, i.e. into an approach stressing the constitutive origin and the structural organisation of perception, as an activity proper to the subject. Considering this development historically, we may say that it manifested itself first in Stumpf's *experimental phenomenology* (1906). Two parallel movements appeared during this period: Gestalt psychology and transcendental or pure phenomenology. As a consequence of the latter, fundamental epistemological problems were raised; these amount to a radical questioning of the value of psychology as a science.

The striking fact about the evolution of psychology since Brentano is that painstaking philosophical analyses should have been needed to focus psychology on the individual and his acts. The 'act' in the Brentanian sense refers to a constitutive relation with objects and events and not to action as such, though action may scarcely be considered psychologically outside the realm of the acts of consciousness. In other words, this concept refers to the modelling of the subject's essential capacity of building up his own world. Thus 'consciousness' acquires in this framework the meaning of an active instance, whatever the particular aspect of the subject's actual existence may be. One may further ask what sense it would make to speak of 'perceptual acts', as some Behaviourists would have it, if action in the observational sense of the word were the sole criterion. Whether perception is considered from the point of view of form qualities as with von Ehrenfels, or from the point of view of constitutive subjectivity as with Husserl, in either case one is concerned with a treatment of phenomena in themselves, as they actually exist for the experiencing subject. In such a perspective, it may be said that the Graz school occupies an intermediate position between element psychology and Gestalt psychology, the latter being itself situated half-way between experimental phenomenology and transcendental phenomenology. Whatever the case may be, the conflict between interiority and exteriority inaugurated by Descartes, and confirmed by the physiological psychology of Wundt, found its resolution in a psychology in which the supposed phenomena of immanent consciousness were dropped in favour of phenomena as they present themselves in the direct experience of the subject. In this sense, the early foundations of phenomenology did away with the classical dichotomy between the objective and the subjective.

The central interest of the Graz school in perceptual acts is therefore entirely different from the interest of the school of Leipzig in perception as a compound of sensory elements. We shall see in the course of our analyses that sensations still received careful consideration in the theoretical constructs of Brentano's pupils, and that they encountered insuperable difficulties in defining the borders between sensation, perception and cognition. Their respective views on these topics, however, essentially converge. As far as Brentano himself is concerned, it is certain that his Act psychology did not achieve a fully-fledged subject-centred discipline of the kind that has been foreseen by phenomenologists since.

To the names of Brentano, Meinong, Ehrenfels and Stumpf – to mention only the most important – that of Mach should be added. His dual role as an initiator of positivism and as a reformer of sensationism deserves special attention. Although the school inspired by Brentano's teachings is associated with the city of Graz, the movement has had representatives in Vienna, Prague and München. We shall consider successively the contributions of the major representatives of this group in order to bring out the deep meaning of their work in relation to the epistemological problems of today's psychology.

2 *Franz Brentano: the founding of intentionality*

As a student of philosophy at Berlin University, Franz Brentano (1838–1917) at first became interested in Aristotelian ideas. This early influence played a determining role in the development of his personal views on the nature of philosophy and psychology, in spite of the fact that he basically rejected Aristotle's system. His works are manifold and include, in addition to his philosophical writings, studies in theology, ethics and politics. His major book, *Psychology from an empirical standpoint* (1874), may be regarded as a critical survey of the entire history of psychology, oriented towards a definition of the object of the new experimental science, independently of the dogmatic positions taken previously by philosophers. With respect to the epistemological nature of the successive conceptions of psychology, either as a special branch of metaphysics or as an autonomous science, this work offers an astonishingly wide range of analyses and illustrations. Thus it becomes obvious to the reader that confusion and arbitrary postulates have steadily led to interpretations of experience not relying on unprejudiced or 'empirical' observations and have consequently prevented direct access to experience as such. From this point of view, the screen of systems is equally misleading in rationalism and in empiricism.[1]

When one considers the breadth of Brentano's interests, one may wonder why psychology is so very prominent in his work. Having rejected Aristotelian philosophy and being dissatisfied with the attempts of the psychologists of his time, Brentano was bound to look for new solutions if he wanted to succeed in his chief undertaking. But, what was his fundamental endeavour? As Spiegelberg (1960) puts it, Brentano was convinced that he had a mission, his ultimate goal being the scientific reformation of philosophy. This objective was itself motivated by deep metaphysical concerns about time and the problem of immortality. Just as Fechner, about fifteen years earlier, became involved in psychophysics for so-called 'animistic' or 'metaphysical' reasons – namely the desire to elucidate the relations between the material and the spiritual – Brentano devoted himself to the search for an epistemologically soundly-based psychology, because 'only after the development of such a psychology would it be possible to approach the final metaphysical questions such as the relation between mind and body and the chances of immortality' (Spiegelberg, 1960: 25).

3   *The meaning of experience*

In order to carry out his programme, Brentano saw no other possibility than experience. He claimed that experience was his 'only teacher',[2] and that 'like natural science, psychology relies on perception and experience'.[3] Such statements should nevertheless be carefully considered in the genuine context of Brentano's philosophical strivings. Taken in its literal sense, 'experience' could easily convey the impression that Brentano is just renewing the attempts of the old empiricists, particularly those of Locke and Hume, for whom sense-data are the ultimate sources of knowledge. Sense-qualities, however, though beyond doubt existing in themselves for the perceiving subject, cannot be invoked as proofs of the existence of the objective external world: they have only a phenomenal existence. Therefore, we may say that *internal perception* is immediate and is warranted by absolute subjective evidence, whereas *external perception* does not offer similar guarantees. Internal perception is in fact

---

[1]This brings us back to the fundamental issue of the *a priori*. Cf. p. 35.

[2]F. Brentano, *Psychologie vom empirischen Standpunkt*, Leipzig, 1874 (French translation by M. dé Gandillac, Paris, Aubier, 1944, p. 21). Translation ours.

[3]*Ibid.*, p. 48. Translation ours.

synonymous with introspection, since it presupposes the possibility of the individual's 'observing' events in consciousness, i.e. in a purely immanent fashion. In this process, consciousness is endowed with a supposedly 'objective' existence since it is defined as the 'object' of perception. As Gilson puts it,

> it seems that, when comparing the empirical starting-point of natural science with that of psychology, all the advantage is on the side of psychology. However, though internal perception is immediately evident, it does not furnish, in other respects, a sufficient basis for scientific study and, from this point of view, psychology is disadvantaged. Indeed, in order to study the objects of what we commonly call perception, we can observe them and focus attention on them.[1]

This basic difference of approach leads Brentano to the conclusion that internal perception cannot possibly become *internal observation*:

> According to a constant psychological law, we cannot direct our attention to the object of internal perception . . . Even psychologists who consider that internal observation is possible, all stress the extraordinary difficulty involved in making it. It is probably for this reason that they admit in most cases, that they did not succeed. But in the exceptional cases where they thought they had succeeded, they have without doubt been the victims of their own illusions.[2]

This last text clearly states the impossibility of introspection, insofar as the latter implies a systematisation of observation which requires that the experience should be present to the individual and, at the same time, analytically available to him as an observer. Brentano sought to overcome this difficulty by proposing the study of psychic phenomena after a given delay, i.e. in the form of memory traces. He insisted also on the value of studying behaviour as it manifests itself in other people and at lower levels of psychical life as, for instance, in children and animals.

'Empiricism' in Brentano's sense differs therefore from classical empiricist teachings with respect to the fundamental priority given to internal experience as opposed to sensations. Every fact which tends to enhance psychological research must be accepted, but not primarily by virtue of its reference to sensory experience as such. In addition to this, Brentano explicitly states in the very first sentence of his *Psychology from an empirical standpoint* that a certain concern for the 'ideal' is not at variance with empirical principles. According to Kockelmans (1967a), this rather vague expression refers to an immediate

---

[1]L. Gilson, *La psychologie descriptive selon Franz Brentano*, Paris, Vrin, 1955, p. 22. Translation ours.

[2]F. Brentano, op. cit., p. 48. Translation ours.

intuition of ideal entities, not to *a priori* knowledge in the Kantian sense.

Although Brentano did not care to give a precise definition of this 'ideal intuition', one can fit it into the general framework of his empiricism by referring to the 'acts'. In criticising the shortcomings of introspective psychology, Brentano unmasked the two major difficulties which prevented the new science from establishing itself as a truly autonomous field of knowledge: immanence and physical reductionism. In his opinion, these could be overcome by recognising at the outset that every psychical phenomenon refers to an object. This basic feature was called *intentionality*, a concept which became extremely important in later developments of phenomenology, and which allowed Brentano to distinguish between psychical and physical phenomena, the latter being, in his view, devoid of any intentional character.

4 Phenomenal existence

Though extremely important historically, and emphasising what is probably the most obvious difference between the psychological and the physical points of view concerning the ultimate nature of phenomena, the theory of intentionality raises difficult epistemological issues. First of all, it should be noted that the intentional relation between the psychological phenomenon and its object goes far beyond perceptual experience: the objects, needless to say, can be those of immediate everyday life, but they can also pertain to contents of judgements and feelings. When coping with objects of judgements, the subject in fact treats physical phenomena on the same level as psychological ones. Which criteria can I indeed invoke to draw a sharp distinction between the nature of a theoretical object, such as space, on the one hand, and the subjective experience of a given size? If we generalise this problem, we shall soon be aware of the fact that intentionality by itself, precisely by virtue of its all-pervading presence, prevents us from establishing categories of things and concepts which would prove sufficiently discriminative, even in the purely practical sphere of being.

But this does not amount to a definite condemnation of intentionality. On the contrary, it demonstrates that everything exists phenomenally for the subject and, more specifically, that the natural sciences and psychology, in the empirical sense, actually rest on identical foundations. This will allow us to understand more fully how Brentano succeeds, through the theory of intentionality, in the difficult task of establishing psychological phenomena as experienced facts in their own right, while requiring at the same time that the science devoted to their systematic study should be empirical. It should be added that, on this point, our analysis will be more an interpretation of Brentano's ideas than a mere outline of them, because it will tentatively try to shed light on some of their necessary implications.

The intentional reference to objects implies that these exist independently of consciousness, but as soon as one considers phenomena psychologically, they are immanent to consciousness. The actual existence of the physical world outside the subject is taken for granted by Brentano and it never became an autonomous epistemological theme in the general framework of Act psychology. According to him,

> Even when we draw the conclusion, from the phenomena of our sensations, that they have their cause in a spatially extended world, we suppose something which has never been grasped as a fact of immediate experience, and it is nevertheless possible that the conclusion may not be unjustified. But why? Only because the hypothesis of such a world, if we refer it to the hypothesis of certain general laws that rule it, allows us to understand and even to foresee, in their relation, the succession of our sensory phenomena, which would remain impossible to understand otherwise.[1]

Much in the same manner as Descartes sought the ultimate foundation of existential reality in the subjective experience of the *Cogito*, Brentano found it in the unavoidable experience of perceived reality, external and internal. The use of the word 'reality' may be rightly questioned in this context because Brentano's conception is foreign to any form of positivistic realism: indeed, the latter implies a basic separation of the human subject and the object, an *a priori* which contradicts the very idea of the act of consciousness. More fundamentally, the problem of 'reality' is a false one, first because the phenomenal existence of external and internal events by itself exhausts the total range of possible experiences, which establish for the subject the existence of a world outside himself, whatever its 'nature' may be; second, because phenomenism – the belief in a reality behind the screen of sensory data – supposes a physical world independent of any physical cue accessible to the observer. Paradoxically, then, this physical world is precisely the mental construct which realists aim at avoiding, when they reject subjective experience as vague, unstructured and unfit for scientific determination.

In brief, Brentano's *phenomenalism* has nothing in common, either with classical *realism* or with *phenomenism*. A solution of the same problem, based on realism, has been offered by Mach, as we shall see later. But, curiously enough, Mach's conception contributed in its own way to the development of phenomenology.

Brentano's empiricism rests on the absolute character of subjective certainty, but it avoids the difficulties of immanence by stressing the

---

[1]F. Brentano, op. cit., p. 119. Translation ours.

intentional character of the psychological act. But in spite of its importance at the epistemological level, one may require that a psychology which calls itself empirical shall furnish the methodological tools necessary to make the actual practice of psychological work possible, particularly when one is reminded that psychology should proceed exactly as do the natural sciences. This point is no doubt a major one and many experimentalists may remark here that these methodological tools were given to them by psychophysics. The same pragmatically-minded experimentalists would even reject the psychophysical model as crude and biologically unacceptable in many respects, and yet declare themselves satisfied with the methods and with the *empirical* progress they made possible.

This general problem will be treated in detail in the last chapter of this book. Suffice it to say at this point that the kind of psychological science which evolved from psychophysics and mechanistic theories is only one of the many possible scientific psychologies that might have appeared. Why then is it that Fechner's psychophysics and Wundt's elementarism are considered to be the founding systems, and not Brentano's Act psychology? The main reason seems to be that the former lent themselves more easily to a direct transfer of physiological concepts and procedures into the 'subjective' field where the results of the activity of the sense-organs were supposed to be observed. However, as we have remarked before, the subjective field cannot be thought of as that immanent reality which motivated introspectionism.

Had Brentano's epistemology only amounted to the destruction of the myth of introspection, it would already deserve consideration, be it only by the historian. But it had deeper and more lasting effects. Even if the concept of intentionality did not provide psychological science directly with an operational remedy against the simplifications of causal immanence, it convinced at least some philosophers and empirical psychologists that the definition of their discipline was not as evident as was imagined by those who tried, after Descartes, to establish observable relations between physiological facts and mental phenomena. Since Brentano's teachings, the suspicion has grown that the typically Cartesian problem raised by Herbart, Fechner, Wundt and their disciples concerned ultimately pure mental constructs and that these could not serve as a basis for an authentic science. But in striving to shift the interests of psychologists from mythical elements of consciousness to intentional objects, Brentano was in fact dismissing the traditional idea of objectivity as inadequate for an empirical study of the observer. From then on, the observer becomes more important to the psychologist than the factual content of what he observes or imagines he observes. The intentional observer is the true starting-point of psychological theory insofar as the latter is empirically based, because it defines the only basic possibility of circumscribing whatever may be meant by the word 'object'. If this is not granted at the very beginning of any psychological investigation, the result is necessarily the construction of an objectivism without an object.

5   *The description of psychic phenomena*

This explains why Brentano divided empirical psychology into two main areas: descriptive, and genetic. The aim of descriptive psychology is precisely to delineate by intuition the actual realm of psychic phenomena. The principle underlying descriptive psychology has often been misunderstood. Many experimentalists have believed that this expression meant purely and simply the rejection of a scientific approach in favour of the intuitive one. They interpreted this as a desire to reintroduce some sophisticated form of introspection. In fact, descriptive psychology is a survey of psychic experience directed towards a definition and a classification of subjective events which deserve to be called psychic phenomena. The final aim pursued in this way is nothing other than the foundation of a scientific psychology. According to Brentano, this latter discipline, which he terms 'genetic', is objective: it tries to establish causal relations between phenomena, and it is closely linked with physiology.

As Gilson remarks,[1] *Psychology from an empirical standpoint* (1874) contains few genetic analyses and is devoted, for the most part, to descriptive developments. However, Gilson notes a continuous evolution in Brentano's thinking from 1874 to 1911, the year of the partial republication of the original work under the new title of *On the Classification of Psychic Phenomena*. It is in this last treatise that the respective tasks of descriptive psychology (also referred to as *Psychognosis* or *Phenomenognosis*) are clearly outlined.

On the basis of descriptive intentional qualities, Brentano proposes a grouping of psychic acts under the headings of (a) representation, (b) judgement, and (c) love and hatred, this last category in fact including all affective phenomena. A detailed justification of these classes of experience is beyond the scope of this chapter.[2] Of interest for our purpose are the following points:

(1)   Bearing in mind Brentano's characteristic attempt to provide an autonomous basis for psychology, his empiricism is essentially epistemological in nature.

(2)   Its philosophical care and its correlative insistence on intuition must be understood as normal constraints in establishing a new science. The starting-point of a field of knowledge can never be criticised by reference to fully-fledged logical systems or to experimentally based theories elaborated in the field under study, since the aim of the innovator is precisely to try to define in the first instance the legitimacy of these systems. Primordial intuition being the rule in the first stage of construction of every kind of systematic knowledge, it is grossly

---

[1]L. Gilson, *op. cit.*, pp. 76f.

[2]Cf. on this problem, L. Gilson, *op. cit.*, passim; H. Spiegelberg, *op. cit.*, pp. 42f and J. Kockelmans, *op. cit.*, pp. 69f.

uncritical to search for basic concepts in already existing sciences, on the assumption that there exists some continuity between those and the newly emerging discipline.

(3)   This procedure was applied to the 'new science' of psychology by Wundt and his followers when they related experimental psychology directly to physics and physiology and attempted to introduce the classical causal principle in their studies of the content of consciousness. In doing so, they excluded the epistemological problem and guaranteed themselves an eidetic model only endowed with face validity, justified purely by external similarities of method. The same holds true for the foundation of psychophysics.

(4)   As a consequence, the unavoidable *a priori* intuitive dimension made its appearance *a posteriori* in the form of introspection. Therefore, it was considered as forming part of scientific method, an implicit assumption that could never be justified and which finally ruined the theory of elements of consciousness.

(5)   Every psychology is first of all a phenomenology. In other words, no psychological system (scientific or not) can escape the *a priori* moment of its constitution. In the case of scientific psychology, the denial of this epistemological constraint is to be referred to historical causes, viz. the monistic physical model and the consequent Cartesian dualism of substances. This particular point was treated as a major problem in the works of Stumpf, Mach and Husserl.

We cannot claim to have given a complete analysis of Brentano's psychology. Many other questions deserve careful attention, in particular his theory of the intentional object, which was considerably developed in various writings, not to mention his experimental work and his studies in ethics, religion and politics. However, what we have said is sufficient to understand the preoccupations of his main pupils. It explains at least the peculiar focusing of the Graz school on topics which all converge on the nature of the perceptual and of the cognitive object. These studies opened the way to both experimental and transcendental phenomenology.

6   *The positivism of Ernst Mach*

An important step towards a non-reductive psychology was made by Ernst Mach (1838–1916). His contribution is particularly significant because he was a mathematician and a physicist as well as a philosopher. Being a strict positivist, Mach unceasingly insisted on the necessity of verification in science. His epistemological rigour was such that he not only excluded metaphysical constructs, but also denied any scientific significance to major concepts of classical physics, such as ether, absolute space and even molecule and atom. As a theorist, his criticism of the Newtonian system may be considered as a

C

preparatory step in the development of Relativity. Mach's contribution to experimental psychology was chiefly concerned with the perception of movement by the body and with the functioning of the semicircular canals. But his main work is *Die Analyse der Empfindungen und das Verhältnis des Physischen zum Psychischen (The Analysis of Sensations and the Relation between the Physical and the Psychical)*. The book, published in 1886, made history. Under its apparently psychophysical title, it deals with the constitution of subjectivity as seen by a physicist and furnishes an entirely novel view of the nature of sensations. The epistemological themes contained in this partly mathematical, partly descriptive short treatise were to be completed in *Erkenntnis und Irrtum (Knowledge and Error)* published some twenty years later. In the *Analysis*, the concept of sensation is given a more radical meaning than in any previous psychological studies. According to Mach, sensations are the fundamental data of every science; they therefore define the starting-point of physics as well as of psychology. To the classical attributes of quality and intensity, space and time should be added. Changing the colour and the size of a circle does not alter its 'circularity', which means that form is independent of quality; nor does transposing a melody into a different key alter its temporal form. In brief, we are bound to admit the existence of sensations of temporal forms and sensations of spatial forms. These forms, which Mach calls *Zeitempfindungen* or *Zeitgestalten* and *Raumemp findungen* or *Raumgestalten*, are not to be confused with the pinpoint sensations abstracted from elementaristic introspections, based on a geometrical reconstruction of the receptors. Sensations exist as given, prior to the subject himself. It is the sensations which build up the subject and not the reverse. Space and time, as *a priori* forms in the Kantian sense, exist in subjective experience as founding dimensions.[1]

Mach's theoretical position in psychology is typically transitional: it brings unexpected support to some elementaristic views by acknowledging the importance of sensation, but destroys the idea of consciousness as an autonomous substance containing mere replications of the external world. At the same time, it foreshadows, in many respects, later teachings of the Gestalt school, especially, perhaps, the phenomenal organisation of space and time. His careful descriptive radicalism has something in common with Husserl's claim to be a true 'positivist' in returning to the 'things themselves' through phenomenology.

7 Form qualities and object theory

Christian von Ehrenfels (1859–1932) has been more generally recognised as the precursor of Gestalt psychology, because of his well-known article

[1] Several of Mach's remarks on the respective subject-matters of physics and psychology may be considered as foreshadowing the phenomenological problem of embodiment. Cf. in particular *Die Analyse der Empfindungen*, Jena, Gustav Fischer, 5th edn, 1906, Ch. I, section 10.

published in 1890 under the title of 'Ueber Gestaltqualitäten' (*On Form Qualities*). The problem can be stated in the following manner: if we consider a square, for instance, we observe that the ultimate analytical elements to which we can reduce it at the sensory level are the four lines of its perimeter. These elements are the 'sensations' subtending the perception of the figure: they are, says von Ehrenfels, the fundamentals (*Fundamente*) whose combination makes the foundation (*Grundlage*) of the perception. As soon as the latter combination exists, the 'squareness' of the figure appears as something distinct from the mere arrangement of elements: this perceptual character of the whole is the 'form quality'. Form qualities emerge in all perceptual fields. They are of spatial or temporal nature, so they will be present in movement as well as in static figures, in tonal fusions, etc.

The best-known example of this process is given by the phenomenon of melody transposition, a case already quoted by Mach. A tune will be recognised irrespective of the key in which it is played because the changes brought in the fundamentals, i.e. separate notes, do not modify their mutual relations. This does not imply any mental activity since the simple organised succession of the notes produces the form quality directly. The latter foreshadows what was to be called *Gestalt* by later theorists. Nevertheless, von Ehrenfels does not endow the form quality with all the descriptive characters that will be progressively attributed to the 'form' in the classical sense. The relations of the parts to the whole developed by Gestalt theorists are not fully expressed by the type of relations existing between *Fundamente* and quality. No less important is the fact that, under Mach's influence, von Ehrenfels teaches that form qualities pertain exclusively to sensations, while insisting on their autonomy in relation to the components of the physical substrate.

The cognitive dimensions of perceptual acts and their role in the constitution of objects are thematised in the theories of Alexius Meinong (1853–1920). Like other major psychologists of the Graz school, Meinong had wide philosophical interests. Logical and epistemological problems in his writings dominate his psychological interests. (Meinong founded the laboratory of experimental psychology at the University of Graz in 1894.)

It would seem at first sight that Meinong simply developed von Ehrenfels' views and limited some of his contributions to a mere change in the vocabulary. But with new words, new thought orientations appear. They are based on the concepts of content and judgement.

Meinong published *Ueber Annahmen (On Assumptions)* in 1902 and *Ueber Gegenstandstheorie (On the object theory)* in 1904. In his highly elaborated analyses, von Ehrenfels' form qualities are termed *fundierte Inhalte (founded contents)* and the *Fundamente* become *fundierende Inhalte (founding contents)*. Founded and founding contents result in *complexes*. Real complexes correspond to organised perceptions, and ideal complexes to conceptions. The founding acts play the determinant role in every emergence of a complex, although ideal complexes are more exclusively dependent on these acts. Extending the process to the logical level, Meinong considers that complexes also designate the relations themselves. In order to ascertain the existence of a complex, it is not sufficient that a certain number of elements should be given together; it is also necessary that the subject should be aware that they are given together. As Gurwitsch (1957) puts it, 'In addition to this "being together in consciousness", there must be a "consciousness of their being together". In other words, objects must be seized as belonging to a whole, as forming a whole, and as parts of this whole.'

Meinong groups relations and complexes in the same class: they belong to the category of 'objects of superior order'. The members of the relation and the quality of the complex are *superiora*, while the objects on which this relation is based are *inferiora*. Superiora and inferiora are bound by logical necessity; the inferiora are a necessary but not sufficient condition of the superiora. Without considering in detail the further problem of the reality or ideality of the various kinds of relations and complexes,[1] it is clear that Meinong's conception is a hierarchical one and that it leads at the same time to a psychology of perception and to a theory of knowledge. The theory of the object is destined to be completed in a theory of logical relations. In such a context, the latter cannot be conceived in a purely formal manner, although Meinong's influence on logical positivism cannot be denied.

But in developing the concept of form quality in this fashion, Meinong laid the foundations both of Gestalt theory and of Husserlian studies of logic. He belongs to that exceptional class of experimentalists who felt the need to question the nature of psychic phenomena, instead of taking them for granted by the sole virtue of factual procedures.

8   *Stumpf's experimental phenomenology*

The same holds true of Carl Stumpf (1848–1936), a prominent figure in post-Brentanian psychology. Stumpf was attracted by natural history and by music. This had a definite influence on his later work, and explains his taste for careful observation coupled with the analysis of subjective experience. Among the numerous books and articles he published, we shall mention principally *Tonpsychologie (The Psychology of Sound;* two volumes published in 1883 and 1890 respectively), and *Erscheinungen und psychische Funktionen (Phenomena and Psychic Functions)* and *Zur Enteilung der Wissenschaften (On the Classification of the Sciences)*, both published in 1907. Stumpf's place in the psychology of the end of the nineteenth century and the beginning of the twentieth is important because of the great amount of work he devoted to epistemological analysis. His theory of tonal fusion (*Verschmelzung*) is akin to the theories of the relations between phenomenal parts and wholes as outlined

[1]For a detailed analysis of this problem, cf. A. Gurwitsch, *Théorie du champ de la conscience*, Paris, Desclée, 1957 (Chapter 3) and J. N. Findlay, *Meinong's theory of objects and values*, Oxford, Clarendon Press, 1963 (Chapter 5).

by von Ehrenfels and Meinong, and it can be ranked accordingly among the main topics of the Graz school. But the basic contribution of Stumpf is what he himself calls his *phenomenology*. As we shall see, this term has a meaning in his system which differs profoundly from the significance given to it by Husserl, though in some manner it prepares the way for it.

As Spiegelberg (1960) remarks, the description of psychic phenomena we owe to Brentano leaves some uncertainty as to the precise line of departure between physical and psychic events. Partly in line with Mach's theory of founding sensations, Stumpf considers that the ultimate basis of every scientific observation is to be found in physical phenomena. However, the latter are of two types: those studied in experimental physics, such as waves, molecules, etc., and those studied in scientific psychology, which all fall into the sub-class of sensations. The object of phenomenology is to analyse the sensations in the sense defined above. The investigations of Stumpf that resulted in the writing of the *Tonpsychologie* were carried out in the fashion of experimental psychology, but the acoustic events experienced by the subject were not tentatively reduced to the abstract entities called sensations in Wundt's physiological psychology. Such experimental work is definitely phenomenological. The underlying descriptive approach of the *Tonpsychologie* is explicitly developed in the epistemological analyses of the *Enteilung* under the name of *experimental phenomenology*.

According to Spiegelberg (1960) and Kockelmans (1967), Stumpf's phenomenology can be characterised as follows:

(1)   The subject-matter of phenomenology includes primary and secondary phenomena. Phenomena may be considered as the objective correlates of Brentano's acts. Stumpf calls the acts *psychical functions*. Phenomena have an autonomous existence. Primary phenomena are the contents of immediate sensory experience. Secondary phenomena are images present in memory.

(2)   The phenomena do not include the contents of mental activity. These contents (corresponding to Meinong's ideal complexes) are the subject-matter of a special discipline which Stumpf calls *eidology*. The relations among contents do not pertain to the field of phenomenology; they are to be studied by another special discipline, *logology* or the science of relations.

(3)   Phenomenology is a neutral science essentially devoted to establishing the foundations of the natural and human sciences. As such, it does not exclude the later causal analyses of the particular sciences.

(4)   Phenomenology is the first of the three preparatory sciences. It therefore has priority over eidology and logology.

(5)   Phenomenology does not exclude *a priori* any methodological approach. The realisation of its objective therefore includes the use of the experimental method. This enlarged conception of scientific

investigation was applied in the *Tonpsychologie*, i.e. at a date when Stumpf had not yet given a complete outline of his epistemological system. Thus, studying the consonance of musical tones, Stumpf proceeds in line with classical scientific method when he controls the physical values of acoustic stimuli, but he adopts a phenomenological procedure when he tries to determine the audibility of partial sounds in relation to attention or previous experience.

In contrast to Husserl's transcendental phenomenology, Stumpf's experimental phenomenology does not involve the process of reduction, i.e. the 'bracketing' of the naturally given. This 'bracketing' has often been considered as a sort of idealistic operation and moreover as a fictitious, factually unrealisable aim. We shall consider this issue more fully in the course of Chapter 5. Suffice it to state here that what Husserl intends by it is an abandonment of the natural point of view in order to establish firmly the task of scientific knowledge. Does man, the subject-matter of psychology, simply belong to nature as physical science defines it? In order to answer this question, an investigation of the concept of nature is needed and the current idea we have of it must be reconsidered. This is, briefly stated, the task of 'bracketing'. Apart from this principal difference, both phenomenologies converge on more than one point. They both strive for a description of phenomena prior to any empirical generalisation, and they draw a basic distinction between psychological acts and logical structures. From this point of view, it could be argued that current experimental psychology is satisfied with eidological and logological analyses, thereby refusing to consider that the inductive material submitted to theoretical explanation should be epistemologically established by a preparatory discipline.

Considering Stumpf's ideas on the place of psychology among the other sciences, one wonders why the problem of the foundations of psychic phenomena did not appear to scientific psychologists as an obvious requirement of their work. A synthetic view of the historical development of their discipline could easily have convinced them that Meinong, Mach and Stumpf had laid the foundations of a theory of the object *and of the subject*, including the logical implications resulting from the relations between perception and cognition.

In addition to this, Stumpf's theory of fusion, by insisting that the total perceptual structure is independent of the constituent sensory components, represents a pre-formulation of the Gestalt concept even more direct than von Ehrenfels' form qualities. Furthermore, Husserl was to adopt Stumpf's point of view on the question of whole and parts in the *Logische Untersuchungen*. In brief, the work of Stumpf is the crossing-point where the basic issues of phenomenology, experimental and transcendental, intermingle with the need for significance resulting from the historical evolution of psychological science.

Nevertheless, as we noted before, the phenomenological trend was more closely associated, in the eyes of psychologists, with the transcendental investigations of Husserl and was therefore interpreted as purely philosophical. Husserl's dominating influence actually masked Stumpf's experimental phenomenology. Very few experimentalists developed their research in this direction. The only prominent scientific psychologists who maintained and enriched this tradition were Michotte and Buytendijk. We shall come back to them in the last chapter of this book. The main conceptual contribution of the Graz school was secretly absorbed by the Gestalt school and disappeared from the scene as a result of the natural regression of isomorphism. In Köhler's (1924) conception, which extends a principle previously formulated by Wertheimer (1912), isomorphism means that neurophysiological and psychological phenomena as they exist in perceptual processes, for instance, are of an identical nature and are basically related to corresponding physical phenomena. Thus, the manner in which physical forces act on a drop of water according to the laws of surface tension is the 'real' model of interaction of electrical potentials in the brain and of the corresponding perceptual structure.

This theoretical integration of phenomena belonging to different orders of reality has been severely criticised both by physicists and by physiologists. In psychology, it appears as a return to classical parallelism, with the sole difference that the so-called simple sensory processes are replaced by more complex perceptual entities. In any case, it overlooks Stumpf's phenomenological teachings in spite of the latter's influence on emerging Gestalt theory (cf. also p. 135).

9   James Ward's system of Act psychology

It is not customary to include James Ward (1843–1925) in Act psychology, although the influence of Brentano can be traced at many points in his system. His *Psychological Principles*[1] must be considered as an important contribution to the epistemological problems raised by psychology and stands as a rather exceptional piece of theory in the midst of British empiricism. His criticism of Cartesian dualism and his insistence on the active character of subjectivity are much in line with the phenomenological standpoint.

'Psychology', he writes, '... we define as the science of individual experience – understanding by experience not merely, not primarily, cognition, but also, and above all, conative activity or behaviour.'[2] The active relation of the subject to objects is called by Ward 'presentation' and has much the same meaning as Brentano's intentionality. Presentation is cognitive when attention is focused in a non-conative manner on sensory events, and conative

---

[1] J. Ward, *Psychological Principles*, Cambridge University Press, 1918 (4th edn, 1952).
[2] *Ibid.*, p. 28 (4th edn, 1952).

when the subject acts to modify his relation to objects through motor changes. Feelings refer to pleasurable or painful consequences of non-conative presentations.

This triadic classification is very similar to the description of psychic phenomena outlined by Brentano (cf. p. 64). Whether such a classification is exhaustive or not is not of interest here. The significant issue is that Ward was able to develop a theoretical psychology of consciousness devoid of introspectionism (introspection, he claimed, was only retrospection) and relying on intersubjectivity. To him, the subjective standpoint is that 'of the living subject in intercourse with his special environment',[1] a position which is not foreign to that of Husserl when he speaks of the constitution of consciousness. In spite of these similarities, Ward remained fairly isolated and did not take part in the phenomenological movement as such, or in the evolution from Act psychology to Gestalt psychology.

10   *Husserl's influence on Gestalt psychology*

In order to understand this evolution more fully, we must now finally consider the work of Edmund Husserl (1859–1938) himself. But in doing so, we shall only take into account that part of his effort which stands in direct relation to the teachings of the Graz group. It corresponds to the first period of Husserl's career, during which he was basically interested in epistemological issues raised by problems of the nature of mathematics and logic. The Husserlian reflection upon psychological issues is therefore based on grounds different from those naturally adopted by empirical or scientific psychology. The questioning of the starting-point of the latter has been a determining factor in the development of holistic systems, and particularly of Gestalt theory, to which Husserl contributed in his own way, as we shall see later. Husserl consistently attempted to unmask the danger of *psychologism*, i.e. the tendency to base every science of man (and of the living in general) on psychology. This being granted, and whatever the historical success of this endeavour may have been, it was not possible legitimately to extend to the totality of psychic life the modes of analysis which the Gestalt psychologists used so widely in their descriptions of perceptual structures.[2]

In fact, if the influence of Husserl's phenomenology is so profound, it is not because it criticises some particular problem studied in scientific psychology, but because it questions the very manner in which the problems are raised. In other words, does the impersonal character of scientific analysis fit the specific requirements of a possible science of subjectivity and intersubjectivity? This, however, is the point of view of the mature transcendental phenomenology

---

[1] *Ibid.*, p. 17.

[2] In his *Logical Investigations* (1900–1901) Husserl criticised his own previous work as still under the influence of psychologism. Historically speaking, however, his role in the founding of Gestalt concepts remains independent of it.

and no definite trace of it is found in Husserl's first work, the *Philosophy of Arithmetic*, published in 1891, or in the previous period (1886–91) during which Husserl was active in experimental psychology under Stumpf's direction. But it is during this same period that we can find the concrete impact of his thinking on the emergence of the idea of Gestalt. At that moment, Husserl looked for materials capable of helping him elaborate his philosophy of mathematics. His main source was Stumpf, especially *Ueber den psychologischen Ursprung der Raumvorstellung (On the Psychological Origin of Space Representation)*. According to Osborn (1949), the first stage of Husserl's reflection is marked by psychological preoccupations, including the possibility of using experimental psychology in the instrumental sense, to attain his philosophical aim, the analysis of the concept of number.[1] The starting-point of Husserl's analysis is the idea that the origin of the concept of number must be found in the concept of multiplicity and that the latter results, from the psychological point of view, from what he calls *collective association*. This kind of association can only be observed 'through a reflection on the psychical act by which totality is realised'. Such an analysis of the genesis of totality leads logically to the study of the actual emergence of wholes. Reflection is therefore related simultaneously to the perceptual and the cognitive aspect of the psychical act. This is consistent with the teachings of Stumpf, especially with that part of his phenomenology devoted to the study of forms and relations which he called logology.

11 Numbers and structures

The *Philosophy of Arithmetic* aims at an 'epistemological study of arithmetic' (p. vi), but it will often bring its author back to strictly psychological considerations. If collective association is sufficient to characterise the phenomena psychologically, multiplicity cannot reach conceptual existence unless a further intuition intervenes to fix its content concretely. The content may be anything insofar as the whole is maintained as univocal. In order to attain conceptual multiplicity, collective association must be completed by the concept of a definite 'something'. At this stage, however, the notion of number is not yet present. It requires a supplementary discrimination between the abstract forms of a given multiplicity with regard to another multiplicity. In this manner the rather vague character of multiplicity disappears and is

---

[1]'The dissertation reveals that the emphasis during the first articulated stage of Husserl's thought was on psychology; they were not logical analyses but psychological analyses that he was attempting in regard to the theory of number. This first period can therefore be characterised as psychological. It was a time in which he attempted to solve logical and mathematical problems through the instrumentality of psychology, a time in which he employed psychology as a way of philosophic clarification. This period, defined in terms of Husserl's published work, began with the inaugural dissertation in 1887 and was completely ended ten years later with the publication of a review of German writings in the field of logic.' (A. D. Osborn, *Husserl and his logical investigations*, Cambridge, Mass., 1949, pp. 32–3.)

replaced by the concept of number proper, which is common to all defined multiplicities expressed as discrete integers: one, two, etc.[1] Having established the theoretical conditions of the appearance of the concept of number, Husserl examines in detail the acts governing its elaboration. This subsequent analysis makes it possible to grasp the impact of the ideas expounded in the *Philosophy of Arithmetic* (particularly in the second part) on the progressive appearance of the idea of 'form' in psychology. Husserl distinguishes at the outset between *real* processes and *symbolic* processes. The former are those at work in the direct grasping of the actual components of a whole; their efficiency is limited, since it is hardly possible to grasp directly more than a dozen elements in a multiplicity, as is known from classical experiments on the span of apprehension. Beyond this limit, collective association needs to be replaced by subjective estimates which are, according to Husserl, necessarily symbolic. The significance of this conversion from real to symbolic is important since it corresponds to the basic operation to which the mathematician must make recourse in order to manipulate quantities that cannot be enumerated. The psychological basis of formalism is thus to be found in a symbolism which encompasses wholes.

Historically speaking, we touch here on an essential articulation in the development of the concept of form, as it was to be used later by Gestalt psychologists. The main issues are set forth in the eleventh chapter of the *Philosophy of Arithmetic*. Let us analyse this chapter in more detail.[2] Husserl insists on the fact that Brentano was the first to stress the difference between the two kinds of apprehension processes and who therefore understood the significance of non-real processes in psychological life as a whole. As we have already seen, the general trend of thinking in the Graz school was oriented in the same direction.

Husserl, however, gives a more schematic definition of symbolisation: 'A symbolic or improperly called representation', he writes, 'is, as its name indicates, a representation by way of a sign'.[3] Such representation is possible not only in the case of apparent objects but also in the case of those which are abstract and universal. In every description of an apparent object, Husserl adds, there is a tendency to substitute a symbolic representation for the real one. The process culminates in all cases in which abstract language refers to symbols and relations between symbols, without ever considering any perceptual correlates which may correspond to the symbols used. In pure logical reasoning, this correspondence is largely irrelevant since actual representation is mostly impossible. In such cases, the symbol exists for itself. In the relation of logical equivalence, for instance, the object of one concept is

---

[1] '[Consequently], the concept of multiplicity is endowed with a certain vague indetermination . . . What it is lacking is what the character of number first realises and which gives to the former its distinctive connotation: the sharply determined "how much"' (*Philosophy of Arithmetic*, p. 89).

[2] For a thorough analysis of this problem, cf. Osborn, *op. cit.*, Ch. 3, pp. 29–42. Translation ours. Original author's quotation marks.

[3] *Philos. Arith.*, p. 215, note.

the object of the other and conversely. The 'object' as such cannot be represented, except by the sign used to define it.[1] These principles are then applied to numbers to clarify the formation of the idea of multiplicity. They furnish the foundations of the unitary intuitions of large numbers to which we have referred above.

The following text illustrates this logico-psychological interpretation: 'when we enter a room full of people, we can judge at a glance: a crowd of people. We look at the starred sky and we judge at a glance: a great number of stars. The same holds true for wholes of totally unknown objects. How are such judgements possible?'[2]

It is worthy of note that Husserl excludes any explanation in terms of pure association for the evident reason that the individual characteristics of the components are not perceptible in isolation by virtue of their belonging to the whole.[3] Consequently, the only solution consists in supposing that in the intuition of the totality, there is a sign which makes it possible to identify the whole as such immediately. Husserl calls this character a sensory quality of second order or *quasi-quality*.[4] Does this quasi-qualitative character of the whole foreshadow the figural character of the later Gestalt theorists? In classical Gestalt descriptions and structural analyses, the figural character is a notion which always stands in direct relation to the actual phenomena of perception, though various types of extensions to the field of intellectual operations were attempted (the 'productive thinking' of Wertheimer) and even to categories of phenomena already reduced to the status of scientific facts, as in Köhler's isomorphism. Husserl's early views are foreign to these interpretations, since symbolic wholes are postulated precisely when real processes fail. In this perspective, the justification of the quasi-quality is purely negative and serves only logical ends. Enumerating is not a primary perceptual experience, but the impossibility of enumeration is always considered by Husserl in concrete situations involving multiplicity. Moreover, Husserl observes that the unity of a whole is not reducible to the sum of its constituent parts: they undergo fusion[5] and it is the fusion which produces the specific character of totality.

Moreover, the case of perceptual structures is considered in a further section of Chapter XI of the *Philosophy of Arithmetic*, where Husserl analyses the limits of objects in the visual field (p. 229). In this part of the work, Husserl appears as a true theoretical founder of the psychological concept of Gestalt.

[1] *Ibid.* p. 217. Translation ours.
[2] *Ibid.* p. 219. Translation ours.
[3] *Ibid.* p. 225. Even if association had explanatory value, it could only be invoked for numbers which can be grasped in their singleness, i.e. for those numbers which can be counted in the span of attention.
[4] *Ibid.* pp. 225–6.
[5] Husserl uses the word *Verschmelzen* which he borrows from Stumpf and stresses the fact that fusion determines the non-additive character of the whole. See on this point the *Philosophy of Arithmetic*, pp. 228–9.

The words 'Gestalt' and 'configuration' are used repeatedly in contradistinction to the purely additive wholes of associations. In previous
chapters, Husserl frequently uses the expression 'figural moment' and gives it
a broader sense than 'Gestalt' in the ordinary acceptance of material form. He
also refers to the figural character of perceived motion, which possesses, in his
opinion, a definite quasi-qualitative aspect. The examples quoted by Husserl
in this important chapter are strikingly similar to those which continually
appear in later Gestalt literature, be it only for the fact that they are nearly
always taken in visual perception (Osborn, 1949: 41). Having proceeded to a
brief historical survey of the psychological trend which developed from
Brentano to Husserl, we must now try to analyse its significance for a
biologically based psychology, i.e. a science of behaviour in the true sense of
the word.

12   Gestalt psychology reconsidered

Let us first consider the case of Gestalt psychology. The movement of thought
which culminated in this important system did not keep its promises in the
theoretical developments of Wertheimer, nor in those of Köhler, because they
professed a misleading conception of the subject in spite of their unceasing
attacks on mental atomism. Their opposition to the latter, and particularly to
the first form of Behaviourism, was an important step in psychological theory.
It stressed the inadequacy of elementarist models of behaviour based on the
conviction that mental combinations of discrete abstract elements, or
associative connections of separate acts, were sufficient to give a realistic
account of the subject's actual adaptive attitudes, movements and conceptual
constructs. But their basic conception of psychological science was still
inspired by physicalism. Integrated wholes simply replaced mental entities
(reflexes in the Behaviouristic sense). Köhler, for instance, painstakingly
elaborated his isomorphic theory of structures by referring exclusively to
physical phenomena of equilibration, e.g. electrical potentials and surface
tension of liquids, but never considered the biological origin of wholes in the
light of evolutionary principles and the specific survival value of such
widespread field characteristics.[1]

It is all the more surprising that perceptual phenomena were one of the
central interests of the Gestalt school. This obedience to physical theory
testifies to the lack of an epistemological foundation which would have
endowed the system with a more concrete and lasting psychological
significance. As it actually developed, it persistently adhered to classical
concepts and proved unable, in spite of its emphasis on descriptive
procedures, to overcome the ancient dualistic pitfalls and their unavoidable
consequence, viz. philosophising on the individual taken as an abstract

[1]On this point, cf. Chapter 3.

being.[1] Nevertheless, the historical existence of Gestalt theory appears to have been an important and even indispensable point of departure for Piaget's biologically inspired system and for some aspects of Lorenz's ethological theory.[2] In conclusion, we may consider that the Gestalt school filled the gap in the psychological scene left by Husserl after 1901, when he turned to transcendental reflection with his *Logische Untersuchungen*. In this dramatic conversion, motivated by his rejection of psychologism, Husserl brought to a sudden end the influence on scientific psychology of the epistemological heritage of the Graz school and of Stumpf's experimental phenomenology. Among experimentalists, Michotte was for a long period the only laboratory psychologist to refer to this tradition in his work on voluntary choice, the perception of causality and amodal complements (although in an indirect manner and with many concessions to the then dominant Gestalt ideas).[3] His influence on some aspects of Gibson's work on perception was unmistakable.[4]

Psychologism, defined as the tendency to consider the particular field of knowledge called psychology as the foundational discipline for all other fields of knowledge, was and is still considered by transcendental phenomenologists to invalidate every kind of empirical study of the human – and eventually the animal – subject.[5] Such a judgement needs to be reconsidered in accordance with the progress accomplished since phenomenology's early days by the psychological study of the organism. The 'return to things themselves' advocated by Husserl gains a completely new significance from this perspective and amounts, in our opinion, to a compelling new realism in the conception of the behaving organism as the object of study. The new objectivity, to which we referred earlier, after Strasser,[6] cannot establish itself

[1]On abstraction in psychology, cf. Chapter 4.

[2]On the influence of Gestalt theory on Piaget's genetic psychology, cf. A. Gobar, *Philosophic Foundations of Genetic Psychology and Gestalt Psychology*, The Hague, Nijhoff, 1968. A more detailed analysis of the epistemological shortcomings of Gestalt theory will be found in G. Thinès, postscript to J. Guiraud, *L'énergétique de l'Espace*, Louvain, Vander, 1970.

[3]Cf. A. Michotte et al., *Causalité, Permanence et Réalité phénoménales*, Louvain, Publ. Univ., 1962, p. 10, and A. Michotte, G. Thinès and G. Crabbé, *Les Compléments amodaux des Structures perceptives*, Louvain, Publ. Univ., 1964.

[4]J. J. Gibson, *The Perception of the Visual World*, Boston, Houghton Mifflin, 1950; *The Senses considered as Perceptual Systems*, Boston, Houghton Mifflin, 1966.

[5]'Husserl calls the totality of objects that each science investigates in its own and typical way, a "region". In this way, he speaks, for instance, of the "region of physical nature", the "region of psychical beings", etc. What all the objects of a certain region have in common and, therefore, what characterizes them is, according to Husserl, fixed in the categories which are germane to each region. Together they co-constitute the "regional categories" or the fundamental and basic concepts of that region ... Because these basic concepts constitute the typical mode of intelligibility and, therefore, also the object-character of the objects of the sciences in question, the sciences in which the categories of a determinate region are discovered are called "regional ontologies".' (J. Kockelmans, *A First Introduction to Husserl's Phenomenology*, Pittsburgh, Duquesne University Press, 1967, pp. 100–1.) The study of these regional ontologies is the ultimate object of epistemology. Psychology depending on a regional ontology among others must therefore be analysed epistemologically before it may claim to be *the* fundamental science.

[6]p. 17.

in psychology, or in the human sciences in general, if the subject is not approached biologically. This endeavour, however, can only be successful if a sort of biologism does not emerge to replace the old psychologism. To state it in an unambiguous fashion, the kind of phenomenological psychology, which could correct and eventually replace an outdated Behaviourism or naïve assimilatory systems mimicking cybernetics or linguistics, must consider as its basic requirement reliance on the actual study of the organism beyond the cultural and even the currently accepted scientific image modern man has formed of himself. In other words, it should become a fundamental anthropology of behaviour, capable of synthesising *Homo* as a species and man as creator of his own images including the philosophical and the scientific ones.

13   *The phenomenological v. the biological standpoint*

A synthesis of the respective conclusions reached in the two preceding chapters is necessary in order to establish whether the phenomenological approach and the biological one are truly compatible. Studying the living subject is the task of a life-science. It has also been the claim of phenomenology since the very beginning of its existence. The outline of its historical development has shown us how different the conceptions of subjectivity were in the empirical tradition inaugurated by Brentano and in classical experimental psychology. Both tendencies focused, however, on problems of consciousness. The work of the Austrian psychologists and of Husserl before the *Logische Untersuchungen* was an important contribution in this respect, because it was inspired by the idea of intentionality. Subjectivity was thought of for the first time as the essential foundational feature (the 'act' of Brentano) of beings in relation to their world.

We left Husserl at the end of the 'psychological' period of his career, i.e. when he was just going to develop transcendental phenomenology. Gestalt psychology was to a great extent the outcome of Act psychology and of Husserl's pre-transcendental work. It ran parallel to pure phenomenology but was always epistemologically at variance with it.

Nevertheless, the careful studies of Gestalt psychology, mainly in the field of perception, testify to the deep influence which early phenomenologists exerted on them. They experimentally analysed the subject's world (as constituted by the 'acts' of consciousness), but their tentative physiological interpretations were mostly inspired by physicalist ideas, as in Köhler's isomorphism. Goldstein's use of Gestalt concepts in psychopathology is a brilliant exception.

The issue is this: can phenomenology be considered as meeting the requirements of a biology of behaviour? Further chapters of this book will deal with this question in a more factual manner. Our immediate task is to answer the possible criticism that phenomenology, even in its least 'philosophical' form, is basically foreign to any biological outlook and that any attempt to reconcile them amounts to mixing up concepts which are radically heterogeneous.

Let us first come back to the idea of intentionality. For the non-philosophical reader, the word may be misleading, since 'intention' seems at first glance to imply some sort of voluntary act. In phenomenology, it means 'reference to something' or 'reference to an object'. The will is undoubtedly intentional, but so is every act of the subject because it always has a productive character. The world of the perceiving and acting being is the necessary correlate of this 'founding' function of consciousness.

Now, quite apart from the problems of consciousness, students of animal behaviour readily speak of intentionality in the sense of 'purpose'. The animal actively exploring its surroundings and even the rat running a maze are behaving intentionally because their perceptions and movements are directed towards a specific goal or result. Non-directed behaviour, i.e. behaviour devoid of external object or aim, is biological nonsense. Even in early molecular Behaviourism, the organism's performance is still related to an object, be it only the stimulus causing the reaction in a purely passive way. In the scheme of operant conditioning, the animal is also acting according to programmes in which reinforcement could not be invoked if the response did not guarantee a minimal rewarding effect.

Thus, in all mechanically inspired models of behaviour, some kind of intentional reference to objects is tacitly assumed. The trouble is that the theories built up to explain the observed phenomena consistently dismiss the intentional aspects of behaviour in favour of an 'inertial' conception of the organism. In other words, activity is considered as a feature of behaviour only when it fits into the general framework of an overall theory of passivity. The same applies to behavioural cybernetics and to the theory of 'purposive' machines.

We see that the intentional character of the living organism is a fundamental concept which is common to the biology of behaviour and to the phenomenological outlook. This is not surprising, since in both fields observation is the absolute starting-point. But, as we noted before, observational or empirical facts are rooted in different forms of *a priori*. The analyses we devoted to this problem led us to the conclusion that its solution required an epistemological clarification of the standpoints pertaining to what Husserl calls the regional ontologies of the various fields of positive knowledge.

However, claiming that biology and phenomenology converge in their basic approaches to living phenomena does not mean that phenomenology is just a particular form of philosophy which fits biological facts better than other philosophical systems. Once again, the issue is not to look for a philosophical interpretation *as such*. It is rather to examine to what extent unavoidable problems belonging to the philosophy of science can be settled and tentatively solved in the framework of phenomenological thinking. The noted convergence is, in our opinion, a strong argument in favour of phenomenology as an adequate reference in our attempt to circumscribe the field of behavioural events.

In relation to this, some additional remarks should be made about dualism in psychology. Dualism is a conception which is related, in a way, to subjective experience. Internal observation in Brentano's sense (cf. p. 60) reveals that a great many biological events occurring in our own organism are entirely independent of our actual decisions. Blood pressure, heart rate, assimilation, in brief, all vegetative and autonomous functions of our body, are regulated by biological systems which escape voluntary control. They are ruled by unconditioned reflexes which are the subject-matter of physiology.

But subjective experience also reveals that we are capable of performing these autonomous functions in a variety of situations which we actually choose or exclude by virtue of decisions. This overall capacity corresponds to the spontaneity of our acts: it defines the realm of behaviour as such and extends from spontaneous bodily movement to abstract thinking.

This duality of levels was perceived by Descartes and led him to postulate two essentially different substances coexisting within the same living organism. It is this coexistence which makes it difficult to characterise psychology's own subject-matter. Descartes' pure deductive way of thinking made him use intellectual experience as the sole criterion of subjectivity as opposed to bodily functions. Once this step was taken, the biological dimension of the living subject *as a whole* was definitely left out. Thus, in following this abstract model in the course of its development, objective psychology was bound in its turn to overlook the subjective aspect of experience as a fundamental part of the biology of the subject.

Along with this process, the relation of psychology to physiology as the source of explanatory processes was bound to meet insuperable difficulties, since, according to the particular Cartesian *a priori*, these two realms of phenomena were radically incompatible. Therefore, as we noted before, the reference of psychology to physiology was not inspired by biological considerations.

Behaviour may be observationally defined as those series of intentional events occurring in the field of the subject which bring the autonomous bodily functions to work in optimal situations. In all behavioural acts spontaneity prepares later automatic responses. In the absence of the former, the latter are deprived of their biological significance.

A sound physiological approach in psychology must therefore rely on this basic descriptive fact. We shall see in the next chapter that Sherrington was the first physiologist to develop an analysis of bodily functions extending to the field of the organism. The relations between his teachings and the phenomenological outlook will be discussed accordingly.

Chapter 3

The Physiology of the Behavioural Field

Earlier, we noted that early experimental psychologists constantly related their subjective findings to analytical physiology and not to biology. They believed that the discovery of mental processes could only find a satisfactory explanation in the functioning of the central nervous system, which they imagined, after Descartes, to be a special kind of complex machinery. Though this image was not entirely false, it was grossly insufficient for giving a realistic account of the organisation of behaviour in terms of operational causes. In a similar fashion, a great amount of speculation is devoted nowadays to the elaboration of models of behaviour mechanisms. Such work may be stimulating and eventually hit on some heuristic hypotheses. However, insofar as it tends to become a substitute for scientific observation, it must necessarily become misleading. No physiologist and no psychologist aware of the difficulties of biological research would ever indulge in the belief that the transformations effected on theoretical postulates of that kind can solve the problems he encounters at the organic level itself. Every model finds its significance and utility in biological description.[1]

The purpose of this chapter is to show how Sherrington made important discoveries in the biology of behaviour not by referring to abstract constructs but, on the contrary, by examining how organisms in their normal life *actually use* the anatomo-physiological systems which are discovered by laboratory experiments. A reference of this kind to physiology is, in our opinion, the only fruitful one, because it stands in direct relation to the biology of the species. This procedure was also followed by many comparative physiologists and ethologists. In this respect suffice it to quote, among others, such major advances as the identification of the 'language' of bees by K. von Frisch, and echo-location in bats by Galambos and Griffin and by Dijkgraaf for instance.[2] When one considers objectively observational work of this kind, one

---

[1] Cf. on this and related issues D. M. MacKay, introduction to 'Neurophysiological aspects of vision' in M. Marois (ed.), *From theoretical Physics to Biology*, Basel, Karger, 1973, pp. 322f.
[2] Cf. K. von Frisch, 'Die Tanze der Bienen', *Ostern. Zool. Zs*, 1946, 1, pp. 1–48; R. Galambos and D. Griffin, 'Obstacle avoidance by flying bats: the cries of bats', *J. Exp. Zool.*, 1942, 89, 3, pp. 775–90; S. Dijkgraaf, 'Die Sinneswelt der Fledermäuse', *Experientia*, 1946 2, pp. 438–49.

might remark that the Behaviouristic relegation of physiological mechanisms to a 'black box' was a scientific option reflecting an unfortunate lack of consideration of biological reality.

1   *Sherrington: the founding of the biology of behaviour*

In studying Sherrington's work, we shall focus our analysis on his theory of subjective space. This will allow us to see the relation between his ideas and some aspects of ethological theory, and to discuss the emergence of perceptual structures, as described by Gestalt theorists, in the context of organic evolution. The starting-point of our analysis may be found in *The Integrative Action of the Nervous System* (1906). The influence of this major work on the conceptual framework peculiar to research on perceptual structures and corresponding motor patterns has not been fully acknowledged by ethologists. Lorenz and Tinbergen rarely refer to the conceptual system elaborated by Sherrington in order to explain the emergence of sensory functions from the anatomy and physiology of receptors. In two studies (1938, 1972), Lorenz only quotes Sherrington with reference to particular physiological phenomena as, for example, spinal contrast.[1] It seems that ethologists were unaware of the fact that one of Sherrington's main contributions was a theory of the biological significance of the perceptual field. Ethologists were first naturalists. As such, they succeeded in reinstating observation in the framework of scientific methodology and were able to shed light on macroscopic events which, until then, had been overlooked by zoologists. Their observations of animal activity enhanced the discovery of behavioural homologies. But, in doing so, they focused on motor organisations and failed to take into account the role of sensory receptors in the constitution of the phenomenal world of the species.

In this fashion the genetic approach to behaviour, peculiar to ethology, amounted to studying exclusively what we could call, in physiological terms, the effects of efferent activity in the behavioural world of the species, without systematically relating the latter to the effects of afferent activity. This was not a consequence of theoretical reductionism as in the case of experimental psychology; the categorising was spontaneous, since the living organism offers itself as an integrated totality which has to be tackled from 'outside'. However, it raised difficulties when ethologists tried to relate behaviour patterns to physiological mechanisms. The solution to this problem must be found, in our opinion, in the framework of von Weizsäcker's theory of the *Gestaltkreis* (cycle of structure) which stresses the functional unity of receptors and effectors. Their reciprocal action results in the constitution of the organism's subjective time and space, these two dimensions defining the modes of relation between the animal and its surroundings.[2] In addition to this, it seems that the Behaviouristic *S* → *R* scheme turned ethologists away from the study of receptors because they considered it a pure mechanistic construct. This scheme was, at the time, the dominant 'conception' of the receptive aspects of behaviour. The ethologists' rejection of reaction psychology as a theory of organic passivity led them unknowingly to overlook the constitutive action of receptors in their own system. But neither did the Behaviourists themselves analyse the receptive aspects of behaviour, and their *S* → *R* model was often not in accord with physiological facts.

On the ethological side, the theory of releasers stated that sign-stimuli are configurations, but it did not aim at clarifying the organisational principles capable of explaining how perceptual structures actually appear in the animal world. Lorenz explicitly rejects Gestalt teachings:

> The conception of 'Gestalt' has assumed, with a good number of Gestalt psychologists, a character dangerously akin to that of a vitalistic factor. To very many authors, 'Gestalt' is something that neither stands in need of, nor is susceptible to, a natural physiological explanation. Also, 'Gestalt' has been very badly overrated as an explanatory principle. The characteristics of 'Gestalt' were uncritically attributed to all 'wholes' and therefore to all organic systems in general.[1]

Köhler's isomorphism must thus be considered as a hasty generalisation and as overlooking particulate elements of systems eventually leading to a physiological explanation. 'This contempt of the particulate element', Lorenz adds, 'is legitimate exclusively in the study of "Gestalt" as a phenomenon of *perception.*'[2] Such restrained appreciation allows Lorenz to select from Gestalt theory the minimum necessary for the elaboration of the concept of sign-stimulus and to relate this to observable behaviour patterns since the function of the sign-stimulus, as a perceptual reality, is precisely to release them. But here again, the constitutive action of the receptor, and the related problem of the biological origin of the subjective field, are left out of consideration.

We can now understand better why early ethologists did not turn to Sherrington's teachings as a basis for their theories.[3] Nevertheless, the numerous experimental facts and original interpretations contained in *The Integrative Action of the Nervous System* are directly relevant to later

---

transfer of physical causation to the behavioural realm. Cf. von Weizsäcker, *Der Gestaltkreis* and F. J. J. Buytendijk, and P. Christian, 'Kybernetik und Gestaltkreis', *Nervenartz*, 1963, 34, pp. 97–104.

[1] K. Lorenz, 'The Comparative Method in studying Innate Behaviour Patterns', *Symp. Soc. Exper. Biol.*, IV (1950), p. 225. Original author's quotation marks.

[2] *Ibid.* Original author's italics and quotation marks.

[3] This neglect has been overcome in more recent texts, as e.g. P. Marler and W. J. Hamilton, *Mechanisms of Animal Behaviour*, New York, Wiley, 1966, pp. 17, 727 and 728.

conceptual developments in both Gestalt theory and comparative ethology, not to mention the fact that they had historical precedence. But neither of these schools acknowledged their debt to this fundamental source.[1]

2   *Central nervous integration*

After a thorough study of reflexes, Sherrington proceeds to analyse the functional aspects of the central nervous system and tries to interpret the phenomenon of cerebral dominance. According to him, the central nervous system cannot be reduced to a crossing-point at which afferent and efferent paths simply conjoin.

> It is, in virtue of its physiological properties, an organ of reflex reinforcements and interferences, and of refractory phases, and shifts of connective patterns; that is, in short, an *organ of coordination*, in which from a concourse of multitudinous excitations there result orderly acts, reactions adapted to the needs of the organism, and that these reactions occur in arrangements (*patterns*) marked by absence of confusion, and proceed in *sequences* likewise free from confusion.[2]

Its integrative action manifests itself in the fact that pluriceptive summation not only connects stimuli pertaining to a single sense-modality, but also 'separate stimuli of even wholly different receptive species'.[3] As examples of integration, Sherrington quotes the mutual reinforcement of the mechanical and chemical responses of the barbels of fishes and of the tentacles of actinians. His theory of nervous integration was to be confirmed in neuropathology by Goldstein thirty years later (1934). Many converging arguments can also be found in Lashley's experiments on the neuropsychology of memory.

Sherrington, however, does more than simply assert the principle of totality. He speaks of *objects* acting as stimuli; what he has in view are thus not stimuli as isolated in the laboratory, but sources of excitation as they occur in the natural context. He adds: 'The simple perceptual image of an object is usually a resultant as regards external stimulations of stimuli applied jointly to several sense-organs . . . The object experimentally regarded as a single object excites a neural reaction that has its starting points in many spatially and qualitatively distinct receptive points.'[4] It is important for our purpose that the notion of integration, understood in this fashion, allows Sherrington not

[1] It is worth noting, among other facts, that the idea of consummatory action was developed in Sherrington's book (p. 329 and *passim*) twelve years before W. Craig's paper ('Appetites and Aversions as constituents of Instincts', *Biol. Bull. Woods Hole*, 1918, 34, pp. 91–107) to which ethologists continually refer.

[2] *The Integrative Action of the Nervous System*, p. 313. Italics ours.

[3] *Ibid.*

[4] *Ibid.*, p. 355.

only to situate the effects of afferent actions in the *field* of the organism at the outset – much in the manner of later ethological theory – but also *in so doing* to indicate the corresponding central organisation. The latter appears therefore as inseparable from peripheral events and necessarily includes, then, the biological significance it presents in the manifest actions of the animal. In such analyses, the causal explanation of behaviour does away with the classical opposition between macroscopic and microscopic structures. *In the latter, behaviour mechanisms are needs invoked as pure constructs and not as real organic causes leading to further observational controls.* As is known, this kind of interpretation was common practice in reflexology, in Gestalt hypotheses on neurophysiological mechanisms of perception and in organic psychiatry.[1] It is still present in the hierarchical models of ethology and in cybernetic models of the nervous network.

3   The anatomical basis of behaviour structures

Sherrington's hypothesis of the behavioural potentialities of organisms is based on their anatomical study. Considering the integrative phenomena at the level of anatomical segments, he notes that metameric segmentation[2] has evolved *pari passu* with a progressive dominance of the synaptic nervous system, as opposed to the diffuse nervous system (that of coelenterates, for instance). The former, he remarks, is the only form of neural organisation which proved capable of realising the functional unity of several anatomically identical organic subparts and which, consequently, made possible the forming of animal individuality in the zoological sense of the word. During the course of evolution, metameric segmentation developed in two main directions, viz. the radial type and the longitudinal. They offer different and even opposite possibilities for nervous integration.

In the radial type, that of echinoderms for instance, the probability of dominance of one segment over another is nearly equal for all of them, and the mouth opening occupies a central position in the body. In the longitudinal type, on the contrary, the relative position of segments determines an anteroposterior anisotropy.[3] The main functional consequence of this is the

[1]Buytendijk describes such uncontrollable abstract models as 'nervous mythology' 'Die biologische Sonderstellung des Menschen', in V. E. Frankl, V. E. F. Von Gebsattel and J. H. Schultz, *Handbuch der Neurosenlehre und Psychotherapie*, Berlin, Urban und Schwarzenberg, 1961, Vol. 5, pp. 119f. Cf. also, with special reference to reflexology, E. Straus, *The Primary World of Senses: a Vindication of Sensory Experience*, New York, Free Press of Glencoe, 1963 (English trans. J. Needleman), as well as Chapter 4 of the present work.

[2]Metameric segmentation refers to the anatomical units (metameres) of pluricellular animals. These units are homologous, i.e. they present an overall similarity of structure so that a segmented organism may be considered in the simplest case, as a repetitive series of such elements, as in the earthworm for instance. In vertebrates and insects, this basic structure has evolved towards much more complicated anatomical patterns. For a detailed discussion of the origin and evolution of metameres, cf. R. B. Clark, *Dynamics in Metazoan Evolution*, Oxford, Clarendon Press, 1964.

[3]A structure, living or inanimate, is said to be *isotropic* when it presents the same characteristics in all directions. It is said to be *anisotropic* when this is not the case.

appearance of a leading segment in locomotion. It is in this segment that the mouth opening is located. Besides, while several successive metameres can accomplish identical functions and form a homogeneous anatomo-physiological whole, others will specialise. In fish, for instance, the neuromasts of the lateral line are distributed over the whole length of the trunk, and their cephalic branchings are rather secondary, but taste-receptors and visual receptors are concentrated in the leading segment. The second type of organisation, which is that of arthropods and vertebrates, is more favourable to neuro-ethological differentiation. It has determined the widespread evolutionary radiation of these two zoological groups.

This, however, is not evident at first sight. Considered from the point of view of its topological potentialities, radial segmentation is in principle an anatomical model endowed with a high degree of spatial adaptiveness. The equidistance of the mouth opening from all metameres is a positive property for efficient predation, since the prey can be detected with equal chances in all directions and brought to the mouth with equal accuracy from any point around the body. In pentaradial Echinoderms, sensory detection is principally effected by mechano-receptors and chemo-receptors. Light-sensitive cells are nevertheless present at the extremity of each arm and thus allow the animal to react to differences in light intensity in all directions. However, Echinoderms show great structural differences from one class to another. Thus, the Holothuridae have a longitudinal axis and the mouth opening occupies a nonventral position during locomotion. If we consider life cycles, we see that the larvae of Asteridae are anisotropic and segmented longitudinally, but that the adults have a pentaradial symmetry.

What, then, we may ask, prevented radially segmented organisms from attaining an evolutionary success comparable to that of longitudinally segmented ones? The only sound explanation must be sought in the *respective locomotory potentialities* of these two types of animals. Radial organisms benefit from biological advantages linked with the sensory equivalence of their multiple body axes, but their displacement capacities are poor. This is compensated for to a certain extent by the neutral position of the mouth, but in such conditions the animal did not evolve in the direction of a behavioural organisation primarily based on active exploratory behaviour. It was neither constrained, nor capable of sensory scanning action at short time intervals. Its readiness remained static from the point of view of varieties of afference, so that its survival was not dependent on the emergence of a subjective field requiring repeated efference to ensure temporary adaptation. It appears that during the course of evolution, the outcome of the competition between a multiplicity of sensory axes and swiftness of displacement was decided in favour of the latter, so that longitudinal anisotropy dominated in the great majority of cases. The consequences of this morphological dominance on the biological organisation of the subjective field can be interpreted as convergent orthogenesis in the major groups of invertebrates and vertebrates.

Sherrington's distinction between exteroceptive, interoceptive and proprioceptive fields has become classical in physiology. He further remarks that the exteroceptive receptive field is (a) *coextensive* with the body surface and (b) richer in specialised receptors. These two facts furnish the basic elements of a biological explanation of subjectivity.

4 Distance-receptors and precurrent reactions

We have seen that the anisotropic organism moves along a preferential vector. Thus, there is a leading segment in locomotion. The animal can only move efficiently in the direction of this leading segment, and the receptors located in it play a predominant role in the taxic orientation of the whole body. These receptors are better developed than other exteroceptors and their anterior position allows them to detect a greater number of stimuli. They can, moreover, detect stimuli *before* they reach the other segments. Their front position has therefore a predominantly spatial and temporal significance. Analysing further the leading segment, Sherrington observes that it is in it that we find the *distance-receptors*, i.e. those 'which react to *objects* at a distance . . . the *sources* of those changes impinging on and acting as stimuli at the organism's surface'.[1]

The biological importance of distance-receptors manifests itself in the constitution of a multimodal subjective field. It is also evident when one considers the evolution of the nervous system and particularly the structure which became dominant in the most autonomous animal form, viz. the brain. This statement may sound rather trite, but it is certainly not the case if one traces the route which led Sherrington to such a conclusion. '*The brain*', he writes '*is always the part of the nervous system which is constructed upon and evolved upon the "distance-receptor" organs.*'[2] In other words, if we want to understand the biological significance of the brain as a highly adaptive organ, we must analyse its functions in relation to the receptors which determined the formation of the subjective field.

The study of metazoans, or multicellular animals, shows that feeding and reproduction are the most important functions of the species. Now, in their actual life, animals can only realise the corresponding physiological actions by incorporating in their bodies certain physical elements of their milieu, which require that a *contact* occur between these elements and the organism. It is an abstract view to define ingestion as energetic supply and fecundation as gametic combination. Neither of these processes can be actualised in the natural life of a species in the absence of bodily contacts. In stating this, we do nothing more than define behaviour. The contacts of one organism with another can have positive as well as negative consequences and the same holds true for contacts between organisms and inorganic objects. They may take the

---

[1] *The Integrative Action of the Nervous System*, p. 324. Italics ours.
[2] *Ibid.*, p. 325. Italics and quotation marks ours.

form of sexual encounter, care of the young, hunting of prey, avoidance of predators and the like. Similarly, the seizing of an absorbable element may bring into the organism edible or non-edible substances. Consequently, if the development of animals had only endowed them with tactile and gustatory receptors, this biological hazard would have been extremely high whenever they perceived anything. For instance, if a predator could only be detected by the tactile sense, the survival value of the sensory information would be very low, since perception would coincide in time with the beginning of actual predation.

Distance receptors have thus been an essential factor in biological progress in the animal series. Since they do not require direct bodily contact to produce specific sensations, they allow the organism to extend its subjective field beyond its own superficial limits and to obtain information from remote *signals*. The responses to these remote signals always occur in time before tactile and gustatory ones. For this reason, Sherrington describes them as *precurrent reactions*. It is thus possible to understand that the segmentary polarisation of the field has taken the form of an anterior dominance of sense-modalities acting at a distance (vision, audition, olfaction) coupled with a high degree of mobility of the organism. The local reflex endowed with a strong affective tone, which was the only possible type of response of non-projicient receptors, has thus been progressively preceded by a general readiness of the organism for a multiplicity of responses to a given situation. In other words, the emergence of the precurrent subjective field was paralleled by a typical increase in autonomous exploratory behaviour. Now, since the latter is anticipatory towards local reflexes, its affective tone is lower. This type of behaviour is therefore controlled by central inhibitory processes which will eventually be lifted when the local adaptive response occurs. The main outcomes of the integrative action of the brain in so-called higher animals are thus exploratory readiness implying central inhibitions and selective discovery of specific stimulating objects in a broad spatio-temporal framework.[1]

5 *Subjective space-time*

The precurrent subjective field is characterised by a remarkable broadening of lived time. This temporal extension includes a lengthening of the time-interval between the moment of stimulus emission and the moment of response; it also includes a lengthening of the response-time itself. Under such conditions, it is possible to understand the appearance of mediating behaviour patterns in organisms endowed with a high degree of autonomy, i.e. sequences of acts reaching a final goal through a number of intermediate steps. This phenomenological trait is common to intelligent and instinctive behaviour.

[1] The anatomo-physiological development of corresponding neural paths is analysed in Chapter IX, Section 9 of *The Integrative Action of the Nervous System*. This issue is beyond the scope of the present book.

The latter is the main behavioural orthogenesis which can be observed in the evolution of metazoans. In instincts as classically described in ethology, we find temporal extension under the form of an appetitive phase which extends as long as the releasers of consummatory action are absent from the subjective field. In a similar fashion Sherrington stresses the preparatory character of precurrent reactions. 'The "distance-receptors"', he writes, 'induce anticipatory or precurrent reactions, that is, precurrent to *final* or consummatory *reactions ... These reactions are all steps toward final adjustments, and are not themselves endpoints.*'[1] Consummatory reactions, i.e. consummatory actions in ethological terms, thus refer to behavioural events which occur when the active subjective phenomena which take place within the field's space-time come to an end. At that moment, reflexes of the non-projicient receptors take over in the overall sequence, i.e. when an animate or inanimate object comes into contact with the body. Tactile and gustatory receptors then initiate the adaptive local efferent patterns. Sherrington gives various examples of this process.[2]

6   *The body as part of the exteroceptive field*

In brief, what we call organised behaviour patterns designates the events of the subjective space-time which take place outside the organism and which are the conditions of events of the subjective space-time occuring inside the organism. The zone between these two realms of organic events is the body surface. Because of its functional significance, it cannot be interpreted as an indifferent portion of space, as a mere area of physical points. Even if a punctate stimulus can act as an adequate one on the tactile surface, the particular point or limited area selected by the observer is always at the intersection of the subjective world and of the physiological mechanisms. The latter, it should be remembered, will ensure their function as *physical* systems even when the subjective constitution of the environment is suppressed, as, for example, in the stimulation of a neuromuscular preparation in experimental

---

[1] *The Integrative Action of the Nervous System*, p. 329. Original author's italics and quotation marks.

[2] 'The reflexes of certain "non-projicient" receptors stand in very close relation to "consummatory" events. Thus, the tango-receptors of the lips and mouth initiate reflex movements that immediately precede the act which for the individual creature viewed as a *conative and sentient agent* is the final consummatory one in respect to nutriment as a stimulus, namely, swallowing. Similarly, with the gustato-receptors and their reactions. The sequence of action initiated by these non-projicient receptors is a short one: their reflex leads immediately to another which is consummatory. Those receptors of the chelae of *Astacus, Homarus*, etc., which initiate the carrying of objects to the mouth, or again the tango-receptors of the hand of the monkey when it plucks fruit and carries it to the lips, give reactions a step further from the consummatory than those just instanced ... The series of actions of which the distance-receptors initiate the earlier steps form series much longer than those initiated by the non-projicient. Their stages, moreover, continue to be guided by the projicient organs for a longer period between initiation and consummation.' (*The Integrative Action of the Nervous System*, p. 329. Original author's italics and quotation marks.)

physiology. The mechanistic interpretation of the organism is only valid under such artificial conditions.

To be sure, the events occurring inside the organism as a result of interoceptive stimulation are encompassed in the subjectively lived. But, as we have seen, their spatio-temporal characteristics are profoundly different from those of the exteroceptive field. Medical auscultation testifies to the lack of differentiation of this internal experience for the subject himself when he is asked to give an account of internal bodily pains and the like. The coenesthesic space-time, though included in the individual body, also offers a peculiar resistance to analysis.[1]

Biologically based psychological descriptions are thus only possible within the subjective organisation of the exteroceptive field. As we have remarked elsewhere, the study of subjective phenomena can only be carried out 'from outside', but we now understand that the observation of behaviour as a realm of external events does not mean registering physical facts in the sense of early Behaviourism. The consummatory act corresponds to the end of the psychic. As Sherrington observed, when we have swallowed food 'the object has passed into such a relation with the surface of the organism that "conation" is no longer of advantage . . . No *effort* can help us to incorporate the food further . . . It is significant that all direct psychical accompaniment of the reactions ceases abruptly at this very point.'[2]

It should be added that the surface of the body with its tactile non-precurrent field is related to the physical through the distance-receptors. Thus, among the various aspects of the exteroceptive field these receptors explore the particular surface of the subject's own body. The latter is *lived* through interoceptive and proprioceptive information, but it is simultaneously *lived and perceived* through visual information. Tactile auto-exploration of the body does not reveal a subjective extension comparable to that furnished by vision. Although both sensory modalities can only partially explore the body surface, the superiority of visual exploration lies in the fact that it places this surface in the perspective of distance. Sherrington's statement that the body surface is co-extensive with the milieu can therefore be fundamentally related to the phenomenological analysis of embodiment.[3]

The distinction between the two spatial orders – that of the body and that of the external world – does not imply that they should be treated separately in the study of behaviour. It is precisely the object of an authentic psycho-physiology to analyse the interactive mechanisms of the body 'interface', by showing, for example, that tactile receptors function differently (by showing quantitative or qualitative modifications of their anatomo-physiological

[1]On the relations between these experienced dimensions of the body and the idea of introspection, cf. G. Thinès, *La Problématique de la Psychologie*, The Hague, Nijhoff, 1968 (Chapter I in particular).

[2]*The Integrative Action of the Nervous System*, p. 332. Italics and quotation marks ours.

[3]On this basic phenomenological problem, cf. R. M. Zaner, *The Problem of Embodiment*, The Hague, Nijhoff, 1964.

properties), according to whether they actively encounter a precurrent source of stimulation or passively undergo mechanical stimulation, i.e. without exploratory involvement of the body segments endowed with mechano-receptors.[1]

7 Perceptual structures from the evolutionary perspective

The study of distance-receptors leads to an approach to the lived body as a structure situated in the subjective field. This may help us to formulate a hypothesis about the origin of object-structures as they appear in perception. We have seen that the phenomena occurring in the interoceptive and proprioceptive fields do not readily lend themselves to description. Judgements about the localisation and intensity of a sensation on the surface of the body are easier, though the purely tactile description of an object may be very difficult. Vision is absolutely necessary in order to define the spatial relations of an object to its environment as well as the precise organisation of its constitutive parts. Besides, tactile identification and structural characterisation, imperfect though they may be, are only possible for tridimensional objects. For bidimensional ones, tactile judgements of surface extension are very vague and rely a great deal on cues such as grain, smoothness, etc. Thus, tactile space presents the same poverty of representation for objects of external space as for the surface of the body. Subjective events occurring inside the body or on its surface are singularly homogeneous. This may be tentatively interpreted as the phenomenal consequence of the various regulatory mechanisms ensuring psycho-physiological autonomy and constancy. In any case, the corresponding sensory fields cannot be analysed from the *perceptual* point of view in the same way as the sensory fields of distance-receptors.

In the latter, perceptions with their structural characteristics exist for the subject with reference to objects as a matter of course. We may attempt to understand the origin and the nature of these phenomenal objects from the biological point of view by referring once more to Sherrington's teachings. Philosophical as well as psychological theories of perception have interpreted them on the basis of sensations by stressing either the external organisation of the stimuli (as, for example, in classical empiricism), or the constitutive effects of the subject's own activity (as, for example, in Act psychology and Gestalt theory). Various intermediate theories were developed, especially in the psychophysiological approach. None of these doctrines, however, considered the significance of *the very emergence* of perceptual structures in the biological context of the organism. An *actual* description of the subjective field with reference to precurrence opens, in our opinion, new perspectives in this domain.

Distance-receptors, we said, are responsible for the formation of a

[1]Cf. on this point F. J. J. Buytendijk, 'Toucher et être touché', *Arch. Neerl. Physiol.*; and R. Zayan, 'Le sens du sens tactile', *J. Phenom. Psychol.*, 1971, 2, 13, pp. 49–91.

subjective field defining the spatio-temporal extension of the specific world of organisms. The development of perceptual structures, though linked with this general phenomenon, is nevertheless an evolutionary process of its own. Vision, audition and olfaction are the three sense-modalities which allow animals to react to sources of stimulation at a distance,[1] but there is an inverse relation between the respective spatial extension and degree of structuring particular to each of them. In some species olfactory signals can be detected at greater distances than acoustic ones and the latter are themselves detected at greater distances than visual ones.[2] From the point of view of differentiation, the olfactory signal acts rather as an all-or-none phenomenon, relatively well specified in direction, but its intensity is not accurately connected with distance. There are no olfactory objects. In audition, structures exist in the form of rhythms and tonal variations, but one can hardly speak of auditory objects.[3] The notion of an object as part of the subjective field endowed with unequivocal meaning (verbal or non-verbal) applies only to vision.

It should also be remembered that vision is the only precurrent sense which is under the control of another modality, viz. the tactile sense. The visual object is, therefore, by its very nature, an intermodal one, and though it may be detected at a great distance, it remains more closely related to the body. It thus establishes special bonds between distance and body-milieu co-extensivity, i.e. between the far and the near. It is true that, if the integrated visual object – and at a further stage, the symbol – replaces signals, visual signalling remains possible at the same level as audition, as, for example, when very brief sections of a body segment act as an efficient releaser.

In conclusion, distance in the visual field remains relatively proximal in comparison with the other precurrent modalities. It is in this relative proximity and consequent body-linkage that we may see the hypothetical evolutionary factor which made perceptual differentiation necessary. Thus, gain of space could only enhance survival, if, at a limited subjective distance, every event was specified with precision as prey, sexual partner, parent, food, inanimate element, etc. All these sources of information were progressively differentiated as structures. Forms in the Gestalt sense are thus the result of an evolutionary counter-chance which defined the limits of security of the

---

[1]To these should be added the lateral line system of fishes and amphibians, which is a mechanical sense, as well as the thermal receptors of some snakes.

[2]Cf. R. G. Busnel, 'On certain aspects of animal acoustic signals' in R. G. Busnel (ed.), *Acoustic Behaviour of Animals*, Amsterdam, Elsevier, 1963. Measurements of the limits of perception of visual, acoustic and olfactory signals in various species show that the olfactory ones are by far those which are detected at the greater distance. There are, however, exceptions, namely in birds. These inter-specific differences must not be interpreted only on the basis of absolute distances, but also in relation to the usual limits of exploration of the species considered.

[3]Except when particular optical forms are associated with corresponding acoustic ones (e.g. the auditory duration and intensity of shape tracing on rough paper). In this case, the inter-modal structure can be identified acoustically (cf. J. H. Dijkhuis, 'Recherches sur les représentations provoquées par l'audition de bruits', *J. Psychol. Norm. Pathol.*, 1953, 46, 2, pp. 188–214.

precurrent field closest to the body step by step. It gave rise to the most 'analytical' releasers of consummatory actions.

8 *Sherrington's teachings and the phenomenological standpoint*

Once again, the striking fact about Sherrington's teaching is that it reaches conclusions, regarding the organisation of behaviour, which dismiss mechanical models that are crude from an anatomical and physiological point of view. His accuracy in observing and his ingenuity in experimenting stand on an equal footing with Pavlov's most refined devices. However, recognition of Pavlov as a pioneer in the field of scientific psychology was undoubtedly broader. What, then, was the difference which turned psychologists to Pavlov rather than to Sherrington when they were looking for physiological explanations of behaviour?

Sherrington and Pavlov were both primarily concerned with the functioning of the central nervous system as such. They both later extended the significance of their findings to behavioural processes. Historically, however, it happened that the Pavlovian theory of conditioned reflexes offered at the right moment a particularly fitting frame of reference for the physiological interpretations of learning that emergent Behaviourism was in need of. Sherrington's contemporary theory of the integrative action of the nervous system was developed into a general theory of the senses, for which there was little demand in psychology at the beginning of the twentieth century. When, some forty years later, ethological theory developed, the demand for a theoretical interpretation of the organism's field had already been met in part by the work of naturalists.

Another important reason for the disregard of Sherrington's views in favour of those of Pavlov in psychological theory is the fact that the Pavlovian concepts were more readily translatable into general psychological vocabulary. In the eyes of psychologists, the teachings of Pavlov seemed more 'obvious' than those of Sherrington because they reminded them of classical association theory, a manifold system to which early psychologists had themselves largely contributed.

Besides, Pavlov himself consistently created new entities in order to explain the behavioural aspects of his experiments; some of them were intended to be used to explain the central mechanisms involved, 'excitation', 'inhibition', 'irradiation', 'concentration' and the like; some others, however, were definitely psychological – 'curiosity', 'distraction', 'attention', etc. But most of these words could be understood physiologically as well as psychologically according to the issue. The very use of such words thus easily gave scientific psychologists the impression that they were performing a kind of work and devising types of theories which were on a par with physiological research from the point of view of technicality.

This has for a long time been the great illusion of psychological objectivism.

What we said before about the cultural transformation of scientific concepts into mere opinions applies particularly well here. When Pavlov was using an ordinary word like 'curiosity' or more elaborate expressions including ordinary words like 'curiosity reflex' or even 'centre of curiosity', he was trying to give a descriptive account of accurate experimental facts with the linguistic means he had at his disposal. In doing so, he was still referring to physiological facts as a matter of course, and he did not consider it his task to elucidate the logical problem of the possible semantic shift which could eventually result from such descriptive expressions or propositions.

But when psychologists – Behaviourists for the most part – were tackling behavioural issues as such and were looking for physiological correlates *not at the outset of their work but when it was completed*, all that remained available to them was the words with their current meanings and not the words with their initially intended physiological significance.

We now see more clearly that some descriptions of behavioural phenomena carried out in the framework of physiological research raise crucial difficulties. We have also noted that when psychologists borrowed descriptive concepts from Pavlovian physiology, they used identical or similar expressions to describe facts belonging to another order of reality, without having comparable criteria of observation at their disposal.

Pavlov was taken as a typical instance not only because of the dual character of his concepts, but also because the part of his work which influenced psychology most was contemporary with that of Sherrington. In Sherrington's work, too, the experimental analysis of physiological phenomena leads to interpretations of behaviour, but of a very different kind.

Pavlov describes the behavioural events he calls conditioned reflexes and related actions and attitudes of his dogs in various experimental situations.[1] He then turns to physiological hypotheses regarding the underlying central mechanisms. Sherrington, for his part, devotes lengthy chapters of his work to the description and interpretation of numerous experiments which deal exclusively with nerve and brain function. He then turns to hypotheses regarding the possible use of these mechanisms in the actual behaviour of organisms. But, in doing so, he sticks narrowly to the bodily structure of living beings and to their observable perceptual and motor capacities. Thus, for instance, the capacity of an animal to perceive objects at a distance is directly related to its capacity to move towards the object or away from it.

In Pavlov's theory, the interpretations are centripetal; they always start from the behavioural act and end in descriptions of brain events. In Sherrington's theory, on the contrary, the interpretations are centrifugal; they start from the physiologically observed fact and end in descriptions of

---

[1] Erwin Straus has very convincingly shown that many aspects of Pavlov's observations did not deal with *reflexes* in the physiological sense of the word. See *The Primary World of Senses*, Ch. 1 and *passim*.

behavioural acts. The respective logics of Pavlov and Sherrington develop on the basis of inversely oriented implications.

The main reason why Sherrington's physiological views are more appropriate for behavioural phenomena is that they lead without discontinuity from descriptions of mechanisms to further descriptions of sensory and motor performances, and ultimately to descriptions of the field or world of the organism.

In other words, the final outcome of Sherrington's physiology is of a phenomenological nature. This last adjective may be used apart from the historical meaning it has been endowed with since Husserl's philosophical achievements. In this case, it would just have the meaning of a purely observational endeavour devoid of interpretational character. But even in this simple form, it would still be based on a specific *a priori*. This brings us back to our previous analyses of the *a priori* and of 'regional ontologies' (cf. p. 77).

Stating that the results of Sherrington's observations and experiments in physiology settle the conditions of a phenomenology of behaviour amounts to saying that they define the framework of a psychology in which theoretical inferences rely on observations of behaviour patterns *and* of corresponding nervous mechanisms. The latter are not mere entities as in classical reflexology, because they are related to the bodily structure of the behaving organism. This, in turn, leads to the study of the subjective world which corresponds to the organism's founding activity. This aspect of subjectivity is called 'constitution' in Husserlian terminology.

In conclusion, we see that a biological approach to behavioural events is closely linked with the requirements of phenomenology. It offers an *objective* solution to the epistemological problems raised in phenomenological analyses of the scientific status of psychology.

In the next chapter, we shall come back to philosophical problems. Our purpose is to show that pure philosophical reflection cannot lead by itself to a positive psychology set free from the dogmas of classical objectivism. We thought that the endeavour of Georges Politzer was a particularly adequate example in this respect, since it claimed, quite apart from the phenomenological movement, to reform classical psychology in a positive way.

Chapter 4

Philosophical and Psychological Realism

In the course of the nineteenth century, a few philosophers and physiologists became dissatisfied with the rationalist discourse on the nature of the mental faculties of man which was traditionally called psychology. They turned to various empirical approaches to these problems and sought solutions in the principles of positivism and in many refined systems of thinking which they intended to refer to experimental science in the naturalistic sense of the word. The forerunner of this endeavour was Christian Wolff who wrote *Psychologia Empirica* as early as 1745; von Wolff occupies an intermediate position between Leibniz and Kant. He did not perform experiments, but was convinced that empirical knowledge was necessary in order to arrive at a correct description of feelings and intelligence. A reading of von Wolff's writings[1] is an astonishing experience. Every sentence of his *Psychologia Empirica* conveys the impression of great rigour in the treatment of psychological issues, and the systematic coherence of questions is very striking. No less striking, however, is the fact that his manifold analysis of sensations, memory and many other classical topics, seems strangely devoid of contact with reality. One is tempted to think that Wundt must have had a similar feeling when, as a physiologist, he decided to look for experimental evidence after reading Herbart's mental mathematics and having compared the latter's equations with Fechner's psychophysical laws. The reader will, we hope, show indulgence for this rather hazy reconstruction, for, after all, there was also much musing in Fechner's writings and of the worst kind in the scientist's eye – animistic musings. The historical context, of course, must be taken into account and it would be absurd to expect that words like 'evidence', 'fact', 'sensations' etc. should have the same technical meaning in an eighteenth-century text as in a contemporary treatise. It is well known that

[1]Ch. Wolff, *Psychologia Empirica*, Gesam. Werke, II Abt., Band 5 (J. Ecole, Ed.), Hildesheim, Olms, 1968. See also J. Ecole, 'Des Rapports de l'expérience et de la raison dans l'analyse de l'âme ou la "Psychologia Empirica" de Ch. Wolff', *Giorn. di Metafisica*, 1966, 21, 4–5, pp. 589–617 and *Idem*, 'De la nature de l'âme, de la déduction de ses facultés et de ses rapports avec le corps ou la "Psychologia Rationalis" de Ch. Wolff', *Giorn. di Metafisica*, 1969, 24, 4–6, pp. 499–531.

fierce philosophical controversies have had – and still have – semantic divergences as their sole origin. But the impression of gratuitousness which we get from reading many psychological analyses, even scientific ones, does not result only from historical distance: it has something to do with the field of knowledge concerned. The concept of 'sensation' already cited furnishes an excellent example in this respect. A physiologist of today would not disagree with the sense given to this word in Helmholtz's *Lehrbuch der physiologischen Optik* (1866), but would hardly be prepared to follow Wundt's development of the concept of sensation in various chapters of his *Physiologische Psychologie* (1873). What, one may ask, motivates these two opposing judgements? The answer is, in our opinion, that Helmholtz, the physiologist engaged in physiology, describes the *seen* (the observed), while Wundt, the physiologist engaged in psychology, uses the same word to describe the *unseen* (the inferred). The former describes an actual fact with a general term; the latter refers to an entity with the same general term. The meaning of abstraction is basically different in physiology and in psychology.

As we remarked in an earlier section of this book (p. 40), this semantic shift of scientific vocabulary in psychology has a pre-scientific cultural origin. It allows psychological discourse to manipulate symbols at a verbal level as if they referred to observable facts. But this reference only exists when psychological work is actually biological. The role of phenomenological epistemology is precisely to establish under which conditions there exists, in the phenomena themselves, an authentic foundation for the concepts used. When no such foundation exists, abstraction exists for itself and pure entities proliferate, free from every tie with organic reality. The task of today's epistemology with regard to the foundation of an adequate biology of human conduct corresponds strictly to the task Husserl set for himself when he became aware of the need for basing logic independently of the conceptual psychology of his time. The motivation is, in both cases, a radical return to the phenomena of the subject as a living, i.e. a simultaneously pathic and constitutive being.

The rest of this chapter will be devoted to the theoretical endeavour of Georges Politzer, who attempted to elaborate a *concrete psychology*[1] in opposition to abstraction devoid of reference. The name of Politzer is practically unknown in Anglo-Saxon psychology.[2] We think nevertheless that

---

[1] 'Concrete psychology' is the literal traslation of 'Psychologie concrète', an expression which we do not feel entitled to alter, since it is consistently used by Politzer to qualify his overall critical endeavour. In doing so, we are aware of the fact that 'concrete' may sound ambivalent and even incorrect in English owing to its use as a substantive. We hope that the reader will forgive us this unavoidable awkwardness of translation and will understand that it is imposed on us by the lack of a more adequate term.

[2] Georges Politzer was born in Nagy-Varad (Hungary) in 1903. He emigrated to France in 1921 and took his degree in philosophy (*agrégé*) in 1926 at the University of Paris. His main work, *Critique des Fondements de la Psychologie*, was published in 1928. The next year he published a violent pamphlet on Bergson's philosophy under the title *La fin d'une parade philosophique: le Bergsonisme*. From 1930 to the outbreak of World War II, Politzer was deeply involved in

D

the study of his work is particularly useful in relation to the main issues of this book, because it exemplifies very convincingly – and mostly by opposition – what may and may not be expected of a theoretical criticism of the foundations of psychology.

1   *A critical analysis of classical psychology*

Politzer's *Critique des Fondements de la Psychologie* (1928) amounts to a condemnation of classical psychology *en masse*. His famous sentence 'psychologists are scientific in the manner that evangelized savages are Christian' testifies to his conviction that classical psychology was only scientific in appearance. In analysing this criticism in detail, we will return, on many occasions, to topics which are now familiar to students of the philosophical conceptual framework underlying psychological epistemology. This was not the case with the great majority of psychologists in the twenties. To this should be added that Politzer was the first to introduce, in official psychology outside Germany, the basic question of the meaning which this approach to knowledge could have for the living subject. Phenomenology appeared on the French philosophical scene only after 1945, but there is no doubt that Politzer exerted an early, though hidden, influence on the initial orientation of Merleau-Ponty's thinking. We shall have to consider whether the *Critique* and other studies written in the same spirit actually tackle epistemological themes akin to those raised by phenomenology.

The expression 'classical psychology', of which Politzer makes abundant use, designates different schools. If the author includes Behaviourism under this heading, his criticisms are principally directed against Elementarism. Gestalt psychology is not analysed thoroughly. Politzer notes, however, in a rather hasty fashion, that the theoretical constructs of this system present the same defects of principle as those of its predecessors.[1] There is little doubt that the harshness of tone which pervades his writings is more than a personal trait; it is enforced by the ideological significance the author wanted to give to his work. And, indeed, the antagonism developed in the *Critique* between classical and 'concrete' psychology masks a more fundamental one: that between materialistic and idealistic psychology. About this, Politzer writes:

> Concrete psychology is materialistic psychology, that is the psychology which adopts in this manner the only attitude capable of assuring to this

---

political action in the French communist party. He took part in 1940 in the formation of a resistance group. Arrested by the German occupation authorities in 1942, he was shot in May of the same year. Politzer was a generous figure intolerant of every attack on individual freedom. His intelligent and aggressive writings reflect an uncompromising personality, well aware of the shortcomings of accepted ideas, both at the theoretical and at the practical level. Four volumes of his collected papers have so far been published (*Editions Sociales*, Paris).

[1]G. Politzer, *Critique des Fondements de la Psychologie,* Paris, Rieder, 1928 (3rd edn, Paris, Presses Universitaires de France, 1968), p. 17.

discipline a scientific future. It is however to contemporary materialism that it is bound, that of Marx and Engels, and which is called *dialectical materialism*. Psychology is in need of a complete materialism and dialectical materialism is the only complete one. It is only from such a starting-point that psychology will be capable of becoming a science.[1]

As we shall see later, the acceptance of a *philosophical* materialism, very different in essence from the general materialistic point of view of objective natural science, will make it difficult for Politzer to establish the positive scientific programme of concrete psychology. But let us first examine his major criticism of classical psychology.

2 The myth of substantialism

The main objective to be pursued in order to renovate psychology is '*the dissolution of the myth of the double nature of man*'.[2] This direct attack on dualism aims at more than defeating Cartesian substantialism; it is directed against the spiritual ideal of a soul within a body, an ideal which made of psychology the 'projection on the theological-dogmatic level of what the "people" must believe so that a social regime can exist'. Considered in this perspective, introspectionism is more than a mere internal examination of the so-called content of consciousness; it is an attempt to penetrate to the 'second nature' of man, into his deep spiritual states. Therefore, the important point is not the actual effectiveness of introspection, nor its value considered from the point of view of experimental control, nor even, as Brentano had remarked, its absolute possibility, but the very fact that it was historically invoked as a method. According to Politzer, this called for a general conception of man rooted in a dualism imposed by the ruling classes as a guarantee of social equilibrium. This well-known Marxist thesis is not of interest for our purpose. But, whatever may be the case, it suggests to Politzer a convincing conclusion about the state of psychology in his time: 'classical psychology strives to consider the same thing twice in the third person:[3] it projects the exterior into the interior, from which it tries next, but in vain, to extract it . . . and while professing a deep disgust for metaphysics, it has not ceased for fifty years to go from one kind of metaphysics to another'.[4]

[1]G. Politzer, *La crise de la psychologie contemporaine*, Paris, Ed. Soc. 1947, p. 90. Translation ours.

[2]*Critique des Fondements de la Psychologie*, p. 7. Translation ours. Original author's italics.

[3]'In the third person' (*en troisième personne*) has become a current expression in existential French texts to designate a mode of approach excluding, by virtue of the impersonal mode of treatment linked with scientific objectivity, every reference to the individual subject, i.e. to the first or the second person ('I' and 'you') as it spontaneously establishes itself in inter-individual communication. Comparison should be made here with Heidegger's use of *das Man* (the one) in the impersonal mode, to describe the merging of the individual in the anonymous. For a further analysis of this depersonalising tendency in the human sciences, cf. E. Straus, *Vom Sinn der Sinne*, Berlin, Springer, 1956 (2nd ed. English translation under the title *The Primary World of Senses*) and K. Holzkamp, *Kritische Psychologie*, Frankfurt/Main, Fischer Taschenbuch Verlag, 1972.

[4]*Critique des Fondements de la Psychologie*, p. 45. Translation ours.

3   *Striving towards the 'concrete'*

Dualism, both at the level of anthropological prerequisites and of scientific constructs, is the price paid for an *abstract* approach to human reality. Abstraction is the central concept of Politzer's criticism; it appears on nearly every page of the *Critique*. 'We say', he writes, 'that a psychology which replaces problems of persons by problems of things, which suppresses man and transforms actors into processes, which relinquishes the dramatic multiplicity of individuals in favour of the impersonal multiplicity of phenomena, is an abstract psychology.'[1] In opposition to this, concrete psychology has as its object the individual 'I'. Therefore, insofar as one may speak of psychological facts, they should be 'homogeneous with the "I" '.[2] 'Now, psychology,' he adds,

> if it has a reason to be, can only exist as 'empirical' science. It must therefore interpret the requirement of the first person and of homogeneity in a manner appropriate to its plan. As it has to be *empirical*, the 'I' of psychology can only be the *particular individual*. On the other hand, this 'I' cannot be the subject of a transcendental act such as apperception, because we need a concept which would be at the same level as the concrete individual and would be simply the act of the 'I' of psychology. Now, the act of the concrete individual is *life*, but the singular life of the singular individual, in brief *life in the dramatic sense of the word.*[3]

This outline of a subject-centred psychology is very different from that of phenomenology, although some verbal similarities may be misleading at first glance. The 'I' of concrete psychology, according to Politzer, is not the conceptual result of transcendental reduction in the Husserlian sense. Nor is the subject empirical in the sense of Hume and later British empiricism. Be it noted, in passing, that there is no explicit reference to phenomenology in the whole text of the *Critique*. Some passages in other texts indicate, however, that Politzer did not ignore an Husserlian influence on psychology, though his quotations refer principally to Heidegger. To him, transcendental phenomenology, insofar as he studied it, must bear the mark of idealism and consequently of the abstractionism he constantly condemned. His remarks on Kant are enlightening in this respect. Kant could not, he contends, agree with Hume's associationist views because the empiricist theory of association was elaborated on the model of Newton's system of universal attraction and it was therefore a doctrine of blind coexistence depending on action 'from thing to

---

[1]G. Politzer, *La crise de la psychologie contemporaine.* Paris, Ed. Soc. 1947, p. 102. Translation ours.

[2]*Critique des Fondements de la Psychologie*, p. 50. Translation ours.

[3]*Critique des Fondements de la Psychologie*, p. 51. Original author's italics. Translation ours. The word 'dramatic' is used here in its primary etymological sense, i.e. in the sense of a concrete fact acted by a subject. This meaning refers thus to common experience and not to exceptional events as in literary contexts.

thing'[1] which did not require a subject. In his theory of synthesis, Kant offers, in principle, a sufficient foundation for a concrete subject, since synthesis is an act in the first person, and the categories of reasoning are distinguished only to specify transcendental apperception. 'But the "I" of Kant', he continues, 'though being a "subject", is the subject of objective and consequently universal thinking; its discovery and its study not only do not require, but exclude concrete experience since we are and must remain at the level of transcendental logic.'[2] The problem raised here, within this broad epistemological framework, extends beyond the limits of our analysis, and amounts to comparing Kant and Husserl from the point of view of transcendental knowledge and to relocating psychology accordingly.[3]

To summarise, Politzer's purpose is to substitute the realism of the subject involved in life situations for the realism of abstract formulations *about* the subject. Thus, his call for concrete psychology converges in a sense with the framework of Straus (1963) and of Buytendijk (1965), although his point of departure is entirely different. The content of his proposals is more akin to the actual strivings of phenomenological psychology than to the preparatory analyses of Husserl which extend from the *Logische Untersuchungen* (1901) to the posthumous *Phaenomenologische Psychologie*.[4] His tone is that of an existentialist although he would certainly have refused this label for epistemological as well as ideological reasons. Finally, he warns against pseudo-concrete psychologies, the best example of which is, according to him, Bergson's theory of intuition.[5]

4   The postulate of conventional meaning

The third major point in Politzer's criticism is directed against the *formalism* of classical psychology. In this context, the word has the double meaning of a pure logical game and of a compliance with traditional standards. The former is the consequence of dualism and abstractionism; the latter results, in the Marxist view of the author, from class notions imposing an ideology of the unreal by virtue of its own conservative mechanisms.[6] The overall picture of classical psychology is then characterised by a peculiar uniformity, in which

[1] *Ibid.*

[2] *Critique des Fondements de la Psychologie, loc. cit.*

[3] Cf. in relation to this point, I. Kern, *Husserl und Kant*, The Hague, Nijhoff, 1964.

[4] The *Phänomenologische Psychologie*, published in 1962 in the series 'Husserliana', under the editorship of W. Biemel, is a set of lectures given by Husserl in 1925. It is thus prior to the *Krisis der europäischen Wissenschaften und die transzendentale Phänomenologie* (1936), Husserl's last great work (republished in 1954 in the series 'Husserliana').

[5] 'The concrete of Bergson is only a concrete in general, for it is impossible to conceive the concrete independently of a particular content: in putting it in quality, in duration and, generally, in the manner and in the form, all that can ever be got is *concrete in general*.' (G. Politzer, *La fin d'une parade philosophique: le Bergsonisme*, 1929. Republished Paris, Pauvert, 1968, p. 44. Author's italics. Translation ours.)

[6] Cf. point 2 p. 99.

Politzer sees the effect of what he calls *the postulate of conventional meaning*.

It amounts to considering, though mostly in an implicit manner, that psychic facts have a conventional and public meaning: 'everything happens as if all individual consciousnesses had exactly the same content of meanings, as if each individual consciousness were only the intuition of meanings always identical and for everybody'.[1] In such a framework, it is only natural that there should exist a tacit agreement that psychology leave the concrete subject in favour of 'mental processes' or any other construct corresponding supposedly to interior life: 'whatever the thing thought may be, only "thought" interests the psychologist'.[2]

The major consequence of this is that psychological abstractionism relies entirely on accepted ideas, i.e. on opinions and not on authentic judgements. Thus, the conceptual translation of psychic experience amounts to a double falsification: not only does it shift from subjective actuality to rationalistic verbalism, but the level of abstraction attained in this manner remains purely at the level of opinion. This conclusion brings us back to our previous analysis of the effect of culturalism on psychology (Chapter 1).

5   Psychoanalysis and the concrete subject

Politzer's negative criticism of classical psychology is completed by a positive plea for concrete psychology. The main thesis defended in the *Critique* and in various other texts is that psychoanalysis in principle furnishes a model for a concrete approach to the subject. We must not forget, however, that Politzer refers to Freud's early ideas and that several deep transformations took place in psychoanalytical theory after the publication of the *Critique*. Nevertheless, the appraisal of the Freudian system is not blindly enthusiastic, and having stressed its concrete aspects, Politzer proceeds to an analysis of its defects, which finally will lead him to conclusions similar to those concerning classical psychology. 'Freud', he writes, 'is as astonishingly abstract in his theories as he is concrete in his discoveries.'[3] We may consider these two aspects successively in order to understand the author's evolution towards his definitive forsaking of psychoanalysis.[4]

Referring to the *Interpretation of Dreams*, Politzer considers that the characterisation of the dream as the realisation of a desire corresponds to the grasping of an authentic psychological fact, because the sense of the dream is found in direct relation to the subject's experience. It is a *concrete* fact of the existence of the individual in the first person. To understand it, no reference to

---

[1] *Critique des Fondements de la Psychologie*, p. 97. Translation ours.
[2] *Ibid.*, p. 86. Translation ours.
[3] *Ibid.*, p. 209. Translation ours.
[4] This critical process took a little more than ten years. The first criticisms appeared in 1928 in the *Critique* and ended in a total condemnation in an article published in 1939 under the title: 'La fin de la psychanalyse', *La Pensée*, No. 3 (reprinted in G. Politzer, *Ecrits 2 – Les Fondements de la Psychologie*, Paris, Ed. Sociales, 1969, pp. 282–302).

organic facts, imagination or pathology is necessary. Thus, Freud is the first to have done away with abstractionism and with impersonal causal explanations, whereas classical interpretations invoking images or affective states had always obliged psychologists to repeat the same general statements about every dream and to elaborate artificial classifications accordingly.

But, in spite of the profound significance of this discovery and of the completely new approach to the subject which it inaugurated, Freud was incapable of developing his theory without falling into the trap of conceptual realism. This survival of classical realism appears in his hypothesis of the unconscious. At this stage (Chapter 7 of the *Interpretation of Dreams*), Freud leaves the interpretation of dreams in order to develop their explanation. This he can only do by referring to the principles of traditional psychological systems. Thus, the explanation proceeds in line with mechanical concepts borrowed from natural science, and the 'process' of the dream is tentatively inserted in the classical mentalistic scheme of sensation and thought. The whole psychic apparatus is reconstructed in terms similar to those of reflexology: transformations of 'energy', displacements of 'intensities', variations in 'levels', etc. In this abstract game of representations, the dream becomes a general entity and the individuality of the subject is finally lost.[1]

To deduce the existence of the unconscious from the latent but real knowledge which is supposed to explain the dream, or from unconscious factors supposedly producing conscious effects, amounts to transforming meanings into things. The theory of the unconscious, however, played a positive role: it definitely excluded any return to the introspective attitude. 'After the introduction of the unconscious, it is impossible to define psychological fact all by itself: the definition of psychological fact is reconsidered *at the psychic level itself.*'[2]

Politzer's position is that of an isolated critic and is paradoxical in many ways. One may wonder what might have been the evolution of his thought if he had lived to the present day to witness psychology continuing unheedingly to create entities not basically different from those he so fiercely fought. Would he have reconsidered his 1939 statement that psychoanalysis already belonged to the past if he had watched the splitting up of the Freudian system into various sub-schools, each of which considers itself to be the seat of orthodoxy? Would he have seen in the new phenomenological psychology a striving towards the concrete akin to his own? Most important of all, would the eventual active growth of his concrete psychology, abruptly interrupted by his death, itself have contributed to changing the classical ideal of objectivity in positive psychological research? This last question calls for a brief critical examination of the main positive issues raised by Politzer.

[1] *Critique*, pp. 126, 139, 148 and 213f.
[2] *Ibid.*, p. 223. Author's italics. Translation ours.

6   *An epistemological appraisal of concrete psychology*

The *Critique des Fondements de la Psychologie* ends with twenty-six propositions which summarise the programme of concrete psychology. In this fashion its author claims to supply future psychologists with the necessary tools of an anti-abstractionist revolution and, consequently, with the theoretical elements of a new scientific psychology. If these propositions make any sense, they must outline an epistemology, i.e. a set of logical principles capable of forming the basis of, but distinct from the actual exercise of, psychology, though essentially motivated by it.

It is hardly possible to admit that the *Critique* (and related writings) amounts to an actual epistemological analysis. Because of his ideological background, Politzer mistakes the hermeneutical problem of the psychological subject for the epistemological one. Indeed, the critical material with which he provides us is an interpretation of the history of psychology, not an analysis of the adequacy of the technical work currently carried out in psychological research. The *Critique* deals with the general psychological mentality of the time, not with actual theories and related problems of validity. As such, however, Politzer's negative statements go straight to the point. Therefore, it is not surprising that his criticisms should converge beyond one's expectations with later phenomenological restatements of classical objective psychology (Straus, Buytendijk, Merleau-Ponty), but only superficial verbal similarities could convey the impression that the contents of these respective analyses are at all identical.

With regard to the 'concrete' subject, the paradox of Politzer's teachings lies in the fact that the 'I' which he places at the centre of every psychological approach has a truly personalistic resonance. Concrete psychology, we are told, aims at studying the individual in ordinary life circumstances. Nevertheless, when this individual subject must be characterised, all arguments against its abstract depersonalisation are found in the collective Marxist framework. This contradiction could have been avoided if Politzer had included an epistemological analysis of intersubjectivity in the constructive part of his *Critique*. Consequently, the subject is said to be 'concrete' when he is immersed in social reality. In interpreting concreteness in this fashion, Politzer fails to avoid the pitfall of culturalism, as analysed in Chapter 1. His criticisms of classical psychology are convincing, but, in considering solely the socio-cultural subject, he can do nothing more than shift the subject from one theoretical framework to another, which finally amounts to deciding in favour of a new kind of abstractionism. This has prevented him, not less than his unavowed hermeneutics, from endowing concrete psychology with authentic scientific significance. We may see in this gap the second great paradox of his endeavour.

In conclusion, Politzer's attempt to free psychology from inadequate abstract constructs has failed in its positive part, because he fights against metaphysics with metaphysical weapons. Now, it is debatable whether establishing psychology as a science requires an absolute exclusion of metaphysical reflection. Historically, the liberating of psychology from philosophical ties was a necessary step in introducing the scientific method as an actual positive procedure. It made psychology focus on the necessity of coping with 'facts' and not with 'ideas', 'mental faculties' and the like. It was, in a sense, the first victory over abstractionism. It soon appeared, however – with Brentano's *Psychology from an empirical standpoint* (1874) – that the so-called psychological facts were still constructs not related to subjectivity. Thus the content and sense of the findings made available by the use of scientific methodology had still to be examined critically. They required an adequate epistemological treatment.

'Concrete' psychology was an epistemological failure precisely because it did not care to elaborate *concretely* the conditions of approach of subjectivity and intersubjectivity. It consistently missed the issues it advocated by neglecting the subject as a biological being. Politzer states explicitly that the problem of concrete psychology is '*to define the psychic as psychic, i.e. to avoid every confusion with physiology, biology or any other natural science*'.[1] But to look for biological foundations does not amount to confusing psychology's own standpoint with that of biology. Sherrington's descriptive analyses of the *actually existing* relations between the anatomo-physiological features of the receptors and the emergence of subjective space-time, which were discussed in Chapter 3, would indeed have prevented a lot of confusion in the study of the living subject if they had not been ignored by the vast majority of psychologists. Politzer with good reason taunts them for their obedience to the myth of man's dual nature and their consequent abstract objectivism. Unfortunately, his concrete subject is just a further abstract construct originating from a social ideology and, strangely enough, devoid of biological reality.

7   Epistemology and ideology

An ideology is a system of beliefs about man and the world which is not only impossible to verify scientifically but also rejects verification as a matter of principle. In psychology and in the human sciences in general, there is a growing tendency to consider ideologies as conceptual systems concerned with the foundations of knowledge. In fact, their role is limited to the spreading of beliefs: they are concerned with opinions, not with technically definable concepts.

The danger of ideologies lies in the fact that, being the source and vehicle of opinions, they are always ethico- or politico-social in nature. Thus, when they interfere with human sciences, they may be taken seriously because they claim

---

[1] *Critique des Fondements de la Psychologie*, p. 223. Original author's italics, translation ours.

to define objectives aiming at development, welfare, peace and the like. One should expect that men of science, and psychologists in particular, are sufficiently critical to draw sharp distinctions between epistemological requirements and ideological beliefs. Experience shows that this is not always the case.

Thus, scientists who readily admit that Lysenko was wrong in stating that Mendelian genetics was a product of capitalist ideology, nevertheless think that teaching systems should be 'democratic' and that something like 'Marxist psychology' exists.[1]

To the epistemologist, such expressions are sheer nonsense. If epistemology has an important role to play in studying the foundations of psychology, it is precisely because it aims at eliminating from it mere cultural or ideological influences.

The failure of Politzer's endeavour is, as we have seen, the result of an ideological interpretation of psychology which he uncritically equated with a scientific programme. Ideological influences threaten the scientific status of today's psychology in much the same way. Epistemology should thus stop psychology from going again 'from one kind of metaphysics to another', though ideologies have little in common with genuine metaphysics.

[1] Cf. *Psychologie et Marxisme*. Collective work (no editor) Paris, Soc. Générale d'Edition, 1971.

Chapter 5

Phenomenological Psychology and the Biological Standpoint

It is customary, in American texts on the history or epistemology of psychology, to refer to phenomenological psychology as the 'third force', the first and second being classical experimental psychology (mostly considered in its Behaviouristic aspects) and psychoanalysis with its various (generally opposing) groups or sub-schools. As Misiak and Sexton remark,[1] the third force entered the American psychological scene around 1950 as a consequence of the pre-war immigration of European psychologists of several German universities who had been under the influence of Husserl's teachings. The point of interest for our purpose is that this historical phenomenon had such powerful consequences that it shook Behaviourism at its very roots and cast doubt upon the value of traditional scientific psychology. According to Misiak and Sexton, however, the 'third force' may have a narrower meaning, designating more specially humanistic psychology in the sense of Maslow (1969).[2] Whatever may be the case, phenomenological psychology has for a long time had more than a philosophical import in the field of psychology proper. It began its autonomous existence, i.e. as distinct from Husserl's transcendental phenomenology, in Europe in the twenties. Katz's *Aufbau der Tastwelt (The World of Touch)*, published in 1925, is generally considered as the first phenomenologically oriented piece of research carried out by a scientific psychologist. Buytendijk turned to phenomenological analysis about 1950, but this new orientation stands in direct continuity with his previous research work as a physiologist and student of animal behaviour.[3] The theoretical developments treated in this chapter will be both technical and historical, since we shall consider the progressive emergence of phenomenological psychology in Husserl's own writings. We shall point out,

[1]H. Misiak and V. S. Sexton, *Phenomenological, existential and humanistic psychologies*, New York, London, Grune and Stratton, 1973, Ch. 3.
[2]More will be found on this topic in J. Cohen, *Homo Psychologicus*, London, George Allen & Unwin, 1970.
[3]Cf. G. Thinès and R. Zayan, 'Buytendijk's contribution to animal behaviour: animal psychology or ethology?' *Acta biotheoretica*, XXIV (1975), pp. 86–99.

wherever needed, to what extent his teachings may be advocated to support our biologically-centred outlook.

The analysis carried out in the previous chapters indicates that if phenomenological psychology aims at a basic change in the approach to subjectivity, it can only achieve this on firm biological grounds. The factual and theoretical issues dealt with in Chapter 3 were meant to convince the reader – and primarily the reader unsympathetic to phenomenology and to epistemological problems of psychology in general – that the point of departure had to be sought in the direct study of the living organism in his adaptive relations with his world. This last sentence should, however, be understood in a sense which differs profoundly from well-known existentially inspired definitions of the subject as 'being-in-the-world'. There is no doubt that this widely used expression describes a fact which was overlooked by objective psychologists for decades and that sensitivity to it is still hard to find in traditional scientific circles. But, as we shall see, this reminder of the basic vital condition of the subject remains to be specified.

1. The life-world

In his analysis of psychology as a human science, Giorgi (1970) stresses its lack of relevance to the life-world (*Lebenswelt* as defined by Husserl) and refers on this point principally to the criticisms of Sanford (1965) and Allport (1947). 'The most obvious implication of such a criticism', he writes, 'is that psychology is not yet adequately dealing with the problem of everyday life . . . Applied psychology does not really fill this need – because it deals with everyday problems on its own terms, i.e., by first translating the problem into a scientific expression, and then solving it'.[1] As we have seen when we dealt with concrete psychology (Chapter 4), Politzer also required that psychology should consider the everyday subject as its central theme. But, to paraphrase Giorgi's quotation, Politzer did not really fill this need either, because he dealt with everyday problems by first translating them into an ideological expression and so missed the obvious concreteness of biological and behavioural givenness.

In trying to outline the new science called phenomenological psychology, the first difficulty we encounter is precisely the need for relying on a definition – however provisional – of the biologically concrete. In other words, we are faced at the outset with the obligation of admitting a certain idea of the given, which amounts to elaborating the concrete *a priori* of the science in question epistemologically. As we have remarked previously, the *a priori* does not designate any kind of preconception or philosophical one-sidedness. It merely refers to the absolute necessity of guaranteeing oneself a starting-point, without which the very intention of securing knowledge in a particular field disappears. The limits of the *a priori* are thus defined by the

[1]A. Giorgi, *Psychology as a Human Science*, New York, Harper & Row, 1970, p. 85f.

constitutive powers of the subject and are ultimately rooted in his perceptual experience. Every area of knowledge is then originally circumscribed by what Husserl calls a regional ontology.[1] The essence of a particular field of knowledge should not be understood as a sort of metaphysical entity 'included' in a thing or a concept in the sense of classical idealism. When Husserl refers to 'essence', he contrasts it with the mere factual existence of a thing considered as the final product of knowledge. The existing thing as such is not understood or explained by the very fact of its existence. If it were, there would be no point in knowledge at all. As knowledge necessarily results from some *a priori*, the kind of *a priori* at work in a given science must be specified. This specification is what Husserl calls the 'regional essence' of the field concerned. It corresponds to the content of the 'regional ontology' of the field in question. It deals with the *material* content of a particular science, as opposed to the *formal* properties of objects in general as studied in pure logic.

All these specific contents are, of course, different from one science to another. In physics, for instance, this content is not the same as in the life-sciences. It is therefore necessary to outline the basic *a priori* assumptions of physical knowledge and to examine those of biological knowledge in comparison. This indicates that the use of physical concepts in biology or in psychology should be justified according to the subject-matter proper to biology or psychology. The transfer cannot be effected as a matter of course.

The elaboration of regional ontologies is, however, a first theoretical systematisation. Although it is not the result of pure logical deduction, it already defines a particular essence and stands therefore at a higher level of knowledge than primary subjective experience. It should be noted that the latter has all too often been interpreted as dealing exclusively with the individual quality of one's personal and incommunicable psychic life, i.e. of private interiority. According to Strasser (1963) this is especially true of French philosophers of existence. 'They crusade', he writes, 'against what they call "objective thought". In their view, "*objective thought*" prevents man from discovering that which is fundamental, genuine and authentic. They appear unaware of the distinction between objectivity and objectivism.'[2] This kind of anti-scientific subjectivism has brought much confusion to the evaluation of phenomenology, which has sometimes for this reason been considered as an 'art of describing impressions'.[3] As the same author remarks, we have to do here with an interpretation of Husserl which the technical analysis of his writings does not in any way allow. What is distorted is the Husserlian

---

[1] 'The system of synthetic truths which have their ground in the regional essence constitutes the content of the regional ontology . . . *All empirical science* [must be] *grounded in their own regional ontologies*, and not merely on the pure logic which is common to all sciences'. (E. Husserl, *Ideen zu einer reinen Phänomenologie und phänomenologischen Philosophie*. Halle, Niemeyer, 1913, 16 and 17. Translated by W. R. Boyce Gibson; *Ideas: General Introduction to Pure Phenomenology*, London, George Allen & Unwin, 1931, pp. 77–79. Original author's italics and quotation marks.)

[2] S. Strasser, *Phenomenology and the Human Sciences*, Pittsburgh, Duquesne University Press, 1963, p. 67.

[3] *Ibid.*

concept of *Lebenswelt*, i.e. the world of everyday life, or the life-world. In attempting to establish to what extent the life-world, considered as the primary basis of an authentic phenomenological psychology, may be approached from the biological standpoint, we must refrain from such oversimplifying interpretations. Let it be clear that indulging in conceptual distortions of this kind would be as harmful to our purpose as the assimilative transfer of analytical physiology to early experimental psychology was detrimental to the formulation of an adequate theory of consciousness. We must therefore examine carefully what exactly Husserl's theory of the *Lebenswelt* amounts to, and the model which can be legitimately found in it for the present analysis.

At the beginning of the second section of his *Ideas*, Husserl expounds the 'thesis of the natural standpoint' as a preparatory step for its 'bracketing' (*Epoche*), the latter being the absolute requirement of the transcendental reduction. The natural world is 'for me simply there'[1] and is revealed to me in ordinary perception; it is to this world-about-me that 'the complex forms and my manifold and shifting *spontaneities* of stand are related'.[2] Thus the subject's internal states are factually related to the world in a primary vital fashion. This relation, Husserl adds, includes every immediate experience which Descartes subsumed under the word *Cogito*.[3] But to be the subject of the *Cogito*, I do not need to express it consciously in speech, i.e. reflectively. It is a constitutive fact granted by my condition as a living being. Moreover, the object of my *Cogito*, i.e. the *cogitatum*, varies in its nature according to whether it refers to the naturally given world, or to another world as present in representation, e.g. to quote Husserl's own instance, the arithmetical world when I am busied with numbers:

> *The arithmetical world is there for me only when and so long as I occupy the arithmetical standpoint*. But the *natural* world, the world in the ordinary sense of the word, is *constantly there for me*, so long as I live naturally and look in its direction . . . The natural world *still remains 'present'*, I am at the natural standpoint after as well as before, and in this respect *undisturbed by the adoption of new standpoints*.[4]

---

[1] *Ideas*, sect. 27, p. 101.

[2] *Ideas*, sect. 28, p. 103.

[3] As we noted above (p. 29), in Descartes' seventeenth-century vocabulary, the word *pensée* (*cogitatum*) refers not only to abstract thinking, but to psychic experience as a whole, including affects and the like. However, the experienced relation to the world does not assess by itself the value of knowledge, it is just its unavoidable point of departure. The theory of knowledge requires therefore that this uncritical attitude should be excluded at the outset. This process is called by Husserl the 'bracketing' of the natural attitude, i.e. of the belief in the existence of the natural world. The act by which this bracketing is effected is called the reduction. The relation between the latter and the standpoint of natural science is discussed in section 7 of this chapter. It should be remarked that this reduction, which Husserl considers as transcendental (because it goes beyond immediate experience), does not amount to a 'negation' of the natural world. The word 'bracketing' indicates by itself that the natural attitude is just left out provisionally, because it is not, as such, an inherent part of analytical knowledge.

[4] *Ideas*, sect. 28, p. 104. Original author's italics.

The natural world described in this fashion has the characteristic of being unavoidable; as such, not only does it not preclude the coexistence of other worlds-about-me, but appears as their condition of emergence, though the latter remain independent of it. Keeping to his arithmetic example, Husserl adds: 'The two worlds are present together but *disconnected* apart, that is, from their relation to the Ego, in virtue of which I can freely direct my glance or my acts to the one or to the other.'[1] It is appropriate to recall here the Cartesian solution regarding the essence of 'reality'. In Descartes' philosophy, the 'disconnection' is so complete that the natural world itself becomes a particular standpoint with which the sceptical thinker *may or may not* be concerned. In order to avoid his total immersion in unreality, the philosopher is then bound to elaborate two conceptual substances corresponding to the physical world and the psychic one, thus opening the way to the irreconcilable dualism of objectivity and subjectivity. At the limit of this process, the natural world and the natural subject have both become mere abstractions.[2]

An important remark is necessary at this point. The characterisation of the natural world which we have considered until now in the context of Husserl's *Ideas* is, as we said before, only analysed in view of the 'radical alteration of the natural thesis' leading to the transcendental reflection (commencing with section 31 of the *Ideas*). In this prolegomenon, there is no mention of the life-world in the sense of the *Lebenswelt* as it will appear much later in Husserl's writings, namely in the *Krisis der europäischen Wissenschaften und die transzendentale Phänomenologie (The Crisis of European sciences and transcendental Phenomenology;* 1936). In his 1913 *Ideas*, Husserl designates the natural world by the words *Umwelt* or *natürliche Umwelt*, which refer to the natural environment of the subject *prior* to reduction, and which consequently express a concept that does not have all the implications of the *Lebenswelt*. The latter will indeed be introduced in a different context, *posterior* to the reduction of objective science. We shall come back to this question in a later section of this chapter.

2 *Husserl's first characterisation of phenomenological psychology*

But, although we may not, for the reason just stated, infer from the analysis of the *Ideas* any epistemological consequence for the possible biological dimension of phenomenological psychology, we find in Husserl's same work some remarks about the nature of the latter. In the Introduction to the *Ideas*, Husserl clearly defines his position with regard to empirical psychology:

In the last decade,[3] there has been much talk of phenomenology in German philosophy and psychology. In presumed agreement with the *Logical*

---

[1] *Ibid.*, p. 105. Original author's italics.
[2] On further psychological consequences of the Cartesian *Cogito* and its relation to the idea of consciousness as interior 'reality', cf. G. Thinès, *La Problématique de la Psychologie*, The Hague, Nijhoff, 1968, p. 65f.
[3] From 1900–1901 (*Logische Untersuchungen*) to 1913 (*Ideen–I*).

studies, phenomenology is conceived as a sub-domain of empirical psychology, as a region containing 'immanent' descriptions of psychical events [*Erlebnisse*] which – such is their understanding of this immanence – remains strictly within the framework of inner *experience* [*Erfahrung*]. My protest against this interpretation has apparently been of little use, and the accompanying elucidations, which sharply delineate some at least of the main points of difference, have not been understood or have been heedlessly set aside. Thence also the completely empty replies – empty because the plain *meaning* of my statement was missed – to my criticism of the psychological method, a criticism which in no way denied the value of modern psychology and in no sense depreciated the experimental work carried out by men of distinction, but exposed certain, in the literal sense of the term, radical defects of method on the removal of which, in my opinion, the raising of psychology to a higher scientific level and an extraordinary extension of its field of work must depend.[1]

In the next section of the text, Husserl states without ambiguity that pure phenomenology '*is not psychology*'.[2]

His purpose was not to substitute pure phenomenology for scientific psychology. However, since his time, epistemological reflections on the value of psychology as a science have resulted in the development of an autonomous phenomenological psychology, and this new approach to the human sciences has thus evolved towards a new characterisation of the object and methods of psychology *at the empirical level itself*. If phenomenological philosophy had any historical (and normative) consequences, it was precisely to modify the conception of the natural world in which psychological research is actually carried out. We could venture to say that, even if he is absolutely ignorant of the phenomenological movement, or if he explicitly rejects any of its teachings, a psychologist of our time cannot possibly adhere to the same *natural* standpoint as before. Hence our attempt to analyse to what extent this natural standpoint can be described in biological terms.

We have seen that Husserl conceived his work as exclusively philosophical. In the preface which he wrote in 1931 for the English translation of his *Ideen*, he specifies the relations that exist between transcendental phenomenology and phenomenological psychology. As is known, he claims to reach the transcendental point of view by means of the 'reduction' which is realised by 'bracketing' the natural world. This philosophical operation should not be confounded with a mere return to pure idealism. What does subjectivity lose in reduction? 'Just', Husserl writes, 'that which makes it something real in the world that lies before us . . . the meaning of the soul as belonging to a body that exists in an objective, spatio-temporal Nature.'[3] The reality of the natural

[1] *Ideas*, pp. 41–2.
[2] *Ibid.*
[3] *Ibid.*, p. 14.

world and of the subject who belongs to it are not questioned, and it is always possible to revert from the transcendental to the natural point of view and conversely. Husserl writes further:

> To each eidetic or empirical determination on the one side there must correspond a parallel feature on the other. And yet, this whole content as psychology, considered from the natural standpoint as a positive science, therefore, and related to the world as spread before us, is entirely non-philosophical, whereas the 'same' content from the transcendental standpoint, and therefore as transcendental phenomenology, is a philosophical science – indeed, on closer view, *the* basic philosophical science, preparing on descriptive lines the transcendental ground which remains henceforth the exclusive ground for all philosophical knowledge. [1]

Husserl's main theme is thus the founding of philosophy – not of psychology – as a science. But if philosophical science exists under this form with all its epistemological consequences, psychology as a science is then radically different from what it is at the natural level. It is noteworthy that when Husserl refers to empirical subjectivity, he has in mind mainly the natural subject as it appears in the Cartesian context and in nineteenth-century 'physiological psychology'. This 'natural subject' or 'natural observer' is that of psychophysics, i.e. a subject considered as natural because it is grasped in the framework of physical science; it is a 'mundane subject' conceived after the model of the science which was capable of conceiving the world in natural terms, rather than the individual of ordinary life in his biological concreteness. Phenomenological psychology as it is developing today considers the psychophysical subject and the related 'body–soul' problem as a mere historical issue. Thus, though relying on the epistemological foundations of pure phenomenology, it does not find a complementary outline in Husserl's early analysis of empirical subjectivity because the psychophysically defined subject is largely irrelevant to the biological outlook. [2]

[1] *Ibid.*, p. 15. Original author's italics.

[2] In section 53 of *Ideas* (pp. 164–5 – Italics ours), Husserl states that 'only through the empirical relation to the body does consciousness become real in a human and animal sense, and only thereby does it win a place in Nature's space and time – the time which is physically measured . . . Thus *on the plane of appearance* the psychophysical natural unity, man or beast, is constituted as a unity that rests on bodily *foundations* and corresponds to the grounding function of apperception.' One should nevertheless not be misled by the word 'psychophysical' as it appears in Husserl's texts. His frequent description of psychological phenomena as related to the body suggest that he uses this term to describe the integrated body-psyche much in the sense of what we today call psychophysiological unity. Nevertheless, as the above-quoted texts indicate, this 'psychophysical' unity, though not understood literally in the Fechnerian sense (i.e. as referring to psychophysical experiments), leaves room for some dualistic interpretation and never invokes any argument taken from the biological situations of behaviour. Our statement that psychophysics is not relevant to biology rests on the fact that psychophysical measurements, past and present, imply an artificial idea of 'consciousness' as distinct from organic reality. In present-day psychophysics, thresholds problems are excluded in favour of models based on hypothetical input-output schemes, for which sensory physiology and physiological ethology have little use.

3 *Further Husserlian analyses of phenomenological psychology*

A further development of Husserl's own conception of phenomenological psychology is to be found in a series of lectures which he gave on this topic between 1925 and 1928 and which was published in a volume in 1962 under the general title of *Phaenomenologische Psychologie.*[1] These texts are of great value for our purpose because in them Husserl studies explicitly the reciprocal relations between transcendental phenomenology and psychology. More-over, as Biemel points out in his preface to the work, in it Husserl devotes lengthy analyses to the world of experience (*Erfahrungswelt*), which may be considered as foreshadowing the concept of life-world (*Lebenswelt*) as he will treat it later in the *Krisis* (1936).[2]

At the end of his introductory lectures, Husserl summarises the main characteristics of phenomenological psychology as he then conceived it. This characterisation is the outcome of a long period of reflection which begins after the publication of the second volume of the *Logical Investigations* (1901) and which finds a first systematic expression in *Die Idee der Phaenomenologie* (*The Idea of Phenomenology*), published in 1907. It is in this work that Husserl had studied the relationship between the 'unreal' objects of logic and mathematics and the subjective acts connected with this kind of pure abstract knowledge.[3] This part of the work (Vol II) was severely criticised because Husserl seemed to revert to the psychologism which he had discarded in the first part of his analysis (Vol. I). Besides, in the *Philosophie als strenge Wissenschaft* (*Philosophy as rigorous science*) published in 1911, the distinction between phenomenological philosophy and eidetic psychology was not clear and gave rise to many misunderstandings, as Husserl himself points out in the introduction to the *Ideas* (1913).[4] Eidetic psychology was in fact the kind of descriptive analysis used in the second part of the *Logical Investigations* to characterise the psychic correlates of acts dealing with unreal logical objects. As Kockelmans says:

'The characteristic of phenomenological psychology consists in the fact that it, unlike empirical psychology, employs an eidetic reduction, whereas it, unlike transcendental phenomenology, does not use a transcendental

---

[1]E. Husserl, *Phaenomenologische Psychologie* (The Hague, Nijhoff, 1962) W. Biemel (ed.), 'Husserliana', Vol. IX. The volume also contains the four versions of the article on Phenomenology which Husserl wrote in 1928 for the *Encyclopaedia Britannica.* Cf. also the already quoted book of H. Drüe, *Edmund Husserls System der Phaenomenologischen Psychologie* (Berlin, De Gruyter, 1963).

[2]*Ibid.*, Einleitung, p. 25.

[3]On this important aspect of Husserl's thinking and its consequences on his later idea of a phenomenological psychology, cf. J. Kockelmans, *A first Introduction to Husserl's Phenomenology* (Pittsburgh, Duquesne University Press, 1967, Ch. 10) and *Idem, Edmund Husserl's Phenomenological Psychology. A historico-critical study* (Pittsburgh, Duquesne University Press, 1967, Ch. 5).

[4]J. Kockelmans, *A first introduction* . . . , p. 290.

reduction . . . Eidetic reduction brings us forth from the realm of the factual into the domain of pure essences, whereas a transcendental reduction cuts us loose from the real, spatio-temporal world.'[1]

Eidetic psychology is concerned with the nature of realities as they exist for consciousness in the natural world and studies them by intuition; as a psychological discipline, it therefore occupies an intermediate position between transcendental phenomenology and pure empirical psychology. Kockelmans concludes that 'a comparison between this eidetic psychology of the *Ideas*, which is also there called rational psychology or psychological phenomenology, with the phenomenological psychology of which Husserl speaks in his later works reveals that both undoubtedly refer to the same discipline'.[2]

Coming back to the main features of phenomenological psychology as expounded by Husserl at the end of his 1925 lectures, we must notice that he tries to work out epistemological principles allowing the establishment of a psychology basically rooted in the natural world but satisfying the requirements of eidetic reduction. These features are as follows:[3]

(1)   The new psychology is an *a priori* science, i.e. it aims at discovering the necessary ontological principles, without which psychological life is unthinkable. Only after completion of this preliminary task can psychology turn to the descriptive analysis of psychological facts and consider the possibility of their theoretical interpretation.

(2)   Intuition furnishes the source of this *a priori*. This means that eidetic descriptions bear on the ontological necessities themselves.

(3)   The result of this procedure amounts to clarifying the intentionality and the intersubjective dimension of consciousness.

(4)   The psychological work carried out in this way prepares the way for radical phenomenological philosophy, i.e. transcendental phenomenology. Husserl insists that this preparatory role is not an absolutely basic one, since such an assumption would mean a return to psychologism.

(5)   Psychological knowledge is, in this sense, a knowledge of the world, which transcends pure empirical induction. It must reach, in its own sphere, the status of an *a priori* science of the psychical, comparable to mathematics as an *a priori* science of natural space and quantity.

We must now ask ourselves whether a scientific programme of this kind allows for the elaboration of concrete observations and experiments in direct relation to the living organism. When Husserl contends that the phenomeno-

---

[1] *Ibid.*
[2] *Ibid.*, pp. 292–3.
[3] *Phaenomenologische Psychologie*, pp. 46f.

logical (or eidetic) psychology he outlines leads to a knowledge of the world, he specifies that it is that world through which the psychic is realising itself. The question is to know whether it includes the biological *Umwelt* (in the sense of von Uexküll) with its morphological and behavioural characteristics. It seems safe to conclude from Husserl's own text that, in his view, the biological as an object of scientific inquiry is entirely defined by the physical nature of the organism. In this sense, scientific psychology must be considered as 'a non-autonomous branch of the more concrete anthropology or zoology, which are also directed towards the study of physical and psycho-physical phenomena'.[1] Thus, we find in *Phenomenological Psychology* a set of analyses of great use for the epistemological grounding of subjective experience in the world. Such an analysis aids a more concrete understanding of the psychological significance of intentionality; but the organism's own world is, *as such*, left out of consideration. Husserl's positive contribution of this period remains, however, that of having achieved a new psychology of consciousness free from introspectionism, and in having laid the foundations of a new scientific psychology. These foundations are those of a regional ontology, as outlined in *Ideas*; they define the principles of analysis of the worlds of living beings – a task which Husserl did not perform himself because he considered it one for empirical scientists.

In the *Phaenomenologische Psychologie*, as in *Ideas* and many other writings, Husserl speaks of the natural world and of the empirical subject by reference to psychophysics and to experimental psychology, especially to perceptual phenomena. He is definitely more conversant with human physiology than with zoology and he rarely quotes facts from general biology or animal psychology. It is worth recalling, in this connection, that von Uexküll's *Umwelt und Innenwelt der Tiere*, which was published in 1909, contains a wealth of factual information and basic methodological reflections – on the situation of the observer as well as on that of animals – which could have considerably broadened Husserl's description of the world of experience (*Erfahrungswelt*). A second edition of von Uexküll's work appeared in 1921. The 1909 first edition was then well known in German scientific circles and it is hardly credible that it should have escaped Husserl's attention. One wonders what would have become of the phenomenology of the embodiment and of Husserl's idea of somatology (particularly developed in *Ideen*–III),[2] if he had included more comparative data in his analysis.[3]

---

[1] *Phaenomenologische Psychologie*, p. 303. Translation ours.

[2] The second and third parts of *Ideen zu einer reinen Phaenomenologie und Phaenomenologischen Philosophie* have been published posthumously under the editorship of Marly Biemel ('Husserliana' Vols. IV and V, The Hague, Nijhoff, 1952). *Ideen–II* is devoted to the problem of constitution, i.e. the relations between nature and subjectivity. *Ideen–III* treats phenomenology and the foundations of science. In a complementary section of *Ideen–II* (Beilage IV, p. 313), Husserl states 'Descriptive psychology offers a proper and natural point of departure for the elaboration of the idea of phenomenology. In fact, this was the way which led me to phenomenology.' (Translation ours.)

[3] Another important source for Husserl's purpose is Köhler's observations and experiments on

4 The problem of 'foreign subjectivity'

These remarks regarding Husserl's attitude towards general biology concern some parts of his major works, in which he deals with the natural world. They may be somewhat tempered if one turns to *Ideen–II* and *Ideen–III* and, above all, to less-known texts, particularly to those which were published posthumously under the title of *Zur Phaenomenologie der Intersubjektivität (On the Phenomenology of Intersubjectivity)*.[1] They include numerous studies on the problem of 'foreign subjectivity', i.e. subjectivity in different individuals and in different forms of living beings. The first study to be considered is that which Husserl devotes to the different ontological structures of the natural worlds (*Umwelten*) of children and lower animals.[2] We are told here once more that the problem considered is included in the framework of the ontology of experience, i.e. the form of a possible nature. Natural experience exists for us as a constitutive fact, but we can apprehend eidetically the essence of nature and of natural experience and examine further whether the natural experience of another individual or of a given animal species fits with this general eidetic model. In doing so, we shall find in all cases different types of apperceptions, which all fall into the general category of natural apperception. Considering the human subject, I can leave aside kinesthetic aspects, for instance, and describe a world of objects which would be purely oculomotor. The same procedure can be applied in order to characterise the successive 'worlds' emerging in ontogenetic development. In other words, there will appear in the descriptions various levels of apperception.

Husserl explains our reconstruction of the natural world of an animal species by assuming that we perceive it as a psychic being by empathy ('Durch Einfühlung fassen wir das organische Individuum als beseelt auf').[3]

This empathic apprehension of an organism different from ourselves allows us to endow it, by analogy, with constitutive characteristics which we derive from our own bodily structure. This analogical operation is effected by each of us as a matter of course in our intersubjective relationships with other human individuals. As far as animals are concerned, the same operation can only be achieved by leaving aside the differences of levels of apperception which we established in the phenomenological description of the species under study. 'If light-sensitive zones are present', he writes,

---

higher primates, the results of which were published during the same period (W. Köhler, *Intelligenzprüfungen an Menschenaffen*, Berlin, Springer, 1921 – first published in 1917 under the title of *Intelligenzprüfungen an Anthropoïden* in the *Abhandlungen der Königl. preuss. Akad. der Wissenschaften*). To my knowledge, Husserl did not make use of it in any of his analyses of the natural world.

[1] Vol. XIII, XIV and XV of 'Husserliana', The Hague, Nijhoff, 1973 (I. Kern, ed.). These studies extend from 1905 to 1935.

[2] 'Husserliana', Vol. XIV, pp. 112f.

[3] *Ibid.*, p. 115.

which may be compared to an eye insofar as they can be considered as subjectively receptive to stimuli, this raises the question of their relationship with the corresponding kinesthetic system which we may consider to be 'at the disposal' of the unknown psychic being. It is in accordance with the rudimentary nature of this system (by derivation from the motivation originating in our own highly organised system), that we interpret the vision of this animal, i.e. we understand accordingly which kinds of 'things' constitute themselves for such a being, in other words, what the optical delineation of the whole 'thing' looks like for it.[1]

The empathic-analogical reconstruction of the foreign subjectivities has a positive result: it allows us to assert the existence of phenomenal worlds corresponding to each particular animal species and endowed with perceptual structures akin to our own. Husserl, however, considers that this reconstruction is vague, even for higher animals, because the limits of analogy are dictated by the possibilities of transposing our own bodily organisation to other living organisms. Nevertheless, the eidetic analysis is ontologically successful, since it forces us to recognise that subjective constitutions differing from our own result in the emergence of natural worlds in which things as such have a status of existence comparable to the things present in the human natural world.

But, although we must agree with Husserl's analysis of the theoretical possibility of providing a basis for comparative psychology in this manner, and although we must recognise the originality of his insights, we cannot agree with him when it comes to strictly biological considerations. When he says that the reconstruction of the world of a given species is necessarily vague, we can object to this contention by referring to the very precise facts established in the field of animal perception by comparative physiologists. The work of von Frisch already quoted on the visual world of the bee demonstrates this point very clearly. In this case and in all experimental studies of colour perception in animals using differential responses based on learning, the spectral limits of chromatic vision can be established with great accuracy. In such experiments, it is true that the observer bases his initial working hypothesis on a vague analogy between his own constitution and that which he empathically perceives in the organism he studies; von Frisch's point of departure is the human visual spectrum, which he experiences for himself in everyday life, but which he can also characterise by referring to the physical laws of colorimetry. In any case, the very possibility of the comparative experiment lies in a primary similarity of structure – however remote it may be – between the animal organism and the human organism, which we readily perceive. The scientific reconstruction itself may be mostly descriptive and

---

[1] *Ibid.*, pp. 116–17. Translation ours.

involve measurements only subsidiarily, as in von Uexküll's representation of the visual space of insects.[1]

But a still more important aspect of the question must be considered. The principle of analogy holds true as constitutive of inter-organic comparisons at the eidetic level of description and we cannot escape the eidetic point of view if we look for an epistemological foundation of a comparative psychology of animal worlds. We also know that in doing so, we do not indulge in anthropomorphism, since the point of the empathic approach is precisely to recognise the existence of differences, and to try to establish to what extent they present themselves *as differences* in our inquiry. However, when we pass to the actual description of organic structures and related 'foreign' world-constitutive potentialities, the principle of analogy becomes insufficient. The comparative point of view is then, unavoidably, that of comparative anatomy and comparative physiology. In this soundly based empirical perspective, homology is prior to analogy, because it rests on an observational basis, in which the physical structures of the organism show point-to-point correspondences from one animal to another, as, for instance, in the pelvic bone in vertebrates. As is well known, very slight differences were found to be sufficiently characteristic to allow the establishment, on such foundations, of divergent processes of orthogenesis in evolution. Similar studies are conducted in comparative ethology, which result in phylogenetic trees based entirely on instinctive motor patterns.

We must insist once more on the fact that it is not Husserl's purpose to outline a programme of biological research, but to characterise the natural world as much as possible from a great variety of standpoints. Our criticisms must therefore be considered as stressing not only the shortcomings of some of his analyses, but also their constructive aspects. In another section of *Zur Phaenomenologie des Intersubjektivität*[2] we find more concrete characterisations of the respective natural worlds of men and animals. The principle of analogy is applied here in the opposite way. The reference is, again, human subjectivity, but Husserl considers the case of animal organisms in the first place and tries to show step by step to what extent animal psychology and human psychology may be eidetically related to one another on a continuum. 'Animals', he writes, 'are, as ourselves, subjects endowed with a consciousness, in which a "natural world" is given to them in a certain fashion as their own in the evidence of being.'[3] But, even if the animal possesses something of an 'I-structure', it is never a *personal* 'I'. Man is not only personalised by his biological individuality, but first and foremost by the fact that his subjectivity is, as such, intersubjectivity. Therefore, when we compare animals and men as subjects of their respective worlds, we are bound

---

[1] J. von Uexküll and G. Kriszat, *Streifzüge durch die Umwelten von Tieren und Menschen*, Hamburg, Rohwolt, 1956, pp. 38f.

[2] 'Husserliana', Vol. XV, pp. 174f.

[3] *Ibid.*, p. 177. Translation ours. Original author's quotation marks.

to recognise that 'man as a person is the subject of a cultural world'[1] and that his subjectivity is that of a historical being. Animals live in a natural world whose psychological constitution may be compared to our own, but they are essentially ahistorical. Each animal generation repeats the natural world of the preceding ones, whereas each human generation creates a new world by virtue of culture.

It is of special interest for the epistemological foundations of phenomenological psychology as it evolves today to note that the transcendental dimension has been analysed by Husserl himself with reference to the concrete natural aspects of living beings. Their characterisation in the framework of eidetic reduction amounts therefore to locating their study in relation to the essence of nature and of organic constitution; it never does take the form, as many superficial readers of Husserl would have it, of an 'escape' from the natural in pure philosophising. The need for an epistemological analysis of these issues appears clearly if one remembers that the very idea of 'nature' is nearly impossible to define in the realm of strictly empirical biology. When we refer, as biologists or comparative psychologists, to the perceptual world of a species, we admit at the outset that the latter is selected by sensory activity and corresponding motor organisation from a basic totality which we call the 'natural world' or 'geographic environment'. Those expressions refer to a synthetic concept, not to an actual quantification of all detailed material elements which can be categorised under these headings, and which should be exhaustively counted and classified if we were to keep to a strictly empirical point of view. Instead we use a vague idea, more vague indeed than that which phenomenology offers us in eidetic descriptions.

The historico-cultural essence of the world of man should not be thought of as a theoretical concept devoid of any bearing on the ahistorical natural world of other organisms. It is by virtue of our own historicity that we are in a position to consider synthetically the series of animal generations as an infinity of moments internally related by a common principle of actualisation. In this sense, the idea of evolution is a specifically human idea, although it required the expression of a great number of factual observations which remained unconnected before the organic world was seen as a whole. The principle of evolution, as expounded by Lamarck and later by Spencer, Wallace and Darwin, was a revolutionary one because it inaugurated a new eidetic point of view in zoological knowledge. The animal's constitution does not possess the framework of historical time. 'We, men, are those who ontologically possess the chains in our world, the infinite series and branchings of generations of ants, etc. The animal has no generative world in which he lives in conscious fashion . . . no factual existence in a world of its own, which we humans ascribe to it by humanising it.'[2]

[1] *Ibid.*, p. 180. Translation ours. For a systematic treatment of this and related issues, cf. *Ideen–II*, sections II and III ('Husserliana'), Vol. IV, pp. 90f. and 173f.

[2] *Ibid.*, p. 181. Translation ours. This statement does not contradict the idea that animals are

It is worthy of notice that, in the same text, Husserl refers to instinct in a way which would not be rejected by today's ethologists. 'Instinct', he writes, 'is first of all a heading for facts which must be characterised from outside and which, seen from inside, raise specific problems which cannot be understood.'[1] He remarks further that the impossibility for an animal of constituting an authentic intersubjective world in the human sense of the word, is due to its lack of a foundational language: 'Animals understand each other, they understand sounds – but they have no language'.[2]

The natural world exists as a biological reality at different analogical levels of subjective constitution, which we can approach in eidetic analyses. In doing so, we are bound to rely fundamentally on our own psychic constitution. Husserl concludes accordingly: 'Psychology as rooted fundamentally and specifically in experience, is therefore human psychology in its very essence. Animal psychology, on the contrary, is purely constructive and presupposes a truly intentional human psychology to legitimise its constructs.'[3]

We need not discuss here all the implications of Husserl's theory of the natural world in relation to comparative psychology and ethology. The aim of our analysis was to establish, by a close examination of relevant texts, that the biological reality of the organism was a primary concern for the founder of transcendental phenomenology. The main argument of this book, that the actually developing phenomenological psychology must be biologically based, therefore finds very strong support in works which are mistakenly considered as excluding this dimension of psychology. Once again, it is an illegitimate oversimplification to jump from *Ideen–I* to the *Krisis* if one wants to have a complete view of the Husserlian epistemology which underlies the phenomenological conception of natural science, and establish phenomenological psychology with accuracy as a positive science of living beings.

5   *The historical nature of man's life-world*

Let us now consider Husserl's last period and its main achievement for our purpose, the theory of the *Lebenswelt* (life-world) as it is outlined in the *Krisis* (1936). In the preceding paragraphs, we found sufficient theoretical evidence

---

endowed with a consciousness peculiar to their own world constitution (cf. Husserl's text quoted on p. 119). It merely stresses the fact that this consciousness lies at a lower level of 'transcendence', devoid of the possibility of grasping the life-situation 'in an open infinity of generations' (*Ibid.*). When Husserl says that we are 'humanising' (*Vermenschlichen*) the animal, he does not have in view the crude anthropomorphism of early animal psychologists, which amounted to endowing it with all characteristics peculiar to man. Here again, he wants to make it clear that it is only by reference to the human constitution of consciousness that we are in a position to characterise the natural world of animals precisely *as different* from ours.

[1] *Ibid.*, p. 183. Translation ours.
[2] *Ibid.*, p. 184. Translation ours.
[3] *Ibid.*, p. 185. Translation ours.

in Husserl's writings prior to the *Krisis* to establish that he did not intend to elaborate pure phenomenology by negating the natural standpoint and that the *Epoche* assumed the latter as an absolute starting-point. In this way, Husserl puts himself in a position which allows him to distinguish between the *natural* and the *objective* in the sense of natural science. This distinction may serve as a basis for evaluating the aim of the *Krisis*. But why does Husserl start, one may ask, from the negative idea of a crisis, and a crisis of the objective sciences in particular? We are accustomed to crises in various domains: political, economic, moral, social and the like. But among the vicissitudes of man's manifold activities, one would be tempted to believe that scientific knowledge remains untouched and that it furnishes, precisely by virtue of its objective character, the final solution to every problem. Even those who think that scientific solutions are not the ultimate ones in many fields, particularly in those which have to do with personal affairs and irrational attitudes, will readily recognise that science is successful in explaining natural phenomena and in generating practical applications. In the last few decades, the idea has often been put forward that a contempt for science is truly scandalous, since those who reject it can only do so because scientific progress ensures for them health, security and many other minor but enviable advantages. The conception of 'technical humanism' is closely linked with the mentality just described. It contends that scientific knowledge is an essential part of modern man's culture in the Western sense of the word, on a par with the historical and literary knowledge of the traditional humanities. All this may be true at the level of general opinion and may find acceptance in educational circles, but the reverse 'truths' are also frequently expressed, viz. that science, by increasing power, entails war and destruction and will ruin humanity in the end. Therefore, however real the advantages or disadvantages of science may be, they remain, as such, foreign to an evaluation of the fundamental meaning of objective science. Nevertheless, it would be careless to draw too sharp a distinction between 'common' problems and 'scientific' problems, since, as we shall see, the crisis evoked by Husserl has a direct bearing on the meaning of everyday life.

The picture of science in Husserl's days was not very different from that of today as far as spectacular achievements and their social impact are concerned. The main change seems to have taken place inside the scientific world itself in the form of a growing interest in epistemology. Scientists as well as philosophers have developed an entirely new attitude towards scientific knowledge, to such an extent that dogmatic positivism has become obsolete. This could not be the case if the living subject – and the living scientist, for that matter – were not in a position to consider objectivity as a debatable concept. The crisis to which Husserl refers has its origin in the basic conception of objective science. In current opinion, objectivity designates what exists for the knowing subject independently of his private attitude. In other words, the object is not only considered as corresponding to reality: it *is* reality.

Therefore, the uncritical observer will not differentiate between the objective world and his life-world. he will naïvely believe that the world described by science is the only possible real world. This naïve attitude is adopted in fact by the theorising scientist when he contends that science can and will express the total reality of the universe. This conviction is that of *objectivism*. Objectivity defines the general principle of a method of investigation. Objectivism is a belief.

The crisis of Western man is a direct consequence of the development of European objective science, since, by implicitly assuming that scientific reality is the only source of facts, the subject loses every possibility of placing himself in everyday life. Scientific facts are theoretical constructs which cannot be grasped in immediate experience; they are 'ideal entities' which are only available to the subject in an indirect fashion. But idealisation can only be effected on the basis of this very same immediate experience. As Kockelmans puts it,

> because of its intrinsic sense as a superstructure, the world of science must have a firm basis upon which it can rest and upon which it is built. This basis cannot be anything other than the life-world and the immediate evidence of our lived experiences – the term 'evidence' referring to immediate self-presentation of the objects involved. And so all theoretical truth, whether logical, mathematical or scientific, has its final justification and roots in evidence which concerns events and happenings in the life-world.[1]

Consequently, if we want to understand the meaning of objective science, we can only hope to do so by returning to its pre-scientific foundation, i.e. to the structure of the life-world, the *Lebenswelt*. This appears as the primary task of a philosophy like phenomenology, which adopts a radical point of view.

But, if we consider the constructive character of science from the epistemological point of view, we have to face, not only the problem of its foundation but also that of its formal rigour as a closed system. The internal coherence of science is the result of an integrative process, which corrects and proves its methodological framework by a critical appraisal of its theoretical results. This has the consequence that scientific knowledge is a transcendental act in ceaseless evolution, but by transcending the *Lebenswelt* in this manner, the latter 'is also concealed without being noticed. It is this failure to notice the concealing action of the sciences which resulted in an "objectivism".'[2] As Husserl puts it, objective science is the result of the mathematisation of nature inaugurated by Galileo, in which the 'real praxis' dealing with immediate life-possibilities is replaced by an 'ideal praxis' at the level of pure thinking.[3] It should not be forgotten, however, that the life-world of Western civilised man

---

[1] *A first introduction to Husserl's phenomenology*, p. 268.
[2] J. Kockelmans, *Edmund Husserl's phenomenological psychology*, p. 267.
[3] *Krisis*, p. 23.

includes science as a cultural phenomenon. In the course of the analysis expounded in the *Krisis*, Husserl repeatedly states that the life-world should not be understood as the mere natural environment with which we come into contact by sensory experience; this world also has a fundamentally historical and social meaning. The evidence of our lived experience therefore includes the historical reality of science as an element of our ordinary life. Nevertheless, submerging ourselves in scientific culture does not grant us direct access to scientific evidence. Referring to Husserl's analysis of the natural world at the time of *Ideas*, it is clear that an eidetic reduction is necessary to uncover the life-world which made scientific knowledge possible. We must here again dispose of a specific regional ontology. This aim is to be attained by a *mundane phenomenology*, which prepares transcendental phenomenology in its own fashion.[1] We shall come back to the problem of reduction in the next paragraph.

We need not analyse the concept of the *Lebenswelt* in more detail in order to justify our thesis that the biological foundation of lived behaviour is an essential part of the still evolving phenomenological psychology. Many thoroughgoing studies have been devoted to the meaning of the life-world in Husserl's works and specially in the *Krisis*.[2] However, we must be aware of the bearing of Husserl's last teachings on our thesis just stated. If we keep strictly to the analysis in the *Krisis*, we must conclude that phenomenological psychology, as outlined in this work, is conceived as a discipline studying the subject in order to prepare the transcendental outcome. Kockelmans remarks that Husserl's final conclusion is not unequivocal and that it is difficult to make a clear-cut distinction between the respective reductions required by phenomenological psychology and transcendental phenomenology. He notes further, by reference to the penultimate section of the *Krisis*, that, in spite of this, it 'does not mean that phenomenological psychology cannot be maintained as a "scientia media" between empirical psychology and transcendental phenomenology'.[3]

A return to the immediate experience of the life-world thus leaves room for scientific psychological investigation. But the latter cannot be scientific in the sense of a natural science because it must base its verification procedures on an

---

[1] *Krisis*, pp. 176f.

[2] In this vast literature, the following titles may be proposed to the reader as sufficient guides for further study: A. Gurwitsch, 'The Last Work of Edmund Husserl', *Philosophy and Phenomenological Research*, 1955–1956, 16, pp. 370–99; L. Eley, *Die Krise des A priori*, The Hague, Nijhoff, 1962; W. Marx, *Vernunft und Welt*, The Hague, Nijhoff, 1970; P. Janssen, *Geschichte und Lebenswelt*, The Hague, Nijhoff, 1970. In addition to this, the two books by J. Kockelmans already quoted, *A first Introduction to Husserl's Phenomenology* (Pittsburgh, Duquesne University Press, 1967) and *Edmund Husserl's Phenomenological Psychology* (Duquesne University Press, 1967) are excellent critical works on Husserl's phenomenology as a whole. Moreover they give detailed analyses of the *Lebenswelt* and of the relation between transcendental phenomenology and phenomenological psychology. On the actual trends in phenomenological psychology, cf. A. Giorgi, *Psychology as a Human Science*, New York, Harper & Row, 1970.

[3] *A first Introduction to Husserl's Phenomenolgy*, p. 311.

epistemology which defines the relation between the life-world and the world of psychological theorising.

As Brand remarks, the crisis caused by objectivism is not harmful to science itself, considered as a closed system of relations, but to man. The confusion between objective reality and lived reality brought about the impossibility of approaching the problems of truth in an adequate manner and consequently of allowing the human subject to live with a firm reference to his world. But, Brand asks, what is truth? The word may designate a great variety of facts and outcomes of judgements, but truth always means adequacy in relation to something. If the true and real are only the objectively true and real, it follows that 'the vital meaning of science is lost and with it, the vital meaning of life itself'.[1] The meaning of the crisis is to be understood ultimately as a drastic change in the behaviour and attitudes of man. Therefore, apart from the general problem of the foundations of science, the concealment of the life-world by objectivism raises a psychological problem of its own.

In the *Krisis*, Husserl offers no solution to this particular difficulty and it would not be legitimate to interpret the function of phenomenological psychology, as he defines it in this work, as a possible means of reintegrating the referenceless subject into the realm of immediate experience. The return to the *Lebenswelt* is a condition of the transcendental accomplishment of phenomenological philosophy. Thus, insofar as phenomenological psychology contributes to it, it prepares the way for a new philosophy of science, but not necessarily for a new readily available scientific psychology.

But the problem can be tackled from a different point of view. We believe that the epistemological change brought about by transcendental phenomenology was the beginning of an organism-centred psychology, *whatever the role of phenomenological psychology may have been in the preparatory phase of the final reduction.* From this perspective, the conceptual framework of the *Lebenswelt* may be considered as less conclusive than some of Husserl's earlier attempts following the *Logische Untersuchungen*. In conclusion, phenomenological psychology as it developed towards an epistemologically based biology of human and animal behaviour (Straus, Buytendijk) owes more to transcendental phenomenology than to Husserl's own phenomenological psychology. In this latter trend, the theory of the life-world appears as a mere implement in an already fully-fledged system. As a fundamentally historical concept, it did not by itself offer a sufficient foundation for a systematic study of organic subjectivity.

6   *The dual meaning of phenomenological psychology*

Thus, the study of Husserl's work dealing explicitly with psychology leads us partly to a negative conclusion. Phenomenological psychology as Husserl

---

[1]G. Brand, *Die Lebenswelt. Eine Philosophie des konkreten A priori*, Berlin, De Gruyter, 1971, p. 8. Translation ours.

views it is a preparatory step towards transcendental phenomenology. In the framework of present experimental and theoretical research, however, it has become something very different. It is a positive science which, though resulting historically from Husserl's initial philosophical impulse, has developed an entirely new approach to observable behavioural phenomena. It is a natural science which is founded on epistemological grounds which are lacking in all areas of scientific psychology still inspired by physicalist concepts.

Such definitions of phenomenological psychology may seem very restrictive in comparison with Husserl's broad undertaking. And indeed, it cannot but be restrictive because what present-day phenomenological psychologists are aiming at is not a radical scientific philosophy but a new scientific psychology capable of coping with specific questions of their discipline in a direct fashion. The main objective is thus to exclude every approach, and even every definition, of psychological phenomena which simply utilises concepts of other sciences without submitting them to an adequate epistemological critical analysis.

Science deals with reality and the verification of reality. Psychology must therefore be in a position to state technically which specific reality it studies and how it intends to verify its findings. The problem of verification has been solved in various ways in psychological methodology. The question of specific reality, on the contrary, remains largely controversial.

As we have seen on many occasions in the preceding chapters, stating that psychology is the science of behaviour is a far too general point of departure. Behaviour cannot be dissociated from the organism's action, but at which point of an action does it actually begin and at which point does it actually end? In Sherrington's description, for instance, it is shown that overall behaviour ceases to exist as an active process when consummatory acts come into play, and a similar view can be found in ethological theory. Thus, even if we keep only to this perspective, the idea of natural events in the organism already has two meanings, according to the level considered. It is therefore no pure philosophical speculation to investigate the idea of natural events. Consequently, if we claim that phenomenological psychology is a natural science, its particular standpoint about facts of nature ought to be made precise.

This is what Husserl did when he elaborated his *Phenomenological Psychology*. We must, however, examine whether the principles laid down in this preparatory set of reflections, which were intended to provide the basis of transcendental phenomenology, may also be used as an adequate foundation for phenomenological psychology as we conceive it today.

7   Reduction and the scientific standpoint

The main difficulty we face in this respect comes from Husserl's concern to perform what he calls reduction, i.e. the suspension of beliefs about natural events. This prerequisite seems at first sight to be fundamentally at variance with our claim that phenomenological psychology should be thought of as a natural science.

The main issue in Husserl's view is that the inquiry into natural events in the current practice of experimental science relies on an uncritical conception of nature. Exact science performs its investigations in the conviction that 'natural facts' result as a matter of course from the application of methods which are elaborated according to its own *a priori*. If one intends to discover the original phenomena which underlie the *a priori* assumptions about the natural, it is necessary to suspend the particular belief about the natural which exact science uses spontaneously as its point of departure. In other words, this belief should be provisionally 'bracketed' or submitted to 'reduction'. Needless to say, if this is required of exact science, it is required, as a consequence, of every discipline striving to comply with its general model, and of scientific psychology in particular.

What justifies reduction is the fact that the phenomena discovered by exact or natural science are dealing with the essence of things. Classical and actual positivists disagree with this. They claim that they are not dealing with essences, but only with relations which they try to verify. But considering relations leading to the discovery of scientific *truths* cannot be solely based on other sets of relations since the latter would have to be justified in their turn, unless the scientist is ready to admit that he is studying relations which may eventually have nothing to do with truths. The search for truths thus always brings us back to an ultimate object or 'essence', distinct from relations as such, and this object is situated in nature. Hence the obligation on the scientist to examine the idea of nature contained in his *a priori*. This critical examination is what reduction is supposed to make possible.

Since each particular science – whether exact or not – elaborates means of investigation which lead ultimately to the discovery of an object of nature, the fundamental idea of nature cannot be considered at the outset as unique and universal for all fields of knowledge. Anyone who claims that there is no difference whatsoever between e.g. the natural as seen by physics and the natural as seen by psychology can only do so if he possesses a universal *a priori* knowledge of nature and if, in this case, the various sub-sections of knowledge have no specific objects. To such a statement, no scientist will subscribe because it ruins the very point of his endeavour.

The Husserlian reduction proceeds in two distinct steps. Starting from the actual existence of the various sciences, Husserl attempts to discover the specific kind of abstraction which allows them to secure essences in their own framework. This reduction is called 'eidetic' because it is directed towards an elucidation of the fundamental point of view or *eidos* of the science concerned. This being achieved, the study of the knowing subject must examine in what way the acts of consciousness generate or 'constitute' the phenomena, again without sticking to the individual as an empirical reality. This defines the task of the phenomenological or transcendental reduction. We immediately see that this latter operation, being concerned with the nature of foundational consciousness, is linked with psychology. The kind of psychology needed here is the phenomenological psychology which we outlined following Husserl in the preceding sections of this chapter. As we said then, its function is to pave the way towards pure or transcendental phenomenology.

Owing to the historical evolution of phenomenology, our actual position towards transcendental reflection has been in fact inverted. The striving towards a new natural science of behaviour, epistemologically based, must indeed rely on a general theory of subjectivity. The general model of it can be found in transcendental phenomenology. A biologically based phenomeno-logical psychology appears therefore in actual circumstances, as the outcome of this epistemological work, not any more as its antecedent. This shows clearly the basic difference between Husserl's undertaking and the scope of the present-day psychologist eager to take epistemological requirements into account.

It remains, however, to ascertain the natural *a priori* of this new psychology. In order to solve this question, the emerging discipline should go through an eidetic reduction. The latter requires the critical choice of a basic set of propositions defining its proper field of investigation, viz. the order of natural reality at which it must exist. As we noted earlier in this book, this reality cannot be thought of outside biology as a general life-science.

Summarising, we may say that phenomenological psychology is a biologic-ally founded science developing from a general theory of subjectivity.

Our appraisal of reduction and its effects on the scope of scientific psychology is but a reminder of the task which stays before us in the context of actual scientific research. We should not forget, however, that similar attempts have been made before by psychologists, some of whom were Husserl's contemporaries. The names of Alexander Pfänder and Max Scheler should be mentioned here, among several others. They, too, had to solve the question of reduction from their own points of view. Pfänder's opposition to objectivism is clearly asserted in his *Phenomenology of the Will* (1900) and his *Introduction to Psychology* (1904). Nevertheless, he only relies on reduction as a safeguard against beliefs and objectivism, without referring to transcendental subjectivity. The case of Scheler is more complex since he was concerned with topics like sympathy, ethics and religion rather than with positive science as such. But here again, the Husserlian conception of reduction is not accepted with all its epistemological consequences; in Scheler's view, rather it is interpreted as a condition guaranteeing the autonomy of metaphysical research.

It is an open question whether the actual evolution of phenomenological psychology should go as far as referring explicitly to transcendental subjectivity. In our opinion, it is certainly less important to psychology than the technical necessity of settling the realm of natural events which should define its subject-matter as against objectivism or any other form of belief. This requirement is undoubtedly closely connected with what Husserl called eidetic reduction.

In the next chapter we hope to show some of the positive contributions of many psychologists and life-scientists, who found basic guiding principles in phenomenology and who carried out their work in this perspective, even if they did not follow Husserl's theory of transcendental subjectivity literally.

Chapter 6

Phenomenological Psychology in Actual Practice

We have seen that in *Phaenomenologische Psychologie* Husserl insists on the necessity of establishing scientific psychology on eidetic foundations whose fuction is to clarify the specific *a priori* governing empirical research. 'Now', he adds, 'it is a different question to establish in what manner the empirical method and especially that which is applied in the search for empirical "laws", should be elaborated in relation to an *a priori* knowledge.'[1] He further warns against the tendency to consider that the same general *a priori* should serve as a common basis for all empirical sciences. Assuming that scientific psychology has found its epistemological point of departure in pure eidetic description, we still have to place the concrete methodological approaches within the various fields of psychological investigation.

1   *The methodological problem*

Psychologists engaged in scientific research governed by traditional standards often find it difficult to imagine what changes the acceptance of a phenomenological framework would bring in their work. As far as they are concerned, the methodological problem is twofold.

In the first place, they are right in asking whether acceptance of the philosophical background of phenomenology would change their procedures. As we noted before, the answer is in the negative insofar as technical experimental devices and methods of calculation are concerned. Preparatory reflections on the realm of natural events to be tackled by psychology do not modify quantitative treatments as such. But they do modify the hypotheses tested and the conclusions drawn from the treatments. Sound mathematical analyses may indeed be used to evaluate the internal relations of results obtained in an experiment devoid of organic significance. Insofar as philosophical reflection contributes to articulating the *a priori* involved, it has effects on the eidetic framework of psychology as a natural science. The

---

[1] *Phaenomenologische Psychologie*, p. 50. Translation ours. Original author's quotation marks.

application of classical scientific methods to problems posed and solved in such a framework necessarily leads to theories from which the ancient physicalist interpretations are excluded. As Bunge (1973) puts it, 'Philosophy can be embraced only insofar as it is consistent with scientific methodology and is furthermore heuristically instrumental in the formulation and evaluation of scientific hypotheses and research programs.'[1] It is only in this manner that the preparatory phase of transcendental phenomenology should be critically considered. The study of psychology's own eidetic is a logical consequence of this initial step.

In the second place, the issues raised by phenomenology in the strict Husserlian tradition amounted in several cases to an actual opposition to experimental psychology in favour of a purely descriptive approach. This trend is obviously unscientific according to classical standards, since it relies on intuitive and deductive means of analysis and does not include physical verification of data. It is not surprising that psychologists eager to arrive at facts resulting from controlled experiments would reject such an approach. Their charge, however, that phenomenologists were simply reinstating in this manner the old introspectionist method, is definitely wrong and merely testifies to their having overlooked phenomenological literature and Husserl's theory of constitution in particular.[2]

Phenomenological psychologists have been well aware of these difficulties since the beginning of their endeavours. The actual practice of reduction and the use of intuition in the discovery of essences were hard to reconcile with the requirements of the scientific method. The most fruitful compromise in this respect was Gestalt theory, since it achieved a peculiar unification of descriptive and experimental aspects in psychological research. However, as we remarked before, it finally went back to the physicalist interpretation. It is, in our opinion, a good example of the weakness of descriptive approaches, when they come into competition with experimental procedures inside the same system.

Transcendental analyses and phenomenological descriptions should nevertheless not be discarded simply because they rest on intuition. The question of whether a method is scientific or not should not be considered from the sole point of view of verification, since we know that verification necessarily implies a reference to reality and truth (cf. p. 127). Given the fact that scientific reality and scientific truth are concepts which are defined according to a particular *a priori*, verification is not independent of the epistemological foundations of science. Transcendental phenomenology is

---

[1] M. Bunge, *Method, Model and Matter*, Dordrecht, Reidel, 1973, p. 178.

[2] 'Constitution', it may be recalled, refers to the acts of consciousness by which an object becomes a part of experience. The object is 'constituted', but as it also exists outside the subject, the idea of constitution should not be interpreted in an idealistic sense. For this reason Husserl distinguishes between 'active' and 'passive' constitution. Therefore, neither is there any possibility of reducing the 'constituted' object to a pure 'content of consciousness' in the elementaristic sense.

therefore not foreign to the problem of verifiability. The error of some phenomenologists, however, was to substitute transcendental reflection for the empirical approach. This indeed amounts to claiming that intuition is the only adequate method in actual research, whereas its role is limited to stating the primary conditions of the *a priori*. In this function, intuition cannot be replaced by any other procedure. It is unavoidable at this incipient stage of knowledge because the latter is, then, still pre-scientific.

In description, the role of intuition is different. Describing phenomena has no foundational function because it presupposes the existence of an already established field of research whose eidetic point of view allows it to be considered as a specific area of knowledge. Within these limits, the opposition between description and experimentation is a classical issue. At this stage, the task of transcendental intuition is completed and intuitive procedures then clash with verification. However, if one considers the successive hypotheses formulated in the course of scientific research it is a fact that intuition is always at work when results have to be interpreted theoretically.

Thus, we see that if we distinguish clearly the successive stages of the scientific act, we come to the conclusion that phenomenological psychology is characterised by a special care in defining the specific type of realism it intends to rely on. Further differences in treatment will of course appear according to whether the problems studied are experimental, clinical, social, etc. These sub-specifications are of importance, if only because phenomenological description, as far as it is accepted as a method of its own, is more appropriate in cases where control is not systematic, as in clinical studies.

This does not mean that psychological issues devoid of rigorous control may be more readily tackled by phenomenological psychology than those requiring control. If this were the case, experimentalists would be justified in claiming that phenomenological psychology is a return to purely qualitative modes of analysis and that no positive achievement can be expected of it.

The first answer to this is linked with the problem of adequacy, i.e. in all psychological issues, it is the *adequate* approach that matters and there are numerous cases in which scientific treatment is out of the question at the outset. Clinical studies provide us with a great many instances of this kind of work and no one would deny their usefulness. Psychoanalysis has contributed in a particularly successful way to the discovery of aspects of human conduct which could not possibly be expressed in scientific vocabulary or solved by scientific techniques. But in the case of psychoanalysis, as in that of experimental psychology, the basic eidetic framework has to be defined. No claim to adequacy can be made if this requirement is overlooked, whatever the domain concerned may be. We should keep in mind that a great deal of psychology *is not scientific*, but that does not mean that it is devoid of meaning. Phenomenological psychology can thus tolerate a non-scientific attitude if the corresponding object of inquiry resists scientific formulation and treatment by its very nature. But *its very nature* should be clearly established, and there is more chance of arriving at a realistic determination of it in phenomenological psychology than in many other conceptual frameworks, since it explicitly raises the question of the foundations of psychological knowledge and evaluates the soundness of methods accordingly.[1]

The second answer must be based on an inquiry into the actual positive achievements of life-scientists who have adopted the phenomenological point of view as the most adequate foundation for a biological study of behavioural processes. What this foundation and its function may be, has been expounded at length in the preceding chapters. Our task now is to examine some typical results of phenomenological psychology. As will be seen, *results* here mean facts and theories due to the work of phenomenological psychologists themselves, not mere reinterpretation by phenomenological philosophers of data gathered by scientists belonging to foreign or even opposed schools.

Such reinterpretative work should nevertheless not be condemned *en masse*, since it often contributed to the unfolding of meanings and theoretical conclusions which had not been fully developed by the original workers. One of the most enlightening instances in this respect is Merleau-Ponty's thoroughgoing analysis of important findings by Goldstein and Buytendijk in the fields of neurophysiology and behavioural processes. Doubtless, both these authors had already furnished original interpretations of their observations, but in the *Structure of Behaviour*[2] and in the *Phenomenology of Perception*[3] Merleau-Ponty showed convincingly that their theoretical framework could still be broadened and lead to a general theory of embodiment and action.

Our sole purpose in stressing this point is once more to meet the current objection according to which phenomenological psychologists would have forsaken experimental work in favour of pure deductive analyses. The historical survey which follows will show that, contrary to this one-sided view of many traditional experimentalists, the practising phenomenologists have discovered a wealth of basic facts. Since the achievements of the phenomenological method in psychopathology are fairly well known, we shall limit our inquiry to some experimental and physiological issues in human as well as in animal behaviour.

2 *Phenomenological experimental psychology*

Several facts of lasting importance in the field of experimental psychology were discovered by physiologists who made an extensive practice of critical

---

[1]Stimulating discussions of the variety of standpoints in psychology and in the human sciences in general, as well as far-reaching appreciations of their relative significance, will be found in J. J. Dagenais, *Models of Man: A Phenomenological Critique of some Paradigms in the Human Sciences*, The Hague, Nijhoff, 1972.

[2]Boston, Beacon Press, 1963 (French edition, Paris, Presses Universitaires de France, 1942).

[3]New York, Humanities Press, 1962 (French edition, Paris, Gallimard, 1945).

self-observation. The work of Purkinje (1819–25) and that of Helmholtz (1856–60) on visual phenomena are the best-known instances of this kind of approach. Hering is another classical example. His many investigations of sensory processes, which were contemporary with Fechner's psychophysics, relied first of all on descriptive observations. It is certainly not legitimate to call these authors phenomenologists, except in a very broad sense. Their results, which were of paramount importance for the understanding of various physiological mechanisms, show, however, that if experimental psychology is to be a fruitful enterprise, its point of departure should be the world of the subject and that technical and mathematical developments can only make sense on this basis.

The history of experimental psychology teaches us an alarming lesson as far as some present trends are concerned. When one considers the actual trends in the field of mathematical psychology and model-making for instance, one is struck by the number of unnecessary assumptions which result from the lack of a suitable description of the organism and its actual biological potentialities. As we noted before (p. 81), any model which does not originate in biological observation and which does not lead heuristically to a further observation or experiment at the biological level must be considered useless from the outset.

The problem of differential studies is also a case in point as far as the value of specific descriptions are concerned. As a result of Galtonian biometry, the psychology of individual traits turned to the investigation of differences in individual characteristics and focused on the statistical analysis of their distributions. The usefulness of such mathematical treatments is not in question since they are the only procedures which allow the establishment of the mode of dispersion of a trait in a given population. However, if the task of differential psychology must limit itself to the quantitative analysis of differences, it may end in sheer comparisons of 'unknowns'.

The difficulty in establishing that the exclusive study of differences amounts to comparing unknowns lies in the fact that differences are relations expressed by numbers. However, it is not the numerical expression itself which casts doubts on the validity of the procedure, but the impossibility of ascertaining what is actually counted with the help of these numbers. Figures are used to express how many times a certain reality has been observed, i.e. the figures stand as a representation of words which, in turn, are used to describe the reality in question. The epistemological criticisms of differential psychology are directed against the ultimate lack of such a description, not against the use of numerical procedures, granted the latter adequately refer to the former.

Whenever this is not the case, experimental psychology overlooks the semantic aspect of the words it uses and performs quantitative operations devoid of observational significance. We shall see that the main effort of experimental psychologists who conducted their researches within the framework of phenomenological epistemology was precisely to go 'back to the things themselves', i.e. to carry out descriptions of phenomena in the first place.

3 Stumpf's acoustical and musical investigations

Early experimental phenomenology is principally represented by Carl Stumpf, to whom we referred in Chapter 2. His work as an experimental psychologist was chiefly devoted to acoustics and to the related field of the psychology of music. In the first volume of his *Tonpsychologie* (1883), he discusses at length the psychophysical aspects of his work, but in his later controversy with Wundt on tonal fusion (1890, the year in which the second volume of the *Tonpsychologie* was published), it clearly appears that the description of subjective phenomena is more important to him than the refinements of laboratory techniques. As far as the latter are concerned, it is worthy of note that he performed all his experiments with the sole aid of musical instruments (piano and organ), though he often complained about the lack of laboratory facilities. Nevertheless, his contribution to tone-perception was fundamental. This should make us reflect, in passing, on the relative importance of the various means which the experimentalist has at his disposal in order to achieve his task. No doubt, in Stumpf's case adequate descriptive hypotheses rooted in a concrete knowledge of perceptual experience allowed him to discover realities which would probably have escaped him if he had been satisfied with pure technical research.

Stumpf's acoustical and musical investigations are only part of his overall psychological work. His philosophical work, to which we referred earlier (p. 68f.) is, however, closely linked with it. His ideas about experimental phenomenology resulted from his actual practice as a scientist studying specific perceptual phenomena from the point of view of the *listener* rather than of the *receptor*, though he devoted much attention to the corresponding physical and physiological aspects of hearing.[1] But the focus of his studies was phenomenal experience, viz. the world of tones as it exists for the subject. And in this respect, he definitely showed that phenomenological psychology is not incompatible with experimental research. As is known, his approach was decisive in the development of Gestalt psychology.

4 The experimental phenomenology of David Katz

A very similar experimental tendency may be found in the work of David Katz. His classical monograph on the modes of appearance of colours (*Die Erscheinungsweisen der Farben*, 1911) is a typical example of a descriptive study which, though phenomenologically inspired, found acceptance

---

[1] Apart from the *Tonpsychologie*, the reader is referred on these points to Stumpf's book on vocal sounds published in 1926 under the title *Die Sprachlaute. Experimentall-phonetische Untersuchungen* (Berlin, Springer).

amongst physicists and colorimetrists. To be logical we should replace *though* by *because*. And indeed, his distinctions between surface colours, volumic colours and film colours are not just refinements in the analysis of subjective impressions; they correspond to actual differences in the physical conditions of light production, surface colours resulting from reflection (which is by far the most common case) and volumic colours from emissive sources having a certain spatial extension, the colour of a hot radiating body being an intermediate case rather akin to a film colour.

In his studies of the tactile sense (*Der Aufbau der Tastwelt*, 1925), he demonstrated that finger-exploration made it possible for the subject to detect specific textures or extended substances such as plasticity, elasticity and viscosity of surfaces. In these experiments, it was the *movements* of the fingers which induced the typical impressions of smoothness or roughness and these phenomenal qualities disappeared as soon as the subjects were prevented from actively exploring the surfaces. Katz considered such perceptions as an aspect of the vibratory sense, for which he determined amplitude thresholds.

The phenomenological hypothesis here was to consider touch as an active sense and not merely as a passive sensory receptive field functioning only *after* physical stimulation was applied to the skin. The difference from the classical psychophysical point of view is evident. These experiments inspired the later investigations of Révész on subjects born blind and of Gibson on tactile constancies of specific objects.[1]

Coming back to phenomenological theory, we are now in a better position to understand, from the experimental evidence quoted above, what Husserl called the constitution of consciousness. It would of course be illegitimate to narrow down this basic issue of transcendental phenomenology to the descriptive or experimental study of the various perceptual fields. These two levels of questions are nevertheless closely linked with each other. As Husserl developed his theory of constitution, he took both these points of view into account and devoted careful analyses to the formation of visual, tactile and kinesthetic space.[2] There is, therefore, in Husserl's own work, no discontinuity between the general theory and the facts which may be observed at the empirical level. Scientific studies on the formation of the subject's phenomenal world, such as those carried out by Katz, are therefore well in line with the fundamental phenomenological approach, at least as far as the problem of constitution is concerned.

In his work on colour and touch, Katz had considered subjective phenomena in relation to the capacities of the corresponding receptors within the framework of active behaviour. In a later study,[3] he extended his

[1]G. Révész, *Die Formenwelt des Tastsinnes*, The Hague, Nijhoff, 1938; J. J. Gibson, 'Observations on active touch', *Psychol. Rev.*, 1962, 68, pp. 477–91.

[2]Cf. on this point U. Claesges, *Edmund Husserls Theorie der Raumkonstitution*, The Hague, Nijhoff, 1964.

[3]D. Katz, 'Zwei Beiträge zur Psychologie der Wahrnehmung', in *Studien zur Experimentellen Psychologie*, Basel, Benno Schwabe, 1953, pp. 117–30.

phenomenology to problems of intersubjective communication and of eye-contact in particular. Eye-contact refers to the expressive aspects of visual fixation as they are experienced by two persons in an encounter or a conversation. Such phenomena are also exemplified by looking at pictures of the human face. In some cases, we have the impression that the face on the picture is looking at us and that its gaze is following us irrespective of our angle of observation. The effect obtains if a painter gives the eyes in the picture an orientation corresponding to that of an observer photographed while looking at the lens of the camera.

In social situations, facial communication rests on the direct subjective estimation of the time of fixation of the gaze, so that looking and being looked at occur subject to reciprocal controls[1] which may be simultaneous or alternating. Katz describes the various sensori-motor factors at play in eye-contact, such as the relative size of the apparent parts of the eyeball, the coordination of eye movements, the position of the eyes relative to the head, etc. He also discusses the effects of perceptual constancies in the apparent invariance of eye-orientation in pictures of faces which seem to 'fixate' us.

In order to stress the exact role of the phenomenological perspective, we ought simply to remark that all Katz's experiments could have been carried out in the form of pure sensory determinations, i.e. without consideration of their significance in behavioural communication. In other words, if one considers them in isolation, they are identical to any current investigation in classical experimental psychology. But we are justified in classifying them as phenomenological because they originated from a description of spontaneous intersubjective relations. In brief, Katz's experimental work is based on an anthropological analysis of embodiment and deals with observable patterns of expressive behaviour.[2]

More recently, an important trend of observational research on non-verbal communication has developed under the joint influence of ethology, cultural anthropology and linguistics. Experimental analyses and phenomenological descriptions of expressive behaviour have much in common with this new field of research.[3]

---

[1] In this context 'control' refers to the spontaneous detection and check of local perceptual clues offered by the body of one person or animal inspected by another as in gazing, sniffing, etc. For a detailed study of such controls in animals, cf. R. Schenkel, 'Ausdrück-studien an Wölfen', *Behaviour*, 1948, 1, pp. 81–130 and R. Schloeth, 'Zur Psychologie der Begegnung zwischen Tieren', *Behaviour*, 1956, 10, pp. 1–80.

[2] A complete discussion of Katz's investigations on eye-contact will be found in G. Thinès and M. Morval, *Recherches sur le Contact Visuel et la Polarisation Faciale*, Trav. Fac. Philos. Lett. Univ. Louvain, 1967, pp. 7–73. The experiments reported in this monograph were devised as a continuation of Katz's original study. See also on this point G. Crabbé-Declève and M. C. J. Deconinck, 'La Perception du Mouvement dans l'Image Picturale', *J. Phenom. Psychol.*, 1974, 4, 2, pp. 425–44.

[3] Cf. R. Hinde (ed.), *Non-verbal Communication*, Cambridge University Press, 1975.

5   *Michotte's conception of experimental phenomenology*

Some ten years of daily contact with Michotte at his Louvain laboratory gave the author of this book ample opportunity to discuss with him the theoretical implications of his work on phenomenal permanence, apparent reality, the perception of causality and amodal aspects of perceptual structures.[1] Michotte was first of all an experimental psychologist, but his working hypotheses were based on philosophical theories, phenomenological as well as neo-scholastic. His early work on voluntary choice[2] is avowedly phenomenological, though in a purely descriptive sense. The methodological position of Michotte remained fairly unchanged since the time when he had been working with Wundt and later with Külpe, which came to an end in 1908.

It seems fair to say that his main concern in experimenting was to stick as strictly and faithfully as possible to phenomenal data. This standpoint, which he repeatedly asserted, was thus very much in line with the experimental phenomenology of Stumpf, who exerted a decisive influence on him when he was at Würzburg. It also testifies to a definite influence of the Gestalt school, though Michotte always refused to be called a Gestaltist because he fundamentally disagreed with the doctrine of isomorphism. However, his training under Wundt and Külpe was not totally obliterated by the works of Act and Gestalt psychologists which were to influence him so deeply in subsequent years.

This remaining tendency is well exemplified by the study which Phelan carried out on the experience of feeling in Michotte's laboratory in the twenties.[3] Subjects were presented with various kinds of stimuli (visual, auditory, tactile, etc.) and were instructed to report the pleasant or unpleasant feelings they experienced by way of introspection. 'The facts of experience', Phelan writes, 'considered as experience, are the prime concern and the starting-point of the psychologist. Whatever may be his private convictions of the objective reference and value of experience, its value for him as a psychologist is purely phenomenal.'[4] This last statement is of particular interest because it shows that, as one of Michotte's pupils, Phelan had been taught to apply introspective techniques in the framework of descriptive phenomenology. Introspection was considered acceptable but the elementaristic interpretation of consciousness had to be rejected. Phelan adds accordingly:

---

[1]Cf. A. Michotte, *The Perception of Causality*, London, Methuen, 1963 (French edition, Louvain, 1946); A. Michotte et al., *Causalité, Permanence et Réalité phénoménales*, Louvain, Nauwelaerts, 1962; A. Michotte, G. Thinès and G. Crabbé, *Les Compléments amodaux des Structures perceptives*, Louvain, Nauwelaerts, 1964; G. Crabbé, *Les Conditions d'une perception de la Causalité*, Paris, CNRS, 1967.

[2]A. Michotte and E. Prüm, 'Etude expérimentale sur le choix volontaire', *Arch. Psychol.*, 1910, 10, p. 194.

[3]G. B. Phelan, *Feeling experience and its modalities,* London, Kegan Paul, 1925

[4]*Ibid.*, p. 19.

The unity of a given conscious moment must be kept constantly in mind. The results of analytic introspection can lead to naught but error unless they are interpreted and understood in the light of that indestructible unity. For the sake of classification and convenience, the various aspects of experience observed by introspection are given names. This is psychological description.[1]

The conviction that the value of experience is 'purely phenomenal' summarises Michotte's conception of subjectivity. The words used by subjects to describe subjective experience are 'differential reagents' corresponding to the modifications of experience, which in turn correspond to physical changes in systems of stimulation.[2] The call on introspection in Phelan's work was fairly unorthodox with regard to the teachings of elementarists. In addition to this, the stress laid on the phenomenal value of experience meant that, in Michotte's eyes, experience was a part of the world accessible to the subject and that the psychologist's task was to give an account of it in objective terms.

These monistic views allowed Michotte to carry out phenomenal descriptions in a rather naturalistic manner and with the help of very elaborate experimental techniques. Introspection as such was explicitly abandoned, so that in his later investigations, he made the constant claim that he was studying 'the world of things as it appeared to the subject on simple inspection'[3] through verbal descriptions. Experimental variations of the spatio-temporal characteristics of events were introduced in order to establish to what extent the impressions reported by subjects corresponded to the situations experienced in everyday life. When the analysis of responses showed constant deviations towards the latter, it could be supposed that they were evidence of laws of organisation of the phenomenal world as such.

In the study of the perception of causality, for instance, it was found that the 'launching' effect was apparently most effective when the impinging moving object had a smaller velocity than the one which was set in motion after the impact. Since, in such experiments, the objects were mere coloured surfaces moving in an observation window, the effects of physical mass could not be invoked. The effect reported was therefore the result of a mere combination of visually perceived movements. The fact that subjects were using terms endowed with a causal meaning to describe such events proved that causal relations existed phenomenally, apart from any knowledge about the laws of mechanics and even contradictory or paradoxical from the point of view of physics.

During his long career as an experimentalist, Michotte designed many sophisticated devices in the same theoretical framework regarding the

[1] *Ibid.*, pp. 20–1.
[2] A. Michotte, 'Réflexions sur le rôle du langage dans l'analyse des organisations perceptives', *Acta Psychol.*, 1959, 15, pp. 70–91.
[3] A. Michotte, *The Perception of Causality*, London, Methuen, 1963, p. 306.

relations between the phenomenal world and the physical world. A detailed account of his extensive work on apparent reality, phenomenal permanence and the like is beyond the scope of this book.[1]

It should be noted that Michotte never considered the epistemological implications of his experiments in an explicit manner, except where the role of language was concerned. In the course of the discussions the author had with him, he often expressed suspicion about transcendental phenomenology, though he valued Husserl's work highly. On the other hand, he disagreed with Behaviouristic interpretations because he thought that mechanistic theories did violence to facts observed in an unprejudiced fashion.

In the last overall discussion of his findings, he defined his general standpoint as that of a psychological or experimental phenomenologist.[2] There is, indeed, no doubt that few experimentalists devoted so much patience to the detailed analysis of the phenomenal world, and we may say that the experimental phenomenology of Stumpf was brought by Michotte to an outstanding level of scientific achievement.

6   *The anthropological physiology of Buytendijk*

The experimental study of central nervous mechanisms underlying perception and movement is the subject-matter of neurophysiology. However, it is well known that the tentative explanation of the relations between physiological mechanisms and behavioural processes has been one of the most difficult tasks psychology ever faced. Neurophysiologists and comparative physiologists became progressively aware of the shortcomings of mechanistic interpretations of the reflex type, as appears from the work of von Holst in particular.[3] Ethologists, for their part, found that reflexological theory was of no use as an explanatory system of innate behaviour patterns.[4]

The same conclusion was reached independently by several physiologists and psychologists who studied sensori-motor patterns and regulation with reference to bodily experience in actual behaviour.

As early as 1927, von Weizsäcker was able to show that behavioural integration resulted not from chains of linear reactions of the organism to external triggers, but from a circular process, namely, regulations of perceptions on movements and conversely.[5] Von Weizsäcker's concept of *Gestaltkreis* is a functional model of the adaptive working of anatomo-

---

[1]A. Michotte, *The Perception of Causality*, London, Methuen, 1963, *passim*.

[2]*Ibid.*, p. 402f.

[3]E. von Holst, *Zur Verhaltensphysiologie bei Tieren und Menschen,* München, Piper Verlag, I: 1969; II: 1970.

[4]Cf. on this point K. Lorenz, 'The Comparative Method in Studying innate Behaviour Patterns', in *Physiological Mechanisms in Animal Behaviour, Symp. Soc. Exp. Biol.* IV, Cambridge University Press, 1950, pp. 221–68.

[5]Reflexgesetz, in A. Bethe (ed.), *Handbuch der Normalen und Pathologischen Physiologie*, 10, 1927.

physiological structures resulting in active responses to external changes, including sensori-motor anticipation. In this respect, this phenomenologically oriented physiological approach is closely linked with Sherrington's teachings on the integrative action of the nervous system and on the anticipatory function of precurrent responses.[1] Besides, this broadened conception of organic regulation foreshadows later cybernetic models of circular causal actions between sensory inputs and motor outputs. It should be remarked, however, that the use of cybernetic concepts in physiology was originally restricted to a mechanical representation of the functioning of nervous networks, whereas, in von Weizsäcker's view, the idea of function includes the modifications of neurophysiological processes via the intentional reference of the subject to external events which modify, in their turn, his bodily situation.

The perspective thus outlined by von Weizsäcker did not simply amount to proposing a new system of relations between internal mechanisms of behaviour. If this had been the case, it would just have added another interpretation of the role of the physiological substrate to the existing ones. The important contribution of the theory of the structure cycle was to bridge the gap between the so-called substrate and overt behaviour patterns by showing that intentionality could actually be observed in bodily acts and attitudes and, still more important, that this intentionality exerted by itself specific retroactive effects on the functioning of the internal mechanisms involved.

Numerous instances of this biological paradigm may be found in two of Buytendijk's major works, *Allgemeine Theorie der Menschlichen Haltung und Bewegung (A general theory of human attitudes and movements)*[2] and *Prolegomena to an Anthropological Physiology.*[3] Important experimental evidence which underlies von Weizsäcker's general theory is to be found in the investigations of some of his close collaborators, such as A. Auersperg and P. Christian.[4]

As Merleau-Ponty remarked,[5] such a phenomenological physiology of human behaviour converges with Buytendijk's similar physiological experiments on the effects of localised cortical lesions on various patterns of behaviour in animals.[6] To a certain extent, the latter are in accordance with Lashley's contemporaneous views on reflex integration and his criticism of the atomistic theory of brain localisation.

Apart from the two extensive works quoted above, which are general

---

[1]Cf. Chapter 3, as well as G. Thinès and R. Zayan, 'La structuration de l'espace biologique. I. Sherrington et la théorie de la distance', *Rev. Quest. Scientif.*, 1975.

[2]Berlin, Springer, 1956.

[3]Utrecht, Spectrum, 1965 (English translation, Pittsburgh, Duquesne University Press, 1974).

[4]Cf. V. von Weizsäcker, *Der Gestaltkreis*, Stuttgart, Georg Thieme Verlag, 1939.

[5]*La Structure du comportement*, Paris, P.U.F., 1942.

[6]'An experimental investigation of the influence of cortical lesions on the behaviour of rats', *Arch. Neerl. Physiol.*, 1932, 17, pp. 370–434; *Idem*, 'Das Verhalten von *Octopus* nach teilweiser Zerstörung des "Gehirns" ', *Arch. Neerl. Physiol.*, 1933, 18, pp. 24–90.

syntheses of a theoretical nature, Buytendijk studied a great variety of topics ranging from motor behaviour and attitudes to the differential psychology of the sexes and the phenomenology of social encounters and ritual gestures. He was the leading figure of the Utrecht school of experimental psychology, whose influence spread in various directions. Thus J. Linschoten investigated problems of visual perception, among other things. His structural analysis of binocular vision is a major piece of experimental phenomenology.[1] D. J. van Lennep and M. J. Langeveld, on the other hand, contributed to problems in psychometry, projective tests and child psychology.[2]

The work of Buytendijk has frequently been misinterpreted, owing to the very diversity of its aspects. His first training under Zwaardemaker, Verworn, Sherrington, Langley and Hill (from 1909 to 1913) was that of a physiologist, a field in which he remained actively engaged until about 1940. From 1923 his work in the field of animal psychology takes a definite turn. While experimenting on various animal species, ranging from insects to mammals, he concentrated increasingly on the subjective dimension of animal behaviour and developed a comparative viewpoint in which the physiological facts are directly related to the bodily experience of organisms. In his last paper dealing with animal behaviour, he elegantly demonstrated in this perspective the difference between active touch, including motor exploration, and passive touch in the motionless organism.[3] This work was carried out on marine animals but its behavioural significance extends far beyond the level of the species used and relates to the general problem of psycho-physiological integration of sensori-motor processes at different phylogenetic degrees. The comparative approach used here is homologous to that of Katz in his studies on human tactile exploration (cf. p. 135).

However, apart from the diversity of the themes tackled, the main source of misunderstanding about Buytendijk's work stems from the fact that he adopted an explicit phenomenological standpoint in the fifties. It was admittedly difficult, both for life-scientists and for philosophical theorists, to grasp the continuity and coherence of a diverse scientific production which gradually led its author from classical nervous physiology to phenomenological psychology and anthropological physiology, through animal behaviour investigations and human psychology studies, some of which were more inspired by existentialism than by phenomenology in the strict sense.

[1] J. Linschoten, *Strukturanalyse der binokulären Tiefenwahrnehmung*, Groningen, Wolters, 1956. Linschoten also devoted a thoroughgoing analysis to William James in which he stresses the 'pre-phenomenological' nature of his conception of psychology. According to Linschoten, William James failed to achieve a fully-fledged phenomenological psychology because he interpreted Brentano's intentionality in a purely immanent sense. Cf. J. Linschoten, *On the Way towards a Phenomenological Psychology*, Pittsburgh, Duquesne University Press, 1968 (Dutch ed., Utrecht, Bijleveld, 1959). See also R. Stevens, *James and Husserl: the Foundations of Meaning*, The Hague, Nijhoff, 1974.
[2] See especially D. J. van Lennep (1948) and M. J. Langeveld (1956).
[3] F. J. J. Buytendijk, 'Toucher et être touché', *Arch. Neerl. Zool.*, 1953, 10, suppl. 2, pp. 34–44.

Buytendijk evidently developed a dual trend of research. A close examination of his publications during his crucial period around the fifties shows nevertheless that his early biological outlook was still present and had not clashed with his epistemological reflection upon the meaning of empirical observations and experimental approaches. Thus, two studies of descriptive phenomenology appeared in 1951, one on the psychology of women[1] and one on the phenomenology of encounter.[2] But in the next year he published his *Traité de Psychologie Animale*,[3] in which he synthesised a conception of animal life which had been in the making since 1920.[4] In this work, and in a later comparative analysis of the human and animal life-situations,[5] the views of the phenomenologist and of the physiologist converge in a striking fashion. As a matter of fact, such views were already the guiding principles of his treatise on animal psychology in 1920, though they were not referred to as phenomenological at the time. In the foreword to the French translation of 1928, Edouard Claparède nevertheless writes: 'Mr Buytendijk's position with respect to psychic life belongs to the major trend which is developing nowadays in various forms, especially in Germany, and which aims not only at *explaining* but also at *understanding* psychic phenomena. Explaining a phenomenon means determining its causes; understanding it amounts to determining its role in the overall behaviour of the individual.'[6] The numerous observations and experiments analysed in this book are strictly factual and no anthropomorphic interpretation ever creeps in, although 'understanding' could have been considered as a non-scientific concept in the psychological world of the twenties, where Loeb's teachings, among others, still attracted wide support.[7] Buytendijk's major point was in fact to show the fruitfulness of a *positive* study of animal behaviour while rejecting the dogmatic *positivism* of mechanistic biologists.

This line of theoretical research can be followed in the successive studies in which he attempted to characterise further the similarities and differences between the respective biological and behavioural traits of man and animals, which range from 1922 to 1958 and intermingle with numerous experimental contributions.[8] Clearly, Buytendijk's biological standpoint about

[1]*De Vrouw*, Utrecht, Spectrum, 1951 (German translation: *Die Frau*, Köln, Bachem Verlag, 1953; French translation: *La Femme*, Paris, Desclée de Brouwer, 1954).

[2]'Zur Phänomenologie der Begegnung', *Eranos Jahrbuch*, 19, pp. 431–86.

[3]Paris, Presses Universitaires de France, 1952.

[4]*Psychologie der Dieren*, Haarlem, Bohn, 1920 (French translation, Paris, Payot, 1928).

[5]*Mensch und Tier*, Hamburg, Rowohlts Enzyklopädie, 1958.

[6]F. J. J. Buytendijk, *Psychologie des Animaux*, trans. R. Bredo, Paris, Payot, 1928. Foreword by E. Claparède, p. 11. English translation ours. Original author's italics.

[7]'Understanding' (*Verstehen*) was introduced in the theory of human sciences by W. Dilthey as early as 1883 in his *Einleitung in die Geisteswissenschaften*. Buytendijk makes no explicit reference to Dilthey in his book.

[8]Apart from his book on animal psychology (1920), the main studies to be considered here are: *De Wijsheid der Mieren*, Amsterdam, Meulenhoff, 1922 (monograph on ants); *Bijdrage tot een onderzoek naar het wezenverschil van mens en dier*, Amsterdam, Kirchner, 1922 (on the essential difference between man and animals); *The Mind of the Dog*, London, George Allen & Unwin,

behavioural processes cannot be dissociated from his phenomenological outlook.

Therefore, we may legitimately consider that Buytendijk's major achievements in phenomenologically oriented experiments are to be found in the field of comparative psychology. A complete analysis of this production is beyond the scope of this chapter, since between 1907 and 1935 Buytendijk published eighty-five experimental papers on physiology and animal behaviour and eleven books on the same subjects. The main topics treated are summarised in the general review by Thinès and Zayan.[1]

We think it is fair to say, to fix the reader's ideas, that such a biological phenomenology has been considered up to now from a philosophical standpoint, based on an ontological distinction between the animal's natural world and man's cultural world. The difficulties raised by this categorisation of living beings have been stressed in the case of Husserl's characterisations of the natural world and the life-world (cf. Chapter 5). But to these early phenomenological views should be added the contributions of hermeneutics and philosophical anthropology. To this latter trend belong M. Scheler, H. Plessner, E. Cassirer, S. Strasser, Ph. Lersch and the philosophical generalisations of Buytendijk's later views on man–animal differences.[2] As we noted before, this kind of positive phenomenology was rarely achieved because there has been a frequent confusion between the epistemological strivings of phenomenological philosophy and the methodological clarification of the levels of empirical knowledge made possible by phenomenological description.

In this respect, we may consider that Buytendijk's experimental work represents an exceptional instance of a sound biological use of phenomenological teachings. This seems due first and foremost to his continual use of scientific methods in the respective fields of physiology, comparative psychology and human psychology. In other words, his originality lies in the fact that he used adequate techniques for each level of factual analysis, i.e. he used for each level of phenomena – or, in Husserlian terms, for each region – a specific explanation, while stressing its limitations and constraints according to the level considered. In his book on attitudes and movements, for instance, both the physiological and the behavioural aspects of motor patterns are plainly taken into account, but at the same time he demonstrates the inadequacy of ultimate explanations of expressive acts in

---

1935; Dutch edn, 1932; *Grondproblemen van het dierlijk leven*, Nijmegen, Dekker & Van de Vegt, 1938 (fundamental problems of animal life); and *Wege zum Verständnis der Tiere*, Zürich, Niehans, 1938 (on understanding animals). This series of monographs was preparatory to the final syntheses to be found in the above-quoted *Traité de Psychologie Animale* (1952) and *Mensch und Tier* (1958).

[1] G. Thinès and R. Zayan, 'F. J. J. Buytendijk's contribution to animal behaviour: animal psychology or ethology?' *Acta Biotheoret*, 1975, 24, 3–4, pp. 86–99.

[2] F. J. J. Buytendijk, *Mensch und Tier*, Hamburg, Rohwolt, 1958, and *Das Menschliche*, Stuttgart, Koehler, 1958.

terms of anatomical structures and corresponding physiological mechanisms. In his opinion, the structures of motor actions are in spatio-temporal continuity with significant, i.e. intentional, perceptions and situations. Their expressive patterning should thus be considered as *functional* sequences of attitudes and not described in terms of *causal processes*.[1]

7 *Intersubjectivity as an ethological problem*

Whatever may be the case, Buytendijk's pioneering and systematic contributions to the *mechanisms* of animal behaviour have been fully acknowledged by comparative psychologists. Moreover, his historical linkage with von Uexküll's teachings, which he shares with K. Lorenz, allows him to be considered, from both the methodological and the factual points of view, as a potential ethologist. As a matter of fact, even his most phenomenologically oriented descriptions of social encounters in animals and men have not been overlooked by contemporary ethologists.[2] *Insofar as ethology defines itself as the biology of behaviour, it would be illogical to dissociate its rejection of mechanistic Behaviourism from phenomenological attempts at grasping the significant relations of the organism to its specific natural world (Umwelt).*

An indirect illustration of this common framework is to be found in the light thrown by A. Portmann, a prominent morphologist and evolutionist, on the phenomenological interpretation of instinctive behaviour and social communication in animals, as described in classical ethological studies. It is worthy of notice that Portmann's approach is one of the few instances in which the phylogenetic dimension appears as the biological outcome of the phenomenological understanding of behaviour patterns and anatomical structures. Of particular importance in this respect are his investigations of the process of cerebralisation during the course of evolution, and his analyses of conspicuous bodily features displayed by animals in mimicry and sexual dimorphism.[3]

More direct links between phenomenology and ethology have been tentatively suggested by the present author in relation to Buytendijk's conception of individual encounters between conspecifics. The main issue here is that of the possible translation of the phenomenological concept of intersubjectivity into terms of behaviour patterns as described by comparative

---

[1] For an experimental approach to sensori-motor regulation from both physiological and behavioural standpoints, cf. R. Zayan, 'Activité proprioceptive et localisation d'une sensation tactile', *Rev. Psychol. Sc. Educ.*, 1971, 6, 3, pp. 293–329.

[2] Cf. e.g. J. Van Hooff, *op. cit.* (1971, 1972), I. Eibl-Eibesfeldt, *op. cit.* (1970). A more specific reference to the phenomenological description of animal encounters is to be found in R. Schloeth, 'Zur Psychologie der Begegnung zwischen Tieren', *Behaviour*, 1956, 10, pp. 1–80.

[3] A. Portmann, *Die Tiergestalt*, Basel, 1948; *Idem, Das Tier als soziales Wesen*, Zürich, Rhein, 1953; *Idem, Neue Wege der Biologie*, Munich, Piper, 1960.

F

ethology.[1] The point is to establish whether the morphological or behavioural patterns of a conspecific are likely to release not only consummatory acts of a stereotyped kind, as a model of a conspecific would, but also reactions which may testify that the animal recognises or looks for a particular conspecific, shows preference for a given sexual partner, etc. If this were the case, the perceptual properties of the conspecific (size, colour, form, movement) would be endowed with an appetitive value requiring the presence of that *particular* conspecific, the individual then being inseparable from a genuine inter-individual relation. Such a relation could be distinguished from mere consummatory interactions having immediate survival value or biological function. The ethological recording of behaviour patterns would then give evidence of a progressive decline of automatic reactions triggered by specific releasers, including those exerting maximal effects, e.g. 'supra-normal' ones.

Conversely, a gradual adaptation or reciprocal synchronisation of the animal to the signal values of the partner encountered could support the idea that an intersubjective relation, in the phenomenological sense of the word, lies beyond the process of causation as observed by ethologists in the sequences of instinctive, viz. reproductive acts as described by Tinbergen.[2] If it can be claimed that, in sexual activities, consummatory reactions can be considered as pseudo-encounters in many species, some observations have shown that the appetitive phase does not exclude the possibility of selection of the partner's properties. Thus, in some bird-species, pair-forming is closely associated with nest-building activities and is independent of copulation; sexual displays which make possible the choice of the individual mate are independent of the sexual cycle. In many birds and mammals it happens that partners form a lasting couple after the consummatory phase, and that parental activities reinforce this intersubjective bond. Kortlandt defines 'encounter' as the most evolved stage of social contacts in cormorants. Thus, in early ontogeny, the animal first displays aggressive behaviour associated with territorial defence; the conspecific is still perceived as a 'signal' releasing general responses. At a second stage, the young bird performs a great number of expressive acts outside its territory; finally, it reaches the stage of the choice of partner and of pair bond.[3]

This gradual maturation of subjectivity characterises sexual behaviour as such. At the outset of ontogeny, this sexual behaviour consists mainly of vacuum activities. It then takes the form of social greeting. Thereafter, expressive acts of appetitive sexual behaviour are directed to *any* other conspecific, male or female. Finally, the active courtship is only performed towards a partner of the opposite sex, chosen for its particular characteristics.

[1]G. Thinès, *Psychologie des Animaux*, Brussels, Dessart, 1966, pp. 287–310; *Idem*, 'The phenomenological approach in comparative psychology', *J. Phenomen. Psychol.*, 1970, I, 1, pp. 63–73.

[2]N. Tinbergen, *The study of instinct*, Oxford, Clarendon Press, 1951.

[3]A. Kortlandt, 'Signal, Ausdrück, Begegnung', *Arch. Neerl. Zool.*, 1953, 10, suppl. 2, pp. 65–78.

Kortlandt has given many other instances demonstrating this increase in perceptual selectivity, and the corresponding regression of the releasing value of general 'specific' sign-stimuli.[1]

It should be further remarked that inter-individual relations in animals can be illustrated from less selective processes, as aggressive interactions and dominance-submission interactions. Thus, Zayan has demonstrated that individual recognition is linked with the stability of hierarchies in viviparous fish of the genus *Xiphophorus* when pair members are placed in an unknown environment.[2] In another experiment, the same author has shown that short-term individual recognition is a more important factor for the establishment of dominance than territorial defence, i.e. aggressive reactions towards an intruder – an instinctive pattern which is very characteristic of that species. It is clear from these data that individual recognition is demonstrable on the basis of strictly ethological criteria, for example, frequencies, time-latencies, etc. of aggressive behaviour patterns in pairs of known fishes and in pairs of unknown ones.[3] The method is that of experimental ethology (using adequate control groups, randomisation, etc.), but the hypothetical framework is in line with the phenomenological standpoint. Katz[4] and Buytendijk[5] referred explicitly to individual recognition phenomena in fishes and birds. Nevertheless, if one defines individual recognition as a perceptual-cognitive process and not merely as an ethological mechanism of reciprocal adaptation (e.g. the physiological synchronisation of partners), the heuristic hypothesis may then be based on the idea of a possible individual relationship as such. The author has therefore found it necessary to demonstrate that behavioural patterns associated with individual recognition are still present when visual cues alone are available during the interactions, i.e. without the actual contacts involved in agonistic communication, e.g. sensory information about the lateral line system, as present in most behaviour patterns such as tail-beats and fights.[6]

The classical ethological hypothesis would have led to the postulation of an adaptive function of individual recognition in ritualising aggressive behaviour and reducing aggression. The author has shown that some patterns of aggressive behaviour are more frequently recorded in known partners than in unknown competitors.

In conclusion, ethological investigations on intersubjective relations may

---

[1] A. Kortlandt, 'Aspects and prospects of the concept of instinct', *Arch. Neerl. Zool.*, 1955, 11, pp. 155–284.

[2] R. Zayan, 'Le rôle de la reconnaissance individuelle dans la stabilité des relations hiérarchiques chez *Xiphophorus* (Pisces, Poecilidae)', *Behaviour*, 1974, 49, 3–4, pp. 268–312.

[3] R. Zayan, 'Défense du territoire et reconnaissance individuelle chez *Xiphophorus* (Pisces, Poecilidae)', *Behaviour*, 1975, 52, 3–4, pp. 266–312.

[4] D. Katz, 'Sozialpsychologie der Vögel', *Ergebn. Biol.*, 1926, 1.

[5] F. J. J. Buytendijk, 'Zur Phänomenologie der Begegnung', *Eranos Jahrb.*, 1951, 19, pp. 431–86.

[6] R. Zayan, unpublished experiments. The same author has reviewed the role of tactile communication in animal intersubjectivity from the phenomenological standpoint in 'Le sens du sens tactile', *J. Phenom. Psychol.*, 1971, 2, 1, pp. 49–91.

fruitfully rely on phenomenological hypotheses while being carried out in a strictly controlled framework. They furnish, in our opinion, a definite proof of the main claim of this book, viz. that phenomenology, understood as a critical approach to the facts of experience, is a heuristic point of departure for an adequate biological analysis of behaviour, and not, as many would have it, a mere hermeneutic discipline.

8   *Subjective phenomena as seen by ethologists*

In the first general texts in which ethologists expounded their doctrine, psychology was severely criticised. Thus in *The Study of Instinct* (1951), Tinbergen stresses the lack of objectivity of the European schools and the disregard of innate behaviour in American Behaviourism. Lorenz, for his part, condemns mechanistic and vitalistic theories and rejects Gestalt theory on the grounds of isomorphism, while considering that the description of structures may be a suitable method in analysing the perceptual patterns of sign-stimuli.[1]

At first sight, such criticisms are akin to those uttered by phenomenologists against classical psychology. On close examination, however, one discovers that ethology and phenomenology are at variance concerning the nature of objectivity. In the former, objective facts are those which are demonstrated by naturalistic observation in the manner of physical science. In the latter, on the contrary, the naturalistic approach is evaluated in the framework of a radical epistemology and is said to call for a specific definition in each objective discipline. Therefore, from the phenomenological standpoint, ethology and classical psychology may equally be charged with objectivism. This, as we have seen before (p. 49), has fundamental consequences for the form in which subjective phenomena are supposed to exist.

The striking fact in this respect is that early ethologists, while doing away with mechanistic psychology, still accepted the ancient introspective concepts as a matter of course. In other words, their biological approach to behaviour was still tainted with traditional dualism. Thus Tinbergen writes: 'Hunger, like anger, fear, and so forth, is a phenomenon that can be known only by introspection; when applied to another subject, especially one belonging to another species, it is merely a guess about the possible nature of the animal's subjective state. By presenting such a guess as a causal explanation, the psychologist trespasses on the domain of physiology.'[2] In a previous paragraph, the author accepted the idea that a hunting animal could be conveniently described as being in search of food but not that it was hunting *because* it was hungry, since 'the scientist . . . wants to know what is happening

---

[1]K. Lorenz, 'The comparative method in studying innate behaviour patterns', in *Physiological Mechanisms in Animal Behaviour*, *Symp. Soc. Exp. Biol.* IV, Cambridge University Press, 1950, pp. 224–7. Cf. also Chapter 3.

[2]*The Study of Instinct*, p. 5.

inside the animal when it is in this state',[1] i.e. which physiological mechanisms are involved.

No scientist, of course, will agree to interpreting a guess as a causal explanation, but neither may he accept that if subjective phenomena refer at all to a reality belonging to the organism's experience, it should simply be approached by guessing. In this case, as in all dualistic interpretations, subjective phenomena are supposed to exist in a purely private mode, i.e. in a manner which excludes communication, by definition. If this is what we must call subjective experience – the 'content of consciousness' in classical terminology – we must, indeed, give up every hope of including it in functional studies of behaviour. But to call on physiological mechanisms does not solve the problem because internal physiological causation is a different issue. We do not suggest that the latter has nothing to do with subjective experience, but it may not simply be equated with it. Referring to the observations and working hypotheses of von Weizsäcker, Buytendijk and several others who have been analysed above, it seems safer to interpret subjective phenomena as a mode of expression functionally included in the behavioural acts themselves (cf. p. 141). Even if ethologists may consider such theories as defective, they seem less inadequate than the traditional dualistic views. The cycle structure hypothesis at least allows the understanding of physiological causation without implying that subjective experience is an epiphenomenon, i.e. an accompanying realm of events devoid of biological significance.

It may be argued that the situation we describe was that of early ethology and that the theory has evolved considerably since. This, as we shall see, is only partly true.

Thus, in a lecture on subjective experience in animals delivered in 1963, Lorenz asserts that 'psychology is the science of the subjective phenomena of experience, which we can only observe directly in ourselves'. Significantly he adds: 'I believe that in German, we should restrict ourselves to calling only that psychology and not, as is usual in America, all other branches of the objective study of behaviour.'[2] In an overall review written in 1969, Baerends holds similar views. He writes: 'In psychology, information about subjective nature – feelings or sensations – has always been considered as an important causal factor in behaviour. In human psychology, it is often possible, by the method of introspection, to obtain information on feelings which coincides with the occurrence of a behaviour. But in the study of animal behaviour, this

---

[1] *Ibid.*, p. 4.
[2] K. Lorenz, 'Haben Tiere ein subjektives Erleben?' in *Über tierisches und menschliches Verhalten* (II), Piper Verlag, 1965, pp. 559–74. Translation ours. In contrasting German and American psychologies in this fashion, Lorenz eliminates with a stroke of the pen all the experimental work of European psychologists and physiologists which did not follow the teachings of Elementarists, including Pavlov, from whom American Behaviourists originally borrowed their physiological explanations of behaviour. Besides, American psychology includes much more than objectivistic Behaviourism, viz., among other trends, psychoanalysis and phenomenological psychology, the latter being already well on its way when Lorenz made the above-quoted statements.

method is useless.'[1] This method is not useless; it is, as Brentano remarked more than a century ago, plainly impossible (cf. p. 60).

Clearly, the views held by some ethologists on subjective experience did not undergo much change over a period of more than twenty years. This static state of affairs is principally due to the belief that psychology *as a whole* is still a mentalistic discipline. Enough has been said in this book about the persistent mentalistic trend in present-day psychology and its biological shortcomings, but our critical evaluation of it applies equally to its survival in ethology.

Such survival is paradoxical indeed. It testifies to a peculiar lack of interest in psychological studies, which led in turn to an overlooking of several objective psychological discoveries. Hence the paradox that some ethologists, who constantly stressed the meaningful relationship between animals and their surroundings, still advocate out-dated mentalistic concepts with regard to subjective experience, in spite of the fact that the issue was approached at the observational level by phenomenological psychologists and comparative physiologists. Special reference should be made again here to the experimental work of von Weizsäcker, Straus, Buytendijk, Portmann and several others (cf. p. 135f).

A very different trend was inaugurated by the interest of ethologists in comparative studies of human and animal communication. Thus Hinde, analysing the qualities of social relationships, considers that terms referring to the latter such as 'demanding', 'competitive' and the like, may be conveniently used to describe some 'intrinsic property of the individual which is exhibited in several types of behaviour . . . These qualities', he concludes, 'refer to modes of interacting, to the manner in which individuals *mesh*, in particular contexts: this is affected, but *not* determined, by intrinsic properties of either individual.'[2] This last statement indicates that the author does not want to suggest that describing subjective aspects of social relationships may be interpreted as a search for internal causes of behaviour. It is an open question whether he would agree to including these qualitative elements in a functional theory of intersubjectivity in the sense of phenomenological psychology.

In any case, it seems safe to conclude that the rapid progress of human ethology as well as the stress laid on non-verbal communication will eliminate dualistic remnants from ethological theory. The main reason for this is that the behaviour patterns observed in these two new fields are closely related to bodily activity. It should be remembered, in this respect, that it was from the descriptive approach of the experienced body – as synthetically outlined in Merleau-Ponty's *Phenomenology of Perception* – that phenomenological psychology was able to elaborate a theory of intentionality directly related to

[1]G. P. Baerends, 'Le rôle de l'éthologie dans l'étude causale du comportement', in M. Richelle and J. C. Ruwet (eds), *Problèmes et méthodes en psychologie comparée* (colloque de Liège, 1969), Paris, Masson, 1972, p. 11. Translation ours.
[2]R. A. Hinde, *Biological Bases of Human Social Behaviour*, New York, McGraw Hill, 1974, pp. 18–29.

organic facts, and stress the overt character of intersubjectivity, as opposed to the mentalistic conception of introspective consciousness. The possibility is therefore not excluded that ethology and phenomenological psychology may converge in the future on the fundamental issues of expressive behaviour.

Concluding Remarks

On completing his manuscript, the author feels that he has left out of consideration many problems of phenomenology, not to mention the science of behaviour since he boldly joined these two concepts together in the title of his book. He nevertheless hopes that the material discussed will, as it stands, contribute towards giving a more precise idea of the phenomenological position concerning the scientific approach to the study of behaviour. The expression 'science of behaviour' has been chosen to stress the fact that we have to deal here with an extensive field of research in which there is – or should be – no monopoly, nor any authoritative attitude as far as objectivity is concerned.

It has been claimed that the integration of all disciplines whose subject-matter is man (psychology, sociology, ethnography, anthropology, human ethology, etc.), under the overall heading of *human sciences* abolished 'schools' defending a particular point of view about the nature of man and his potentialities as a living being. In our opinion, this is still a wish, not a fact. Psychologists, for instance, keep on asserting, since the appearance of Behaviourism, that their science is the objective study of behaviour, but ethologists use the same definition for their domain and think that laboratory studies have not taught us much about behaviour mechanisms.

Sociologists, for their part, frequently confuse the study of social facts with politics and commit themselves in pragmatic battles which have little to do with science. Economists develop abstract systems in very different national contexts and become enslaved to their own beliefs, to the point of seeing no other solution to urgent public questions than a vague hope of spontaneous historical improvements. Meanwhile, they all present themselves as specialists of a field of human sciences.

In this puzzling diversity of standpoints and attitudes, who is objective and who is not? In most cases, the answer is sought in some ideology. But can the scientist accept that objectivity should be defined on the basis of beliefs? And if he does, is he entitled to criticise philosophers for the one-sidedness of their standpoints?

When the founder of phenomenology urged empirical and theoretical workers to go 'back to the things themselves', he was at least aware of the basic difficulty encountered in human sciences, namely that objectivity is a matter of definition, i.e. that it is grounded in some sort of pre-scientific *a priori* and that the nature of the various *a prioris* should be investigated. In this sense, phenomenology appears as the minimum of philosophising we are bound to accept in order to justify the standpoint we choose when we tackle scientific work in whatever domain in which man is the ultimate subject-matter.

This basic philosophy need not be phenomenology as it developed historically; it may be any kind of reflection upon the scientific act which resolutely tackles the problems pertaining to the foundations of knowledge. In other words, no human scientist is justified in refusing to consider the epistemological implications of his endeavours.

Since this book is devoted to phenomenology in the framework of behaviour studies, the author has done his best to present it in a systematic fashion and to stress what he considers its most significant achievements. In doing so, he has not intended at any moment to 'convert' his sceptical readers. His only purpose has been to show, first, that the phenomenological trend has contributed to the study of problems which, in his opinion, cannot be avoided in the human sciences, even if it must be admitted that phenomenology is far from having offered ideal solutions to these issues; second, that there are serious reasons for thinking that phenomenological psychology, considered as a specific positive approach to the study of man, has given a new impetus to many classical problems and therefore deserves the attention of life-scientists.

The concrete achievements which have been reviewed in the course of the last chapter should not be considered as a series of arguments on behalf of the cause. As was repeatedly stressed, the life-scientists who adopted the phenomenological standpoint did so because they found no more adequate point of departure within their own field of investigation. Whether their choice was a sound one can be appreciated either from their actual contributions as valued by specialists, or again from an epistemological standpoint, which brings us back to the preceding paragraph.

However, beyond doubt they provided evidence for phenomena which would have escaped their attention if they had not turned to new sets of hypotheses that they recognised as phenomenological. If their opponents are convinced that such a framework is not valid, it remains for them to prove that the observations and experiments it made possible are artifacts devoid of organic significance.

Historically speaking, we insisted on the fact that the phenomenological trend which is now gaining in importance, both in Europe and in the United States, is the continuation of a psychological approach which appeared in the same epoch as the experimental psychology of the Leipzig school. We mentioned briefly the reasons why it remained largely unexploited for a long time and why Gestalt psychology, which evolved directly from it, did not become a fully-fledged phenomenological psychology. This, of course, should have been more fully developed, but a thorough study of this problem was beyond the scope of this work. Let us just remind the reader that this temporary failure was mainly due to the parallel development of transcendental phenomenology. The new phase which we are watching now is a sign that psychologists and other human scientists appreciate better the relationship between epistemological analyses and the methodological requirements of their own disciplines. The idea that phenomenology is aiming at substituting philosophical reflection for scientific work is, in our opinion, fading, as a result of more technical information about the objectives of phenomenological psychology.

This book is simply intended to show what may be expected from this approach in the biological study of behaviour.

Bibliography

Aguirre, A. *Genetische Phänomenologie und Reduktion*, The Hague, Nijhoff, 1970.

Alapack, R. J. 'The physiognomy of the Mueller-Lyer figure', *J. Phenom. Psychol.*, 1971, 2, 27–47.

Allport, G. W. 'Scientific models and human morals', *Psychol. Rev.*, 1947, 54, pp. 182–92.

Altner, G. (ed.). *The nature of human behaviour*, London, George Allen & Unwin, 1976.

Apter, M. J. *The computer simulation of Behaviour*, London, Hutchinson, 1970.

Apter, M. J. 'Cybernetics: a case study of a scientific subject complex', *Soc. Rev. Monog.*, no. 18, 1972, 93–116.

Apter, M. J. 'Systems and structures', *Technol. and Soc.*, 1972, 1, 2, 55–8.

Arcaya, J. 'Two languages of man', *J. Phenom. Psychol.*, 1973, 4, 315–29.

Argyle, M. 'Non-verbal communication in human social interactions' in R. A. Hinde (ed.), *Non-verbal communication*, Cambridge University Press, 1972, 243–69.

Arnold, M. B. 'Motives as causes', *J. Phenom. Psychol.*, 1971, 1, 185–92.

Auersperg, A. *Schmerz und Schmerzhaftigkeit*, Berlin, Springer, 1963.

Baerends, G. P. 'Le rôle de l'éthologie dans l'étude causale du comportement' in M. Richelle and J. C. Ruwet (eds), *Problèmes et méthodes en psychologie comparée*, Paris, Masson, 1972, 11–28.

Bannon, J. F. *The Philosophy of Merleau-Ponty*, New York, Harcourt, Brace & World, 1967.

Barrell, J. J., and Barrell, J. E. 'A self-directed approach for a science of human experience', *J. Phenom. Psychol.*, 1975, 6, 63–73.

Barton, A. *Three worlds of therapy. Freud, Jung and Rogers*, Palo Alto, National Press Books, 1974.

Bayer, W. von, and Griffith, R. M. (eds), *Conditio humana. Erwin W. Straus on his 75th birthday*, Berlin, Springer, 1966.

Berger, G. *Le Cogito dans la philosophie de Husserl*, Paris, Aubier, 1941.

Berlyne, D. E. 'American and European psychology', *Amer. Psychologist*, 1968, 23, 447–52.

Beshai, J. A. 'Psychology's dilemma: to explain or to understand', *J. Phenom. Psychol.*, 1971, 1, 209–23.

Beshai, J. A. 'Is psychology a hermeneutic science?', *J. Phenom. Psychol.*, 1975, 5, 425–39.

Bieliauskas, V. J. 'Existential philosophy and psychoanalysis' in R. W. Russell (ed.), *Frontiers in psychology*, Chicago, Scott & Foresman, 1964.

Biemel, W. (ed). *Phänomenologie Heute. Festschrift für Ludwig Landgrebe*, The Hague, Nijhoff, 1972.

Binswanger, L. *Grundformen und Erkenntnis menschlichen Daseins*, Zurich, Niehans, 1942.

Binswanger, L. *Being-in-the-world*, New York, Harper, 1968.

Blankenburg, W. 'Provokation und Revokation im psychiatrischen Interview', *J. Phenom. Psychol.*, 1975, 5, 405–17.

Boehm, R. *Vom Gesichtspunkt der Phänomenologie. Husserl-Studien*, The Hague, Nijhoff, 1968.

Brand, G. *Die Lebenswelt. Eine Philosophie des konkreten A priori*, Berlin, De Gruyter, 1971.

Brandt, L. 'Phenomenology, Psychoanalysis and Behaviorism (E ≡ S) vs (E ≢ S)?', *J. Phenom. Psychol.*, 1970, 1, 7–18.

Brandt, L. W., and Brandt, E. P. 'The alienated psychologist', *J. Phenom. Psychol.*, 1974, 5, 41–56.

Brentano, F. *Psychologie vom empirischen Standpunkt* (Vol. I), Leipzig, Duncker and Humbolt, 1874 (posthumous ed., 3 vols, O. Kraus, ed., Leipzig, Meiner, 1924–1928).

Broekman, J. M. *Phänomenologie und Egologie*, The Hague, Nijhoff, 1963.

Brown, S. C. (ed.). *Philosophy of psychology*, London, Macmillan, 1974.

Bühler, C. 'Some observations on the psychology of the third force', *J. Hum. Psychol.*, 1965, 5, 54–6.

Bühler, C., and Allen, M. *Introduction to humanistic psychology*, Monterey, Brooks & Cole, 1972.

Bunge, M. *Foundations of Physics*, New York, Springer, 1967.

Bunge, M. 'Le concept de modèle', *L'âge de la science*, 1968, 1, 165–80.

Bunge, M. 'The metaphysics, epistemology and methodology of levels', in L. L. Whyte, A. G. Wilson and D. Wilson (eds), *Hierarchical structures*, New York, Elsevier, 1969, 17–28.

Bunge, M. *Problems in the foundations of physics*, New York, Springer, 1971.

Bunge, M. (ed.). *Exact philosophy: problems, methods and goals*, Dordrecht, Reidel, 1972.

Bunge, M. *Method, model and matter*, Dordrecht, Reidel, 1973.

Busnel, R. G. (ed.). *Acoustic behaviour of animals*, Amsterdam, Elsevier, 1963.

Busnel, R. G. 'On certain aspects of animal acoustic signals' in R. G. Busnel, *Acoustic behaviour of animals*, Amsterdam, Elsevier, 1963, 69–111.

Buytendijk, F. J. J. 'An experimental investigation of the influence of cortical lesions on the behaviour of rats', *Arch. Neerl. Physiol.*, 1932, 17, 370–434.

Buytendijk, F. J. J. 'Das Verhalten von *Octopus* nach teilweiser Zerstörung des "Gehirns" ', *Arch. Neerl. Physiol.*, 1933, 18, 24–90.

Buytendijk, F. J. J. *Wesen und Sinn des Spiels*, Berlin, Kurt Wolff Verlag, 1933 (first Dutch ed, 1932).

Buytendijk, F. J. J. *The mind of the dog*, London, Allen & Unwin, 1935 (first Dutch ed, 1932).

Buytendijk, F. J. J. *Wege zum Verständnis der Tiere*, Zurich, Niehans, 1938.

Buytendijk, F. J. J. *Over de pijn*, Utrecht, Spectrum, 1943.

Buytendijk, F. J. J. 'The phenomenological approach to the problem of feelings and emotions' in M. L. Reymert (ed.), *Feelings and emotions*, New York, McGraw-Hill, 1950.

Buytendijk, F. J. J. 'Zur Phänomenologie der Begegnung', *Eranos Jahrbuch*, 1951, 19, 431–86.

Buytendijk, F. J. J. *Traité de Psychologie animale*, Paris, Presses Universitaires de France, 1952.

Buytendijk, F. J. J. 'Toucher et être touché', *Arch. Neerl. Zool.*, 1953, 10, suppl. 2, 34–44.

Buytendijk, F. J. J. *Allgemeine Theorie der menschlichen Haltung und Bewegung*, Berlin, Springer, 1956 (first Dutch ed., 1948).

Buytendijk, F. J. J. *Das Menschliche*, Stuttgart, Koehler, 1958.

Buytendijk, F. J. J. *Mensch und Tier*, Hamburg, Rohwolts Enzyklopädie, 1958.

Buytendijk, F. J. J. 'Die Bedeutung der Phänomenologie Husserls für die Psychologie der Gegenwart: la signification de la phénoménologie husserlienne pour la psychologie actuelle' (trans. G. Thinès) in H. L. Van Breda (ed.), *Husserl et la pensée moderne*, The Hague, Nijhoff, 1959.

Buytendijk, F. J. J. 'Die biologische Sonderstellung des Menschen' in V. E. Frankl, V. E. F. von Gebsattel and J. H. Schulz (eds), *Handbuch der Neurosenlehre und Psychotherapie*, Berlin, Urban & Schwarzenberg, 1961, Vol. 5, 119f.

Buytendijk, F. J. J. 'Les catégories fondamentales de l'organisation et de la désorganisation de l'existence animale' in A. Brion et H. Ey, *Psychiatrie Animale*, Paris, Desclée de Brouwer, 1964, 113–20.

Buytendijk, F. J. J. 'Some aspects of touch', *J. Phenom. Psychol.*, 1970, 1, 99–124.

Buytendijk, F. J. J. *Prolegomena to an anthropological physiology*, Pittsburgh, Duquesne University Press, 1974 (first Dutch ed., 1965).

Buytendijk, F. J. J., and Christian, P. 'Kybernetik und Gestaltkreis als Erklärungsprinzipien des Verhaltens', *Nervenartz*, 1963, 34, 97–104.

Buytendijk, F. J. J., and Plessner, H. 'Die Deutung des mimischen Ausdrucks', *Phil. Anz.*, 1925, 1, 72–126.

Cairns, D. 'Results of Husserl's investigations', *J. Philos.*, 1939, 36, 236–8.

Cairns, D. *Guide for translating Husserl*, The Hague, Nijhoff, 1973.

Carafides, J. L. 'H. Spiegelberg on the phenomenology of C. G. Jung', *J. Phenom. Psychol.*, 1974, 5, 75–80.

Claesges, U. *Edmund Husserls Theorie der Raumkonstitution*, The Hague, Nijhoff, 1964.

Clark, R. B. *Dynamics in metazoan evolution*, Oxford, Clarendon Press, 1964.

Cohen, J. *Humanistic psychology*, London, Allen & Unwin, 1958.

Cohen, J. *Homo psychologicus*, London, Allen & Unwin, 1970.

Cohen, J. 'Charles Bell and the roots of physiology', *New Scientist*, 1974, 498.

Colaizzi, P. F. 'The phenomenology of Merleau-Ponty and the serial position effect', *J. Phenom. Psychol.*, 1971, 2, 115–23.

Conrad, T. *Zur Wesenslehre des psychischen Lebens und Erlebens*, The Hague, Nijhoff, 1968.

Corriveau, M. 'Phenomenology, Psychology and radical behaviorism: Skinner and Merleau-Ponty on behavior', *J. Phenom. Psychol.*, 1972, 3, 7–34.

Crabbé, G. *Les conditions d'une perception de la causalité*, Paris, Editions du C.N.R.S., 1967.

Crabbé-Declève, G., and De Koninck, M. C. J. 'La perception du mouvement dans l'image picturale', *J. Phenom. Psychol.*, 1974, 4, 425–44.

Craig, W. 'Appetites and aversions as constituents of instincts', *Biol. Bull. Woods Hole*, 1918, 34, 91–107.

Craik, K. J. W. *The nature of psychology* (S. L. Sherwood, ed.), Cambridge University Press, 1966.

Dagenais, J. *Models of man. A phenomenological critique of some paradigms in the human sciences*, The Hague, Nijhoff, 1972.

Darwin, C. *The expression of the emotions in man and animals*, London, 1872 (Reedit. University of Chicago Press, 1965).

Declève, H. *Heidegger et Kant,* The Hague, Nijhoff, 1970.

Dempsey, J. R. P. *The psychology of Sartre*, Westminster, Newman Press, 1950.

De Waelhens, A. *Phénoménologie et Vérité*, Paris, Presses Universitaires de France, 1953.

De Waelhens, A. *La philosophie et les expériences naturelles*, The Hague, Nijhoff, 1961.

Dijkgraaf, S. 'Die Sinneswelt der Fledermäuse', *Experientia*, 1946, 2, 438–49.

Dijkhuis, J. H. 'Recherches sur les représentations provoquées par l'audition de bruits', *J. Psychol. Norm. Pathol.*, 1953, 46, 2, 188–214.

Dilthey, W. *Einleitung in die Geisteswissenschaften*, Vol. 1, Stuttgart, Teubner, 1966 (6th ed., first pub. 1883).

Drüe, H. *Husserls System der phänomenologischen Psychologie*, Berlin, De Gruyter, 1963.

Dublin, J. E. 'Language and expression of upright man: toward a phenomenology of language and the lived-body', *J. Phenom. Psychol.*, 1972, 2, 141–60.

Dufrenne, M. *Phénoménologie de l'expérience esthétique*, Paris, Presses Universitaires de France, 1953 (2 vols).

Dufrenne, M. *Jalons*, The Hague, Nijhoff, 1966.

Eckartsberg, R. von, 'Experiential psychology: a descriptive protocol and a reflection', *J. Phenom. Psychol.*, 1972, 2, 161–73.

Ecole, J. 'Des rapports de l'expérience et de la raison dans l'analyse de l'âme ou la "Psychologia empirica" de Ch. Wolff', *Giorn. di Metafisica*, 1966, 21, 4–5, 589–617.

Ecole, J. 'De la nature de l'âme, de la déduction de ses facultés et de ses rapports avec le corps ou la "Psychologia rationalis" de Ch. Wolff', *Giorn. di Metafisica*, 1969, 24, 4–6, 499–531.

Edmund Husserl 1859–1959, Recueil commémoratif publié à l'occasion du centenaire de la naissance du philosophe (Van Breda, H. L. and Taminiaux, J., eds). The Hague, Nijhoff, 1959.

Ehrenfels, Chr. von. 'Ueber Gestaltqualitäten', *Vtljsch. Wiss. Philos*, 1890, 14, 249–92.

Eibl-Eibesfeldt, I. *Ethology, the biology of behaviour*, New York, Holt, Rinehart & Winston, 1970.

Eibl-Eibesfeldt, I. *Der Vorprogrammierte Mensch*, Vienna, Verlag Fritz Molden, 1973.

Einstein, A. *Relativity, the special and general theory*, London, Methuen, 1946.

Eley, L. *Die Krise des A priori in der transzendentalen Phänomenologie Edmund Husserls*, The Hague, Nijhoff, 1962.

Ellis, W. D. (ed.). *A source book of Gestalt Psychology*, London, Kegan Paul, 1938.

Erikson, R. W. 'Some historical connections between existentialism, daseinsanalysis, phenomenology and the Würzburg school', *J. Gen. Psychol.*, 1967, 75, 3–24.

Fahrmeier, E. D. 'The validity of the transactionalist's assumed world: a critical reinterpretation of an experiment in size constancy', *J. Phenom. Psychol.*, 1973, 4, 261–70.

Farber, M. *The foundation of phenomenology*, 2nd edn., New York, Paine & Whitman, 1962.

Findlay, J. N. *Meinong's theory of objects and values*, Oxford, Clarendon Press, 1963.

Fink, E. *Studien zur Phänomenologie*, The Hague, Nijhoff, 1966.

Fischer, W. F. 'The faces of anxiety', *J. Phenom. Psychol.*, 1970, 1, 31–49.

Fischer, W. F. 'On the phenomenological mode of researching "Being anxious" ', *J. Phenom. Psychol.*, 1974, 4, 405–23.

Freund, P. 'The visible and invisible: a look at the social psychology of Gustav Ichheiser', *J. Phenom. Psychol.*, 1974, 5, 95–111.

Frisch, K. von. 'Die Tänze der Bienen', *Osterr. Zool. Zs.*, 1946, 1, 1–48.

Galambos, R., and Griffin, D. R. 'Obstacle avoidance by flying bats: the cries of bats', *J. Exp. Zool.*, 1942, 89, pp. 475–90.

Geraets, T. F. *Vers une nouvelle philosophie transcendentale. La genèse de la philosophie de Maurice Merleau-Ponty jusqu'à la phénoménologie de la perception*, The Hague, Nijhoff, 1971.

Gibson, J. J. *The perception of the visual world*, Boston, Houghton Mifflin, 1950.

Gibson, J. J. 'Observations on active touch', *Psychol. Rev.*, 1962, 68, 477–91.

Gibson, J. J. *The senses considered as perceptual systems*, Boston, Houghton Mifflin, 1966.

Gilbert, G. S., and Rappoport, L. 'Categories of thought and variations in meaning', *J. Phenom. Psychol.*, 1975, 5, 419–24.

Gilson, L. *La psychologie descriptive selon Franz Brentano*, Paris, Aubier, 1944.

Giorgi, A. 'Phenomenology and experimental psychology' (I), *Rev. Exist. Psychol. and Psychiat.*, 1965, 5, 228–38.

Giorgi, A. 'Phenomenology and experimental psychology' (II), *Rev. Exist. Psychol. and Psychiat.*, 1966, 6, 37–50.

Giorgi, A. 'A phenomenological approach to the problem of meaning and serial learning', *Rev. Exist. Psychol. and Psychiat.*, 1967, 7, 106–18.

Giorgi, A. *Psychology as a human science. A phenomenologically based approach*, New York, Harper & Row, 1970.

Giorgi, A. 'Toward phenomenologically based research in psychology', *J. Phenom. Psychol.*, 1970, 1, 75–98.

Giorgi, A. 'The meta-psychology of Merleau-Ponty as a possible basis for unity in psychology', *J. Phenom. Psychol.*, 1974, 5, 57–74.

Giorgi, A., Fischer, W., and von Eckartsberg, R. (eds). *Duquesne studies in phenomenological psychology*, I, Pittsburgh, Duquesne University Press, 1971.

Giorgi, A., Fischer, C., and Murray, E. (eds). *Duquesne studies in phenomenological psychology*, II, Pittsburgh, Duquesne University Press, 1975.

Gobar, A. *Philosophic foundations of genetic psychology and Gestalt psychology*, The Hague, Nijhoff, 1968.

Goldstein, K. *The organism: a holistic approach to biology derived from pathological data in man*, New York, American Book, 1939 (first German ed., 1934).

Goldstein, K. *Selected papers* (A. Gurwitsch, E. M. Goldstein Haudek and W. E. Haudek, eds), The Hague, Nijhoff, 1971.

Gordy, M. 'The transcendent ego and the emptiness of consciousness', *J. Phenom. Psychol.*, 1972, 2, 175–94.

Graumann, C. F. *Grundlagen einer Phänomenologie und Psychologie der Perspektivität*, Berlin, De Gruyter, 1960.

Graumann, C. F. 'Conflicting and convergent trends in psychological theory', *J. Phenom. Psychol.*, 1970, 1, 51–61.

Graumann, C. F. 'Psychology and the world of things', *J. Phenom. Psychol.*, 1974, 4, 389–404.

Greidanus, J. H. *Fundamental physical theory and the concept of consciousness*, London, Pergamon Press, 1961.

Grene, M. *Approaches to a philosophical biology*, New York, Basic Books, 1968.

Guiraud, J. *L'énergétique de l'espace*, Louvain, Vander, 1970.

Gurwitsch, A. 'The last work of Edmund Husserl', *Philos. and Phenom. Res.*, 1955–1956, 16, 370–99.

Gurwitsch, A. *The field of consciousness*, Pittsburgh, Duquesne University Press, 1964 (first French ed. 1957).

Gurwitsch, A. 'Husserl's conception of phenomenological psychology', *Rev. Metaphys.*, 1965, 29, 689–727.

Gurwitsch, A. *Studies in phenomenological psychology*, Evanston, Northwestern University Press, 1966.

Gusdorf, G. *Introduction aux sciences humaines*, Paris, Belles-Lettres, 1960.

Hannush, M. J. 'Adorno and Sartre: a convergence of two methodological approaches', *J. Phenom. Psychol.*, 1973, 4, 297–313.

Harriman, P. L. *The new dictionary of psychology*, New York, Philosophical Library, 1947.

Held, K. *Lebendige Gegenwart. Die Frage nach der Seinsweise des transzendentalen Ich bei Edmund Husserl, entwickelt am Leitfaden der Zeitproblematik*, The Hague, Nijhoff, 1966.

Hinde, R. A. (ed.). *Non-verbal communication*, Cambridge University Press, 1972.

Hinde, R. A. *Biological bases of human social behaviour*, New York, McGraw-Hill, 1974.

Holenstein, E. *Phänomenologie der Assoziation*, The Hague, Nijhoff, 1972.

Holst, E. von. *Zur Verhaltensphysiologie bei Tieren und Menschen*. Munich, Piper Verlag, 1969 and 1970 (2 vols).

Holzkamp, K. *Kritische Psychologie*, Frankfurt/Main, Fischer Taschenbuch Verlag, 1972.

Husserl, E. *Philosophie der Arithmetik. Vol. I. Logische und psychologische Studien*, Halle, Pfeffer, 1894 (reprinted in 'Husserliana' XII, L. Eley, ed., The Hague, Nijhoff, 1970).

Husserl, E. *Logische Untersuchungen*. Halle, Niemeyer, 1900–1901 (2 vols). (First vol. reprinted in 'Husserliana' XVIII, E. Holenstein, ed., The Hague, Nijhoff, 1975. English trans. J. N. Findlay. *Logical investigations*, New York, Humanities Press, 1970).

Husserl, E. *Die Idee der Phänomenologie* (1907) (Reprinted in 'Husserliana' II, W. Biemel, ed., The Hague, Nijhoff, 1950).

Husserl, E. *Ideen zu einer Reinen Phänomenologie und Phänomenologische Philosophie* (I, 1913). (Reprinted in 'Husserliana' III, W. Biemel, ed., The Hague, Nijhoff, 1950. English trans. W. R. Boyce Gibson. *Ideas: general introduction to pure Phenomenology*, London, George Allen & Unwin, 1931).

Husserl, E. *Ideen zu einer Reinen Phänomenologie und Phänomenologische Philosophie* (II, 1924–1928). (Reprinted in 'Husserliana' IV, M. Biemel, ed., The Hague, Nijhoff, 1952).

Husserl, E. *Ideen zu einer Reinen Phänomenologie und Phänomenologische Philosophie* (III, 1924–1928). (Reprinted in 'Husserliana' V, M. Biemel, ed., The Hague, Nijhoff, 1952).

Husserl, E. *Phänomenologische Psychologie*. Vorlesungen Sommersemester 1925. 'Husserliana' IX, W. Biemel, ed., The Hague, Nijhoff, 1962.

Husserl, E. *Vorlesungen zur Phänomenologie des inneren Zeitbewusstseins*. Halle, Niemeyer, 1928. (Reprinted in 'Husserliana' X, R. Boehm, ed., The Hague, Nijhoff, 1966).

Husserl, E. *Cartesianische Meditationen* (1929). (First publ. in French, 1931. Reprinted in 'Husserliana' I, S. Strasser, ed., The Hague, Nijhoff, 1950. English trans. D. Cairns, *Cartesian meditations*, The Hague, Nijhoff, 1960).

Husserl, E. *Zur Phänomenologie der Intersubjektivität* (1905–1935). (Reprinted in 'Husserliana' XIII, XIV and XV, I. Kern, ed., The Hague, Nijhoff, 1973 (3 vols).)

Husserl, E. *Die Krisis der europäischen Wissenschaften und die transzendentale Phänomenologie* (1935–1937). (Reprinted in 'Husserliana' VI, W. Biemel, ed., The Hague, Nijhoff, 1954. English trans. D. Carr. *The crisis of the European sciences and transcendental phenomenology*, Evanston, Northwestern University Press, 1970).

Illies, J. *Zoologie des Menschen*, Munich, Piper Verlag, 1971.

Ingarden, R. *On the motives which led Husserl to transcendental idealism*, The Hague, Nijhoff, 1975.

Janssen, P. *Geschichte und Lebenswelt. Ein Beitrag zur Diskussion von Husserls Spätwerk*, The Hague, Nijhoff, 1970.

Jaspers, K. *General psychopathology* (trans. J. Hoening and M. W. Hamilton), Chicago, University of Chicago Press, 1963 (first German ed., 1913).

Katz, D. *Der Aufbau der Tastwelt*, Leipzig, J. A. Barth, 1925.

Katz, D. 'Sozialpsychologie der Vögel', *Ergeb. Biol.*, 1926, 1, pp. 447–77.

Katz, D. *The world of colour* (trans. R. B. MacLeod and G. W. Fox), London, Kegan Paul, 1935 (first German ed., 1930).

Katz, D. *Gestalt psychology. Its nature and significance*, New York, Ronald Press, 1950.

Katz, D. *Studien zur Experimentellen Psychologie*, Basel, Benno Schwabe, 1953.

Katz, D., and Katz, R. (eds). *Handbuch der Psychologie*, Basel, Benno Schwabe, 1960.

Keen, E., 'The five-year-old changes her mind: a phenomenological analysis', *J. Phenom. Psychol.*, 1973, 3, 161–71.

Kern, I. *Husserl und Kant. Eine Untersuchung über Husserls Verhältnis zu Kant und zum Neukantianismus*, The Hague, Nijhoff, 1964.

Kersten, F., and Zaner, R. *Phenomenology: continuation and criticism*, The Hague, Nijhoff, 1973.

Kestenbaum, V. 'On a certain blindness in Jean Piaget: sensing and knowing in Piaget and Dewey', *J. Phenom. Psychol.*, 1974, 5, 81–94.

Kockelmans, J. J. *Phenomenology and Physical Science*, Pittsburgh, Duquesne University Press, 1966.

Kockelmans, J. J. *A first introduction to Husserl's phenomenology*, Pittsburgh, Duquesne University Press, 1967.

Kockelmans, J. J. *Edmund Husserl's phenomenological psychology. A historico-critical study*, Pittsburgh, Duquesne University Press, 1967a.

Kockelmans, J. J. (ed.). *Phenomenology*, New York, Doubleday, 1967b.

Kockelmans, J. J. 'Phenomenological psychology in the United States: a critical analysis of the actual situation', *J. Phenom. Psychol.*, 1971, 1, 139–72.

Köhler, W. *Intelligenzprüfungen an Menschenaffen*, Berlin, Springer, 1921 (English trans. E Winter. *The mentality of Apes*, London, Routledge & Kegan Paul, 1925).

Köhler, W. *Die physischen Gestalten in Ruhe und stationärem Zustand*, Erlangen, Philosophische Akademie, 1924.

Köhler, W. *Gestalt psychology*, New York, Liveright, 1929.

Köhler, W. *The place of value in a world of facts*, Philadelphia, Liveright, 1938.

Kortlandt, A. 'Signal, Ausdrück, Begegnung', *Arch. Neerl. Zool.*, 1953, 10, suppl 2, 65–78.

Kortlandt, A. 'Aspects and prospects of the concept of instinct', *Arch. Neerl. Zool.*, 1955, 11, 155–284.

Kracklauer, C. 'Exploring the life-world', *J. Phenom. Psychol.*, 1972, 2, 217–36.

Kuenzli, A. E. (ed.). *The phenomenological problem*, New York, Harper, 1959.

Kvale, S. 'The technological paradigm in psychological research', *J. Phenom. Psychol.*, 1973, 3, 143–59.

Kvale, S. 'The temporality of memory', *J. Phenom. Psychol.*, 1974, 5, 7–31.

Kwant, R. C. *The phenomenological philosophy of Merleau-Ponty*, Pittsburgh, Duquesne University Press, 1963.

Langeveld, M. J. *Studien zur Anthropologie des Kindes*, Tübingen, Niemeyer, 1956 (first Dutch edition 1953).

Lapointe, F. H. 'A bibliography on Jean-Paul Sartre for the behavioral sciences', *J. Phenom. Psychol.*, 1971, 1, 237–61.

Lapointe, F. H. 'Phenomenology, psychoanalysis and the unconscious', *J. Phenom. Psychol.*, 1971, 2, 5–25.

Lapointe, F. H. 'Merleau-Ponty's phenomenological critique of psychology', *J. Phenom. Psychol.*, 1972, 2, 237–55.

Lapointe, F. H. 'A selected bibliography on the existential and phenomenological psychology of Maurice Merleau-Ponty', *J. Phenom. Psychol.*, 1972, 3, 113–30.

Lapointe, F. H. 'A selected bibliography on the existential and phenomenological psychology of G. Marcel and Paul Ricoeur', *J. Phenom. Psychol.*, 1973, 4, 363–73.

Lapointe, F. H. 'The phenomenology of desire and love in Sartre and Merleau-Ponty', *J. Phenom. Psychol.*, 1974, 4, 445–59.

Lapointe, F. H. 'The evolution of Merleau-Ponty's concept of the body', *J. Phenom. Psychol.*, 1975, 5, 389–404.

L'Ecuyer, R. *La genèse du concept de soi. Théories et recherches*, Sherbrooke, Naaman, 1975.

L'Ecuyer, R. 'Self-concept investigation: demystification process', *J. Phenom. Psychol.*, 1975, 6, 17–30.

Levi, B. L. 'Critique of Piaget's theory of intelligence: a phenomenological approach', *J. Phenom. Psychol.*, 1972, 3, 99–111.

Levy, C. E. 'Toward primordial reality as the ground of psychological phenomena', *J. Phenom. Psychol.*, 1973, 3, 173–86.

Levy, S. M. E. 'Personal constructs and existential *a priori* categories', *J. Phenom. Psychol.*, 1975, 5, 369–88.

Linschoten, J. *Strukturenanalyse der binokulären Tiefenwahrnehmung*, Groningen, Wolters, 1956.

Linschoten, J. *Idolen van de psycholoog*, Utrecht, Bijleveld, 1964.

Linschoten, H. *On the way toward a phenomenological psychology*, Giorgi, A. (ed.). Pittsburgh, Duquesne University Press, 1968 (first Dutch edn, 1959).

Lorenz, K. 'The comparative method in studying innate behaviour patterns', *Sympos. Soc. Exp. Biol.* IV, Cambridge University Press, 1950, 221–68.

Lorenze, K. 'Haben Tiere ein subjektives Erleben?' in Id., *Ueber tierisches und menschliches Verhalten* (II), Munich, Piper Verlag, 1965, 559–74.

Lorenz, K. *Ueber tierisches und menschliches Verhalten. Gesammelte Abhandlungen*, Munich, Piper Verlag, 1965 (2 vols).

Lorenz, K. 'Vergleichende Verhaltensforschung', *Verh. Deutsch. Zool. Gesell. Rostock. Zool. Auz.*, 1939, Suppl. 12, 69–102. (Reprinted in K. Lorenz and P. Leyhausen, *Antriebe tierischen und menschlichen Verhaltens*, Munich, Piper Verlag, 1968, 15–47).

Lorenz, K. 'Zur Naturgeschichte der Angst', *Pol. Psychol.*, 1967, 6. (Reprinted in K. Lorenz and P. Leyhausen, *Antriebe tierischen und menschlichen Verhaltens*, Munich, Piper Verlag, 1968, 272–96).

Lorenz, K. *Die Rückseite des Spiegels*, Munich, Piper Verlag, 1974.

Lyons, J. *Psychology and the measure of man: a phenomenological approach*, New York, The Free Press of Glencoe, 1963.

Lyons, J. 'The hidden dialogue in experimental research', *J. Phenom. Psychol.*, 1970, 1, 19–29.

McCurdy, J. D. 'Synergic perception', *J. Phenom. Psychol.*, 1973, 3, 217–46.

McGill, V. J. 'Behaviorism and phenomenology', *Philos. and Phenomen. Res.*, 1966, 26, 578–88.

Mach, E. *Die Analyse der Empfindungen und das Verhältnis des Physischen zum Psychischen*, Jena, Gustav Fischer, 1885.

MacLeod, R. B. 'Phenomenological approach to social psychology', *Psychol. Rev.*, 1947, 54, 193–210.

MacLeod, R. B. 'David Katz, 1884–1953', *Psychol. Rev.*, 1954, 61, 1–4.

MacLeod, R. B. 'Phenomenology: A challenge to experimental psychology' in T. W. Wann (ed.), *Behaviorism and Phenomenology*, Chicago, University of Chicago Press, 1964.

MacLeod, R. B. *The persistent problems of psychology*, Pittsburgh, Duquesne University Press, 1975.

Marcel, G. *Being and Having* (trans. K. Farrer), London, Collins, 1965 (first French ed, 1935).

Marler, P., and Hamilton, W. J. *Mechanisms of animal behavior*, New York, Wiley, 1966.

Marois, M. (ed.). *From theoretical physics to biology*, Basel, Karger, 1973.

Marx, W. *Vernunft und Welt*, The Hague, Nijhoff, 1970.

Maslow, A. H. 'Toward a humanistic biology', *Amer. Psychologist*, 1969, 24, 724–35.

Meinong, A. (ed.). *Untersuchungen zur Gegenstandstheorie und Psychologie*, Leipzig, Johann Ambrosius Barth, 1904.

Meissner, W. 'The implications of experience for psychological theory', *Philos. and Phenom. Res.*, 1966, 24, 503–28.

Merleau-Ponty, M. *The Structure of Behavior*, Boston, Beacon, 1963 (first French edn, 1942).

Merleau-Ponty, M. *Phenomenology of perception*, New York, Humanities Press, 1962 (first French edn, 1945).

Merleau-Ponty, M. *The visible and the invisible*, Evanston, Northwestern University Press, 1968 (first French edn, 1964).

Meyer, M. W. 'Toward a phenomenological theory of learning: the contribution of B. F. Skinner', *J. Phenom. Psychol.*, 1975, 5, 335–68.

Michotte, A. *The perception of causality* (trans. T. R. and E. Miles), London, Metheun, 1963 (first French edn, 1946).

Michotte, A. 'Réflexions sur le rôle du langage dans l'analyse des organisations perceptives', *Acta Psychol.*, 1959, 15, 70–91.

Michotte, A. et al. *Causalité, permanence et réalité phénoménales*, Louvain, Nauwelaerts, 1962.

Michotte, A., and Prüm, E. 'Etude expérimentale sur le choix volontaire et ses antécédents immédiats', *Arch. Psychol.*, 1910, 10, pp. 119–299.

Michotte, A., Thinès, G., and Crabbé, G. *Les compléments amodaux des structures perceptives*, Louvain, Nauwelaerts, 1964.

Minkowski, E. *Lived time* (trans. N. Metzel), Evanston, Northwestern University Press, 1970 (first French ed, 1933).

Mischel, T. 'Merleau-Ponty's phenomenological psychology', *J. Hist. Behav. Sc.*, 1966, 2, 172–6.

Misiak, H., and Sexton, V. S. *Phenomenological, Existential and Humanistic Psychologies. A Historical Survey*, New York, Grune & Stratton, 1973.

Mitchell, G. 'Looking behavior in the Rhesus Monkey', *J. Phenom. Psychol.*, 1972, 3, 53–67.

Mohanty, J. N. *Edmund Husserl's theory of meaning*, The Hague, Nijhoff, 1964.

Mohanty, J. N. *Phenomenology and ontology*, The Hague, Nijhoff, 1970.

Moncrieff, D. W. 'Heuristic ambiguities in Maslow's "creativeness" ', *J. Phenom. Psychol.*, 1972, 2, 257–69.

Moustgaard, I. K. 'Phenomenological descriptions after the manner of Edgar Rubin', *J. Phenom. Psychol.*, 1975, 6, 31–61.

Murray, E. L. 'Language and the integration of personality', *J. Phenom. Psychol.*, 1974, 4, 469–89.

Natanson, M. *Literature, philosophy and the social sciences*, The Hague, Nijhoff, 1962.

Nel, B. F. 'The phenomenological approach to pedagogy', *J. Phenom. Psychol.*, 1973, 3, 201–15.

Nogué, J. *La signification du sensible*, Paris, Aubier, 1936.

Ortega y Gasset, J. *The modern theme*, London, Daniel, 1931.

Osborn, A. D. *Husserl and his logical investigations*, Cambridge, Mass., 1949.

Parsons, A. S. 'Constitutive phenomenology: Schutz's theory of the We-relations', *J. Phenom. Psychol.*, 1973, 4, 331–61.

Pazanin, A. *Wissenschaft und Geschichte in der Phänomenologie Edmund Husserls*, The Hague, Nijhoff, 1972.

Pfänder, A. *Phänomenologie des Wollens*, Leipzig, J. A. Barth, 1900.

Pfänder, A. *Einführung in die Psychologie*, Leipzig, J. A. Barth, 1904.

Phelan, G. B. *Feeling experience and its modalities*, London, Kegan Paul, 1925.

Phenomenological perspectives. Historical and systematic essays in honor of Herbert Spiegelberg (no editor), The Hague, Nijhoff, 1975.

Piaget, J. *Logic and psychology*, Manchester University Press, 1953.

Piaget, J. *Biology and knowledge*, Chicago, University of Chicago Press, 1971.

Piaget, J. *Insights and illusions of philosophy*, New York, World Publishing Co., 1971.

Politzer, G. *Critique des fondements de la psychologie*, Paris, Rieder, 1928 (3rd edn, Paris, Presses Universitaires de France, 1968).

Politzer, G. *La fin d'une parade philosophique: le Bergsonisme*, Paris, Pauvert, 1968 (1st edn, 1929).

Politzer, G. *La crise de la psychologie contemporaine*, Paris, Editions Sociales, 1947 (first publ. 1929).

Politzer, G. *Ecrits 1 – La philosophie et les mythes*, Paris, Editions Sociales, 1969.

Politzer, G. *Ecrits 2 – Les Fondements de la psychologie*, Paris, Editions Sociales, 1969.

Portmann, A. *Die Tiergestalt. Studien über die Bedeutung der tierischen Erscheinung*, Basel, Verlag Friedrich Reinhardt, 1948.

Portmann, A. *Das Tier als soziales Wesen*, Zürich, Rhein, 1953.

Portmann, A. *Neue Wege der Biologie*, Munich, Piper, 1960.

Psathas, G., and Becker, P. 'The experimental reality: the cognitive style of a finite province of meaning', *J. Phenom. Psychol.*, 1972, 3, 35–52.

Psychologie et Marxisme (collective discussions, no editor). Paris, Soc. Gén. d'édition, 1971.

Rancurello, A. *A study of Franz Brentano. His psychological standpoint and his significance in the history of psychology*, New York, Academic Press, 1968.

Rencontre, Encounter, Begegnung. Contributions à une psychologie humaine dédiées au professeur F. J. J. Buytendijk, Utrecht, Spectrum, 1957.

Révész, G. *Die Formenwelt des Tastsinnes*, The Hague, Nijhoff, 1938.

Richardson, W. J. *Heidegger. Through phenomenology to thought*, The Hague, Nijhoff, 1963.

Richelle, M., and Ruwet, J. C. (eds). *Problèmes et méthodes en psychologie comparée*, Paris, Masson, 1972.

Ricoeur, P. *Husserl: an analysis of his phenomenology* (trans. E. G. Ballard and L. E. Embree), Evanston, Northwestern University Press, 1967.

Robinet, A. *Merleau-Ponty, sa vie, son oeuvre avec un exposé de sa philosophie*, Paris, Presses Universitaires de France, 1962.

Rogers, C. R. 'Some thoughts regarding the current philosophy of the behavioral sciences', *J. Hum. Psychol.*, 1965, 5, 182–94.

Romanyshyn, R. D. 'Method and meaning in psychology: the method has been the message', *J. Phenom. Psychol.*, 1971, 2, 93–113.

Romanyshyn, R. 'Copernicus and the beginning of modern science', *J. Phenom. Psychol.*, 1973, 3, 187–99.

Romanyshyn, R. D. 'Metaphors and human behavior', *J. Phenom. Psychol.*, 1975, 5, 441–60

Rosen, S. M. 'A case of non-euclidean visualization', *J. Phenom. Psychol.*, 1974, 5, 33–9.

Roth, A. *Edmund Husserls Ethische Untersuchungen*, The Hague, Nijhoff, 1960.

Sandford, N. 'Will psychologists study human problems?', *Amer. Psychologist*, 1965, 20, pp. 192–202.

Saraiva, M. M. *L'imagination selon Husserl*, The Hague, Nijhoff, 1970.

Sardello, R. J. 'Behaviorism (versus?) (and?) (or?) phenomenology?', *Amer. Psychologist*, 1970, 25, 567–8.

Sartre, J. P. *The emotions: Outline of a theory*, New York, Philosophical Library. 1948 (1st French edn, 1939).

Sartre, J. P. *The psychology of imagination*, New York, Philosophical Library, 1948 (1st French edn, 1936).

Scheler, M. *The nature of sympathy* (trans. P. Heath), New Haven, Yale University Press, 1954 (1st German edn, 1913).

Schenkel, R. 'Ausdrück-studien an Wölfen', *Behaviour*, 1948, 1, 81–130.

Schilpp, P. A. (ed.). *The philosophy of Karl Jaspers*, New York, Tudor, 1957.

Schloeth, R 'Zur Psychologie der Begegnung zwischen Tieren', *Behaviour*, 1956, 10, 1–80.

Schubert, J. 'S—R theory and dynamic theory', *J. Phenom. Psychol.*, 1971, 1, 173–84.

Schumann, K. *Die Fundamentelbetrachtung der Phänomenologie*, The Hague, Nijhoff, 1971.

Schumann, K. *Die Dialektik der Phänomenologie (I)*. *Husserl über Pfänder*, The Hague, Nijhoff, 1973.

Schumann, K. *Die Dialektik der Phänomenologie (II)*. *Reine Phänomenologie und phänomenologische Philosophie*, The Hague, Nijhoff, 1973.

Schutz, A. *Collected papers (I)*. *The problem of social reality* (M. Natanson, ed.). The Hague, Nijhoff, 1962.

Schutz, A. *Collected papers (II)*. *Studies in social theory* (A. Brodersen, ed.), The Hague, Nijhoff, 1964.

Schutz, A. *Collected papers (III)*. *Studies in phenomenological philosophy* (I. Schutz, ed.), The Hague, Nijhoff, 1966.

Schwankl, P. 'Alexander Pfänder's Nachlasstexte über das virtuelle Psychische', *J. Phenom. Psychol.*, 1972, 3, 69–97.

Sexton, V. S., and Misiak, H. (eds). *Historical perspectives in psychology, Readings*, Belmont, Brooks and Cole, 1971.

Sherrington, C. *The integrative action of the nervous system*, London, Scribner, 1906 (republished Cambridge University Press, 1947, 1948 and 1952).

Sherrington, C. *Man on his nature*, Cambridge University Press, 1940 (2nd edn. 1963).

Simmel, M. L. (ed.). *The Reach of Mind*, New York, Springer, 1968.

Simondon, G. *L'individu et sa genèse physico-biologique*, Paris, Presses Universitaires de France, 1964.

Sinha, D. *Studies in phenomenology*, The Hague, Nijhoff, 1969.

Smith, F. J. 'Musical sound as a model for Husserlian intuition and time consciousness', *J. Phenom. Psychol.*, 1973, 4, 271–96.

Smith, J. H. *Introduction to special relativity*, New York, Benjamin, 1965.

Smith, K. *Behavior and conscious experience. A conceptual analysis*, Athens, Ohio, Ohio University Press, 1969.

Smith, K. C. P., and Apter, M. J. *A theory of psychological reversals*, Chippenham, Picton, 1975.

Snygg, D. 'The need for a phenomenological system of psychology' in A. E. Kuenzli (ed.), *The phenomenological problem*, New York, Harper, 1959.

Sokolowski, R. *The formation of Husserl's concept of constitution*, The Hague, Nijhoff, 1964.

Solomon, R. C. (ed.). *Phenomenology and existentialism*, New York, Harper and Row, 1972.

Souche-Dagues, D. *Le développement de l'intentionnalité dans la phénoménologie husserlienne*, The Hague, Nijhoff, 1972.

Spiegelberg, H. *The phenomenological movement. A Historical introduction*, The Hague, Nijhoff, 1960. 2 vols.

Spiegelberg, H. *Phenomenology in psychology and psychiatry: A historical introduction*, Evanston, Northwestern University Press, 1972.

Spiegelberg, H. *Doing Phenomenology. Essays on and in phenomenology*, The Hague, Nijhoff, 1975.

Stachowiak, H. *Denken und Erkennen im kybernetischen Modell*, Vienna, New York, Springer, 1965.

Stevens, R. *James and Husserl. The foundations of meaning*, The Hague, Nijhoff, 1974.

Strasser, S. 'Phenomenological trends in European psychology', *Philos. and Phenom. Res.*, 1957–1958, 18, 18–34.

Strasser, S. *Phenomenology and the human sciences*, Pittsburgh, Duquesne University Press, 1963.

Straus, E. *Psychologie der menschlichen Welt. Gesammelte Schriften*, Berlin, Springer, 1960.

Straus, E. *The primary world of senses: a vindication of sensory experience* (trans. J. Needleman), New York, Free Press of Glencoe, 1963 (1st German edn., 1935).

Straus, E. *Phenomenology: pure and applied*, Pittsburgh, Duquesne University Press, 1965.

Straus, E. *Phenomenological psychology*, New York, Basic Books, 1966.

Straus, E., Aug, R. G., and Ables, B. S. 'A phenomenological approach to dyslexia', *J. Phenom. Psychol.*, 1971, 1, 225–35.

Straus, E., and Griffith, R. M. (eds). *Aisthesis and aesthetics*, Pittsburgh, Duquesne University Press, 1970.

Straus, E., and Griffith, R. M. (eds). *Phenomenology of memory*, Pittsburgh, Duquesne University Press, 1970.

Straus, E., Natanson, M., and Ey, H. *Psychiatry and philosophy*, Berlin, Springer, 1969.

Streiffeler, F. 'Phänomenologische Philosophie oder Phänomenologische Psychologie?', *J. Phenom. Psychol.*, 1972, 2, 195–216.

Stumpf, C. *Tonpsychologie*, Leipzig, Hirzel, 1883–1890 (2 vols).

Stumpf, C. Erscheinungen und psychische Funktionen. *Abhand. König. Preuss. Akad. Wiss.*, 1906, Berlin. 1907, Abh. IV, 1–40.

Stumpf, C. Zur Einteilung der Wissenschaften. *Abhand, König. Preuss. Akad. Wiss.*, 1906, Berlin, 1907, Abh V, 1–94.

Stumpf, C. *Die Sprachlaute. Experimentell-phonetische Untersuchungen*, Berlin, Springer, 1926.

Tellenbach, H. 'On the nature of jealousy', *J. Phenom. Psychol.*, 1974, 4, 461–8.

Thinès, G. *Psychologie des animaux*, Brussels, Dessart, 1966.

Thinès, G. 'Le langage de l'expérience et le langage de la théorie en psychologie' in *Hommage à André Rey*, Brussels, Dessart, 1967, 199–221.

Thinès, G. *La Problématique de la Psychologie*, The Hague, Nijhoff, 1968.

Thinès, G. 'The phenomenological approach in comparative psychology', *J. Phenom. Psychol.*, 1970, 1, 63–73.

Thinès, G., and Lempereur, A. (eds). *Dictionnaire Général des Sciences Humaines*, Paris, Editions Universitaires, 1975 (see especially the following entries: Anthropologie philosophique; Causalité; Compréhensives (sciences); Corporéité; Expression; Fonction; Gestaltkreis; Intentionnalité; Intersubjectivité; Isomorphisme; Modèle; Objectivisme; Objectivité; Pathique; Physicalisme; Psychologie phénoménologique; Rencontre; Sens; Signification; Spatialité; Structure; Subjectivité; Temporalité; Motif; Motivation).

Thinès, G., and Morval, M. 'Recherches sur le contact visuel et la polarisation faciale', *Trav. Fac. Philos. Lett. Univ. Louvain*, 1967, 7–73.

Thinès, G., and Zayan, R. 'Buytendijk's contribution to animal behaviour: animal psychology or ethology?', *Acta Biotheoret.*, 1975, 24, 3–4, 86–99.

Thinès, G., and Zayan, R. 'La structuration de l'espace biologique. I. Sherrington et la théorie de la distance', *Rev. Quest. Scientif.*, 1975, 146, 209–32.

Thinès, G., and Zayan, R. 'La structuration de l'espace biologique. II. La précurrence et l'organisation spatio-temporelle du comportement animal: Sherrington et la conception éthologique', *Rev. Quest. Scientif.*, 1975, 146, 295–336.

Thinès, G., and Zayan, R. 'La structuration de l'espace biologique. III. La précurrence et l'individualité biologique', *Rev. Quest. Scientif.*, 1975, 146, 433–53.

Tinbergen, N. *The study of instinct*, Oxford, Clarendon Press, 1951.

Uexküll, J. von. *Umwelt und Innenwelt der Tiere*, Berlin, Springer, 1909.

Uexküll, J. von. *Niegeschaute Welten*, Munich, Paul List Verlag, 1957.

Uexküll, J. von, and Kriszat, G. *Streifzüge durch die Umwelten von Tieren und Menschen*, Hamburg, Rohwoltsenzyklopädie, 1956.

Van den Berg, J. H. *The phenomenological approach to psychiatry*, Springfield, Ill., Thomas, 1955.

Van den Berg, J. H. *The changing nature of man: introduction to a historical psychology*, New York, Norton, 1962.

Van den Berg, J. H. 'On hallucinating', *J. Phenom. Psychol.*, 1975, 6, 1–16.

Van Hooff, J. A. R. A. M. *Aspecten van het sociale gedrag en de communicatie bij Humane en hogere niet-Humane Primaten*, Rotterdam, Bronder, 1971.

Van Hooff, J. A. R. A. M. 'A comparative approach to the phylogeny of laughter and smiling' in R. A. Hinde (ed.), *Non-verbal communication*. Cambridge University Press, 1972, 209–41.

Van Kaam, A. L. 'The impact of existential phenomenology on the psychological literature of Western Europe', *Rev. Exist. Psychol. and Psychiat.*, 1961, 1, 63–92.

Van Kaam, A. L. *Existential foundations of psychology*, Pittsburgh, Duquesne University Press, 1966.

Van Lennep, D. J. *Psychologie van Projektieverschijnselen*, Utrecht, Nederl. Sticht. voor Psychotechniek, 1948.

Van Spaendonck, J. A. S. 'An analysis of the metabletical method', *J. Phenom. Psychol.*, 1975, 6, 89–108.

Wann, T. W. (ed.). *Behaviorism and phenomenology: contrasting bases for modern psychology*, Chicago, University of Chicago Press, 1964.

Ward, J. *Psychological principles*, Cambridge University Press, 1918.

Weizsäcker, V. von. 'Reflexgesetz' in A. Bethe (ed.), *Handbuch der Normalen und Pathologischen Physiologie*, X, 1927.

Weizsäcker, V. von. *Der Gestaltkreis*, Stuttgart, Thieme, 1939.

Wertheimer, M. *Drei Abhandlungen zur Gestalttheorie*, Erlangen, Weltkreis, 1925.

Wertheimer, M. Experimentelle Studien über das Sehen von Bewegung, *Zeit. für Psychol.*, 1912, 61, pp. 161–265.

Wertheimer, M. *Productive thinking*, New York, Harper & Brothers, 1959 (enlarged edn; first publ. 1945).

Wetherick, N. H. 'Can there be non-phenomenological psychology?', *The Human Context*, 1972, 4, 50–60.

Wiener, N. *Cybernetics, or control and communication in the animal and the machine*, Paris, Hermann, 1948.

Williame, R. *Les fondements phénoménologiques de la sociologie compréhensive: Alfred Schutz et Max Weber*, The Hague, Nijhoff, 1973.

Wilshire, B. W. *William James and phenomenology. A study of 'The principles of psychology'*, Bloomington, Indiana University Press, 1968.

Winthrop, H. 'Some considerations concerning the status of phenomenology', *J. Gen. Psychol.*, 1963, 68, 127–40.

Wolff, Chr. *Psychologia empirica*, Gesam. Werke, II Abt., Band 5 (J. Ecole, ed.), Hildesheim, Olms, 1968.

Wolff, Chr. *Psychologia rationalis*, Gesam. Werke, II Abt., Band 6 (J. Ecole, ed.), Hildesheim, Olms, 1972.

Wong, E. 'Visual and tactile perception reconsidered: from an empirical-phenomenological perspective', *J. Phenom. Psychol.*, 1975, 6, 75–87.

Wundt, W. *Elements of folk psychology* (trans. E. L. Schaub), New York, Macmillan, 1916 (1st German edn., 1900).

Wundt, W. *Grundzüge der Physiologischen Psychologie*, Leipzig, Engelmann, 1873–4.

Zaner, R. M. *The problem of embodiment. Some contributions to a phenomenology of the body*, The Hague, Nijhoff, 1964.

Zaner, R. M. 'Criticism of "Tensions in psychology between methods of behaviorism and phenomenology" ', *Psychol. Rev.*, 1967, 74, 318–24.

Zaner, R. M. *The way of phenomenology. Criticism as a philosophical discipline*, New York, Pegasus, 1970.

Zayan, R. 'Activité proprioceptive et localisation d'une sensation tactile', *Rev. Psychol. Sc. Educ.*, 1971, 6, 3, 293–329.

Zayan, R. 'Le sens du sens tactile', *J. Phenom. Psychol.*, 1971, 2, 49–91.

Zayan, R. 'Le rôle de la reconnaissance individuelle dans la stabilité des relations hiérarchiques chez *Xiphophorus* (Pisces, Poecilidae)', *Behaviour*, 1974, 49, 3–4, 268–312.

Zayan, R. 'Défense du territoire et reconnaissance individuelle chez *Xiphophorus* (Pisces, Poecilidae)', *Behaviour*, 1975, 52, 3–4, 266–312.

Zhinkin, N. I. 'An application of the theory of algorithms to the study of animal speech: methods of vocal intercommunication between Monkeys' in R. G. Busnel, *Acoustic behaviour of Animals*, Amsterdam, Elsevier, 1963, 132–83.

Subject Index

Abstraction 97, 127
Abstractionism 100, 102, 103, 104, 105
Acoustics 135
Act psychology 57, 58, 62, 63, 71, 78, 91, 138
Acts: consummatory 84, 89, 90, 146; intentional 78; perceptual 36, 67; psychic 73; scientific 36
Adaptation 86; reciprocal 147
Affective tone 88
Afference 86
Aggression 147
Algorithmic theory 48
Analogy 119
Anatomy 85, 145
Animals 85, 87, 117, 119, 120, 121, 143
Anisotropy 85, 86, 87
Anthropology 116, 137; concrete 100; philosophical 78, 100
Anthropomórphism 119, 121, 143
Anticipation 141
A posteriori 65
Apperception 117
A priori 32, 33, 35, 36, 37, 40, 51, 62, 65, 80, 95, 108, 109, 115, 127, 128, 130, 131, 132, 152
Aristotelism 58, 59
Arithmetic 110
Aspects: ontogenic 45, 48; qualitative 20
Association 75, 76, 93; collective 73, 74
Atomism 39, 76, 141
Attitude 141
Attributes 66
Audition 92

Behaviourism 13, 16, 18, 31, 40, 41, 43, 57, 76, 78, 79, 82, 83, 90, 93, 94, 95, 107, 126, 140, 145, 148, 149, 152
Behaviour 40, 93, 128; aggressive 147; anatomical basis of 85; animal 79, 141, 149; appetitive 89; exploratory 86, 88; expressive 137, 144, 146, 151; instinctive 88, 145; intelligent 88; motor 141, 142, 144; non verbal 137; patterns 140; sexual 87, 146; see also Mechanism, Model
Being (structure of) 97
Bell-Magendie law 30, 31
Biologism 78
Biology 35, 105, 107, 109, 112, 117, 118, 119, 120, 128; intuitive 34, 42, 45; of behaviour 45, 54, 56, 78, 79, 81, 82, 95, 124, 125, 133, 145, 154
Biometrics 16, 30

Body 18, 28, 29, 30, 89, 90, 91, 92, 95, 113; axes 86; co-extensive 90; exploration 90; lived 18, 90, 140, 141, 150; segments 85, 86; surface 87
Bracketing 70, 110, 112, 127
Brain 94; biological significance 87; dominance of 87; localisation 141

Cartesianism 14, 53, 99, 111, 113
Case: clinical 15, 46, 132; individual 15; private 46; single 46
Causality 17, 18, 47, 82; perceptual 77, 138, 139
Children 117
Cogitatum 110
Cogito 31, 110, 111
Cognition 147
Colour 118, 135, 136
Communication 137
Complexes 67, 68; ideal 67, 69; real 67
Conation 90
Concrete 101, 102
Conditioning: operant, 79; pavlovian 53, 93, 94, 95
Configuration 76
Consciousness 14, 16, 17, 62, 67, 68, 111, 113, 115, 116, 121, 128, 131; act of 57, 62, 63, 69, 79; constitution of 72, 136; content of 99; elements of 65; immanent 60; theory of 57
Conspecific 145, 146
Constancy 137; tactile 136
Constitution 54, 116, 118, 120, 131; of objects 67; organic 83; sensory 83; subjective 58, 89, 118, 121; temporal 54
Constructs 36
Contact: bodily 87; visual 137
Contents: founded 67; founding 67
Controls 137
Convergence 86
Coordination 84
Courtship 146
Crises of modern man 125
Culturalism 38, 44, 45, 50, 55, 94, 104; psychological 40, 41, 42
Culture 35, 120, 122, 124
Cybernetics 52, 53, 78, 79, 85, 141
Cycle of structure, see Gestaltkreis

Deduction 34
Description 64, 76, 91, 94, 95, 117, 131, 132, 134, 135, 137, 143, 144, 145; eidetic 115, 119, 120, 130; of impressions 109, 136, 139; of psychic phenomena 64; tactile 91

Name Index